D1737879

AMERICAN CIVIL WAR GUERRILLAS

Recent Titles in
Reflections on the Civil War Era

AMERICAN CIVIL WAR
GUERRILLAS

CHANGING THE RULES OF WARFARE

DANIEL E. SUTHERLAND

Reflections on the Civil War Era
John David Smith, Series Editor

AN IMPRINT OF ABC-CLIO, LLC
Santa Barbara, California • Denver, Colorado • Oxford, England

Copyright 2013 by Daniel E. Sutherland

Library of Congress Cataloging-in-Publication Data

Sutherland, Daniel E.
  American Civil War guerrillas : changing the rules of warfare / Daniel E. Sutherland.
        pages cm. — (Reflections on the Civil War era)
  Includes index.
  ISBN 978-0-313-37766-2 (hardback) — ISBN 978-0-313-37767-9 (ebook)
1. United States—History—Civil War, 1861–1865—Underground movements.
2. United States—History—Civil War, 1861–1865—Campaigns.   3. Guerrilla
warfare—United States—History—19th century.   4. Guerrilla warfare—
Confederate States of America.   5. Guerrillas—United States—History—
19th century.   6. Guerrillas—Confederate States of America.   I. Title.
  E470.S889   2013
  973.7'3—dc23   2013024075

ISBN: 978-0-313-37766-2
EISBN: 978-0-313-37767-9

17   16   15   14   13   1   2   3   4   5

This book is also available on the World Wide Web as an eBook.
Visit www.abc-clio.com for details.

Praeger
An Imprint of ABC-CLIO, LLC

ABC-CLIO, LLC
130 Cremona Drive, P.O. Box 1911
Santa Barbara, California 93116-1911

This book is printed on acid-free paper ∞

Manufactured in the United States of America

For the new wee one,
Jane Victoria Sutherland

CONTENTS

SERIES FOREWORD

"Like Ol' Man River," the distinguished Civil War historian Peter J. Parish wrote in 1998, "Civil War historiography just keeps rolling along. It changes course occasionally, leaving behind bayous of stagnant argument, while it carves out new lines of inquiry and debate."

Since Confederate general Robert E. Lee's men stacked their guns at Appomattox Court House in April 1865, historians and partisans have been fighting a war of words over the causes, battles, results, and broad meaning of the internecine conflict that cost more than 620,000 American lives. Writers have contributed between 50,000 and 60,000 books and pamphlets on the topic. Viewed in terms of defining American freedom and nationalism, western expansion and economic development, the Civil War quite literally launched modern America. "The Civil War," Kentucky poet, novelist, and literary critic Robert Penn Warren explained, "is for the American imagination, the great single event of our history. Without too much wrenching, it may, in fact, be said to *be* American history."

The books in Praeger's *Reflections on the Civil War Era* series examine pivotal aspects of the American Civil War. Topics range from examinations of military campaigns and local conditions, to analyses of institutional, intellectual, and social history. Questions of class, gender, and race run through each volume in the series. Authors, veteran experts in their respective fields, provide concise, informed, readable syntheses—fresh looks at familiar topics with new source material and original arguments.

"Like all great conflicts," Parish noted in 1999, "the American Civil War reflected the society and the age in which it was fought." Books in *Reflections on the Civil War Era* interpret the war as a salient event in the hammering out and understanding of American identity before, during, and after the secession crisis of 1860–1861. Readers will find the volumes valuable guides as they chart the troubled waters of mid-19th-century American life.

John David Smith
Charles H. Stone Distinguished Professor of American History
The University of North Carolina at Charlotte

INTRODUCTION

Historians have grown aware over the past few years of the decisive impact that guerrillas had on the conduct and outcome of the American Civil War. Considered a mere sideshow during the centennial celebration of the war, guerrillas have become a major attraction as Americans commemorate the war's sesquicentennial. The reasons for the change are several. The nation's long involvement in Vietnam, frequently defined by irregular operations, caused scholars to reconsider their impact on that conflict. Subsequent involvement in what has become known as *asymmetrical, compound,* or *hybrid* warfare in the Middle East has extended the trend. Deeper inquiry into the social dimensions of the Civil War itself, especially the Confederate home front has also confirmed the significance of the guerrilla's role.

Central to these issues are the ways that the guerrilla war changed the rules of the game. By 1865, the American Civil War had become a far bloodier, more destructive, and brutish affair than anyone imagined in 1861. The latest statistical analysis of its human cost suggests that at least 752,000 soldiers and civilians died in the war, perhaps as many as 851,000. I lean toward the latter figure, as it seems certain that the number of civilian deaths is underestimated. More tens of thousands of survivors carried physical, emotional, or psychological scars for years and decades thereafter. The South incurred hundreds of billions of dollars in physical damage at modern valuations. Much of this carnage could be blamed on changes in battlefield tactics, weaponry, and logistics. Armies had simply become more adept at killing people. But the guerrilla conflict, operating in more subtle, less visible ways, undermined the very standards and expectations of wars, affecting not only the armies, but also untold numbers of noncombatants.

No one knows how many guerrillas fought in the conflict. A West Virginian estimated that at least 1,000 rebel guerrillas, divided into companies of 12–100 men, operated in a seven-county area near his home by late 1861. Even if he exaggerated the numbers, it must have seemed that irregulars prowled at will. A report by the Confederate government showed that 96 companies had been mustered in eight states by the end of 1862, but everyone knew that number was low. For one thing, it did not credit a single company to Arkansas, Kentucky, Missouri, or Tennessee—states where guerrilla warfare raged most intensely. In truth, we do not know how many bands of guerrillas operated during the war, much less the number of individuals. One scholar has estimated the latter to be 26,000, but a more likely tally is 50,000. All that may be said with certainty is that the impact guerrillas had on the war outweighed their numbers.

The guerrilla war also infested a far larger part of the country than has been assumed. Looking at accounts of irregular warfare written in the 1950s and the 1960s, it would seem that guerrillas operated almost exclusively in Missouri and Virginia, with perhaps a sprinkling in Tennessee. In fact, the guerrilla war raged from Iowa to Florida, from the Ohio River Valley to Texas. It began, like the conventional war, in the Upper South, but it grew as the war progressed and Union armies threatened to invade or occupy ever more parts of the Confederacy. For example, the Deep South, with only its sea coasts open to invasion initially, saw very little guerrilla activity before 1862. However, by the end of that year, with the northern portions of Mississippi and Alabama exposed and the upper and lower Mississippi River virtually under Union control, guerrilla resistance kept pace. The federal advance also emboldened Southern Unionists, and insofar as the guerrilla war was as much a battle between armed bands of neighbors as between irregulars and conventional troops, this also helped to spread the struggle.

Equally untidy were the dividing lines between combatants and noncombatants, legitimate military actions and terrorism, just retaliation and personal vengeance, wartime necessity and banditry. Such considerations are especially pertinent in light of the world's fixation on terrorism and counterterrorism since September 11, 2001. Past events that we thought we understood, and about which we presumed to know all that could be known, suddenly evoke new interpretations. Terrorists now seem to lurk everywhere in the past. We have only failed to see them. Of course, any dramatic event in contemporary life often gives history a different look, but in the case of the Civil War, this shifting focus is more than fashionable.

There was terrorism during the American Civil war, plenty of it. Indeed, that very word—*terror*—was used at the time; but what did it mean? Who were the terrorists? What were their objectives? Whom did they terrify? Terror is inherent in wartime. Soldiers and noncombatants alike can be both targets and agents of random terror. Yet, within wartime's cocoon of violence, there can be purposeful terrorism, targeted action designed to breed fear. One finds their roots during the American Civil War in the guerrilla conflict that raged between 1861 and 1865, a conflict that caused either directly or indirectly most of the terrorism and counterterrorism that we associate with that war.

Historians have been aware for some time that all this occurred, but very few of them have understood the significance of the pattern or the scope of the problem. They have either dismissed Civil War terror and guerrilla violence as minor distractions from the main fighting or tried to fit them into some preconceived structure of conventional military operations. For instance, one book, published just months after 9/11, insisted that guerrillas in any war should not be defined as terrorists because they do not target civilian populations. Not only was this an extraordinarily narrow definition of terrorism, but it also did not take into account the variety of ways that the guerrilla war manifested itself in the American South between 1861 and 1865. Its admittedly brief treatment of that war assumed both that the guerrilla conflict was primarily a military operation and that there was some sort of central control and direction over the guerrilla war, neither of which was true. Indeed, the guerrilla war, especially on the rebel side, was very much out of control and ran amok almost from the start.

Not that Americans in 1861 could have anticipated the chaos about to overwhelm them. No one foresaw settled communities becoming targets for destruction, neighbors killing neighbors, or soldiers acting as arsonists and executioners. Yet, for citizens caught in the snares of the conflict, this became the real war. For them, the battles and campaigns, in a very genuine sense, represented the sideshow. The rules of engagement excluded no one, and Americans spent much of the war trying to understand the sort of war that had engulfed them and seeking ways to tame its worst excesses. ·

ONE

CONFEDERATE PERCEPTIONS, 1861

As Union armies massed on their northern border in the spring of 1861, Confederate citizens found themselves in peril. They knew it would be weeks, perhaps months, before their nation's armies were outfitted, trained, and prepared to fight. Even then, there could not possibly be enough men to cordon off the entire Upper South, from Maryland and Virginia to Missouri and Arkansas. Indeed, Union troops marched into Maryland only days after the firing on Fort Sumter and rapidly swelled the federal presence in St. Louis. In between Maryland and Missouri sat Kentucky and Tennessee—two other slave states that had thus far refused to secede. That meant internal enemies, a fifth column of Southern Unionists that could undermine secession and pave the way for a Union military advance across the Ohio River.

Consequently, Confederates in endangered states mounted whatever resistance was possible to thwart military occupation and quash grassroots unionism. Most importantly, they turned to "irregular" warfare, a form of combat employed since the first Neanderthal hurled a rock at a bothersome neighbor or suspicious-looking intruder. In more recent days, it had allowed American colonists to defend their homes against hostile Indians, European foes, and, ultimately, the British Empire. Southerners, especially, recalled how such bold "partizans" as Francis Marion and Thomas Sumter had served the patriot cause.

Prominent citizens reminded people of their heritage and of the natural advantages of partisan resistance. Edmund Ruffin, the fire-eater who legend says fired the first shot at Fort Sumter, organized a home guard to defend his Virginia community "as a guerrilla force." Heartened by the response, he declared in June 1861, "It is only necessary for the people generally to resort to these means to overcome any invading army, even if we were greatly inferior to it in regular military force." Another Virginia fire-eater, George Fitzhugh, issued a national call to arms in the widely read *DeBow's Review.* He warned that if enemy troops gained the interior of the country, the Confederacy's "chief reliance . . . must be on irregular troops and partisan warfare."[1]

Even poets raised their voices. Reminding Southerners of their Revolutionary heritage, William Gilmore Simms, of South Carolina, published "King's Mountain" in mid-1861. The poem's narrative described the great American victory of 1780, but it was also meant to inspire a new partisan war:

> Swift snatching down the rifle from the wall,
> And, with the boarspear, and knife in belt,
> Grasp'd for the keen occasion; our brave men,
> Rose at the bugle's summons; o'er the hills
> Resounding lonely as an eagle's scream.

Toward the end of the year, Simms extolled the wisdom of the Confederacy's guerrilla war in "The Border Ranger":

> My rifle, pouch, and knife!
> My steed! And then we part!
> One loving kiss, dear wife,
> One press of heart to heart!
> Then for the deadliest strife,
> For freedom I depart!
> I were of little worth,
> Were these Yankee wolves left free
> To ravage 'round the hearth,
> And bring one grief to thee!

By then, Virginians, first in the line of fire along the Eastern seaboard, had answered the call. Spurred on as well by the Richmond press, hundreds of men volunteered for irregular service. They lacked most of the accouterments of war, many men being armed only with squirrel guns, knives, and hatchets, but they were resolved to defend their communities. There was no question of serving for pay. Their reward would be to see the Union army in flight.

While much of Virginia's war would be fought between Richmond and Washington, one of the most contentious and continuous focal points for the guerrilla war was in the northwest corner of the state. Populated by the largest block of antisecessionists in Virginia, but with a nearly equally determined core of Confederates, it became an early testing ground for citizens on both sides. That it also provided a convenient corridor for invading Union armies out of Ohio and Pennsylvania guaranteed that the blood would flow early and often.

Rebels and Unionists in Virginia formed guerrilla parties for protection, though, thanks to the arrival of the federal army in force, Unionists gained the early advantage. As one Union army officer recalled, "They worked their farms, but every man had his rifle hung upon his chimney-piece and by day or by night was ready to shoulder it, . . . and every neighborhood could muster its company or squad of homeguards to join in quelling seditious outbreaks." The Confederates, caught off guard by the swiftness of the revolt, feared for their lives. Unionists boasted "that there had never bin but one seceder and that was the devel and he . . . was Banished and that is the way that the secessionist aut to be done drove out of the commonwealth."[2]

Similar passions roiled on the western edge of the South. Missourians were accustomed to irregular warfare by 1861. They had been participating in just such a conflict between proslavery and antislavery forces in neighboring Kansas since 1856. The fighting between Kansas "jayhawkers" and Missouri's "border ruffians" had been so fierce in the 1850s because the outcome would define their way of life and decide the leadership of their communities. Ultimately, too, it was a matter of law and order, of suppressing a rival faction that threatened violence to one's family and property. The stakes were equally high in 1861.

The fact that Kansans, as Northerners, shared the spotlight in their territory's bloody struggle shows that Southerners did not hold a monopoly on guerrilla warfare, but when the Union army secured its hold on St. Louis and backed a pro-Union state government, Missouri Confederates were the first to respond. Irregular bands organized to burn bridges, rip up railroad tracks, and cut telegraph lines. Meriwether Jeff Thompson, who would instigate much of the partisan warfare to come, described the public mood. "[E]very Southern man in the State," he claimed, "from the Iowa line to Arkansas was picking his flint, cleaning his gun, and sharpening his knife to be ready for the coming storm." Thomas C. Reynolds, the ousted pro-Confederate lieutenant governor, informed President Jefferson Davis that the state's Southern men had vowed to throw Missouri "into a general revolution" and oppose the Federals in "a *guerilla* war."[3]

The situation in Missouri became even deadlier when Kansas jayhawkers exploited the chaos that summer. "They have a grudge against Missouri and the South," observed one Kansan of his neighbors, "that they will never forget until it is wiped out in blood." Raids across the border destroyed or confiscated all sorts of property, including, in the latter instance, slaves. While most Americans in 1861 saw the war as a contest between Union and secession, the majority of Kansans, having been at war against slavery since 1856, decided earlier than most Northerners that the national political divide could never be healed without slaying that beast. Jayhawkers such as Charles R. "Doc" Jennison and James Montgomery called themselves practical abolitionists, and all were well-versed in guerrilla warfare.[4]

While not so embroiled as Missouri, Kentucky held enormous political and military significance. For one thing, it was the birthplace of both Abraham Lincoln and Jefferson Davis, and so, for both sides, to control it was a point of pride. In purely military terms, Kentucky had enormous strategic advantages. With its Northern border formed by the Ohio River, the state obstructed invasion in either direction, but should it fall to the rebels, the lower Midwest would be up for grabs. "I think to lose Kentucky is nearly the same as to lose the whole game," Lincoln declared. "Kentucky gone, we can not hold Missouri, nor as I think, Maryland." Also worth noting, the value of Kentucky livestock, especially horses and mules, surpassed every other state in the Union. What complicated matters was a desire by Kentuckians to remain neutral, endorsing neither secession nor the Union. They had voted for John Bell in the presidential election of 1860, and saw no reason to become embroiled in a devastating war.[5]

Tennessee would play a role in Kentucky's fate, much as Kansas did in determining events in Missouri. Tennessee left the Union in June, delayed by a vocal Unionist population in the eastern third of the state. Not knowing which side Kentucky might eventually join, the Volunteer State required guerrilla defenders for the home front. "If the people are armed, and have powder, ball and caps *in their homes, ready for use*," emphasized one advocate, "they will rise *en masse* and the whole country will be filled with armed men to repel the enemy at every point." If need be, those same men could carry the war into Kentucky as effectively as columns of rebel soldiers. As early as May 1861, bands of Tennessee plunderers crossed the border to sack the railroad depot at Paducah. By summer, independent military commanders on both sides routinely entered Kentucky in search of recruits, weapons, and supplies.[6]

Confederates in the Deep South, if not immediately threatened by invasion, were so eager to join the action that they rushed to serve "as partisans . . . on the border." As a South Carolinian phrased it, "[W]e want to be destructive warriors." Even before his state seceded, another Carolinian, who had seen the effectiveness of guerrilla warfare while fighting jayhawkers in Bleeding Kansas, volunteered to raise a partisan company of up to 100 men. "[We will] do more effective service by hampering the enemy than could 1000 men by the usual mode," he vowed.[7]

A resident of Helena, Arkansas, located on the Mississippi River, recruited a company of 30 men to wage a "guerrila campaign" in Missouri. If the Federals could not be stopped in that state, he reasoned, Arkansas communities would then be endangered. A band of 50 Georgians vowed to go as far north as Tennessee to suppress rebellion and repel "vandal hordes of lawless men and unprincipled fanatics." Sixty-five Mounted Forest Rangers in that same state, armed with "country Rifles" and double-barrel shotguns, promised the same spirited response.[8]

Men unable or disinclined to rush to the border still wished to be doing *something*, anything, to engage actively in the nation's defense. A band of Louisianians, "mounted men, on the guerilla order," volunteered to patrol the state's southern parishes. In Georgia, a Guerrilla Corps of 45 men, armed with shotguns, was prepared to "meet the enemy on the *coast* . . . at a few hours notice." In Mississippi, companies of scouts patrolled the Gulf coast in anticipation of invasion.[9]

Texans, perhaps the people least threatened by invasion, were also keen to serve as guerrillas, and better prepared than anyone, save Missourians and Kansans, to wage war. Texas rangers had patrolled the frontier and guarded against Indian attacks as early as 1823, well before Texas became an independent republic or state. They became skilled guerrilla fighters by adopting the "art of plains warfare" from their foes. Texans had no ties to the American Revolution of 1776, but many of them recalled the Texas Revolution of 1836—an experience no less powerful than the memory of Francis Marion's partizans among seaboard Confederates. Consequently, if not preparing for frontier defense in their own state, scores of Texans volunteered to serve in more vulnerable parts of the South as "sort of Guerillas, like warriors, men of old times."[10]

But if this enthusiasm for guerrilla warfare grew mainly from apprehension about invasion, Confederates also knew to beware of internal enemies. Much of the political opposition came from the hill country of the Deep South. In Georgia, citizens reported "tories and traitors" lurking everywhere. "[S]ome of our countys, just above us, are now making threats . . . to plunder and devastate our little county town," declared one citizen. Home guards, "vigilance committees," and "guerilla companies" stood ready to quell insurrection. In the uplands of Alabama, divisions between pro- and antisecessionists were rooted in political battles of the 1830s.[11]

Slave rebellions posed another potential danger to public safety. A Georgia militia officer foresaw a crisis as early as June. "Our country is infested with runaway slaves," he reported to the governor, all of them armed. He knew of three camps of runaways with a combined 40 slaves. "Not a night passes," he swore, "that does not witness robbery from farms, smoke-houses etc. The ladies are very much frightened, as runaway negroes have committed two rapes & two murders the last week."[12]

People were also mindful of possible alliances between Unionists and slaves. "[I]t is thought by the most of people that the Negroes & Robers will Broke out and plunder and Steel," a worried Georgian insisted, "as there is a heep of Union men that says [they] will not fight for the south." A Louisianian feared an uprising in his state's Gulf parishes, where, he claimed, disloyal elements could not even speak English. They included "all sorts," he said, disreputable men who could be "bought and sold; negroes from different Southern States of ungovernable tempers ready for the blackest deeds, suitable fuel for the enemy."[13]

Here again guerrillas could be useful, for in many neighborhoods, they filled the role of antebellum slave patrols. Floridians formed home guards to monitor the "negro population" as early as May, when the first threats of violence surfaced. Georgians thought irregular companies an excellent way "to suppress any insurrection of Slaves or other hostile movements" against the citizenry. A band of Mississippians organized for the purpose of "repelling insurrection among the negroes."[14]

Unsettling evidence of the possibilities of internal conflict had appeared in parts of Missouri, Kentucky, and Virginia by the end of 1861. In Missouri, Unionist home guards and militia companies struck ruthlessly at rebels. Sounding very much like many aspiring Confederate irregulars, a resident of Hannibal asked permission from the U.S. War Department to raise a mounted battalion of 400 men to "ride the Scoundrels down from one side of our state to the other." When all the traitors had been forced from Missouri, he vowed, he would to "go thro Arkansas & eat green peas in New Orleans under the Stars & Stripes" by February.[15]

With rebel bushwhackers responding in kind, a vicious war of retaliation and counterretaliation had ensued by midsummer. A resident of southwest Missouri moaned to his absent wife, "Missouri is in a deplorable condition. We have civil war in our midst. We have union men & secessionists and there is a deadly hostility existing between them. . . . Men seem to have lost their reason and gone mad." A worried Edward Bates, the U.S. attorney general, warned Missouri's provisional Unionist governor, Hamilton R. Gamble that a "social war" would soon destroy the state. Julian Bates, a son of the attorney general, and on the scene, agreed. "There will be hard fighting in Mo," he informed his father, "[but] not between the soldiers, & in many of the Counties there will be ugly neighborhood feuds, which may long outlast the general war."[16]

This became the essence of the guerrilla war everywhere. Local control meant political dominance. This, in turn, meant ridding communities of both outsiders and wrong-headed neighbors. Neighborhood divisions sometimes went back to political and personal feuds begun years before the war. The violence unleashed and sanctified by war intensified those ancient quarrels, especially where the peace and security of a community were at stake.

Clearly, the political and military position of the South in 1861 cried out for guerrilla defenders, but something should also be said about the type of men who preferred this "irregular" service to life in the conventional army. Common wisdom once had it that guerrillas were cutthroats and ne'er-do-wells and that the guerrilla war was a breeding ground for the restless and disaffected, the paranoid and pathological. Such men most certainly joined the irregular war, but they could scarcely account for the large numbers that eventually participated. While the lack of such official records as enlistment papers, muster rolls, and discharges makes it impossible to create a profile of the typical guerrilla, the available evidence at least suggests that the majority were something less than homicidal brutes. The striking thing about many guerrillas, at least on the rebel side, was their respectable, middle-class status. Their bands included prosperous, educated, and respected leaders of the community. Many men also appear to have fought for well-considered political and economic reasons.

For example, in western Virginia, Pennsylvania-born Daniel Duskey was a 52-year-old farmer and justice of the peace when Union soldiers arrested him for being a guerrilla. Forty-two-year-old Perregrine "Perry" Hays, arrested as a notorious partisan, was a man of property, a former postmaster, and a former state legislator. Peter B. Rightor, in his mid-fifties, was a "well-to-do farmer and grazier." Only when his home was burned in June 1861 did he become a bushwhacker who thirsted for revenge. Over half of the 15 guerrillas in a Fayette County band came from landholding families and at least four of them were over 40 years old.[17]

In southeastern Missouri, a largely illiterate farmer named Sam Hildebrand had already shot or hanged a dozen men by 1864, but in that same year, a band of quite different bushwhackers was formed just north of his stamping grounds to protect families and property. Seventeen of those men owned between them 2,580 acres, an average of 152 acres per man, with all of the land valued at a minimum of two dollars per acre. Two of the men operated grist mills, and two more were preachers. Indeed, not a few Missourians joined the guerrilla ranks because they had been dispossessed of their lands by Unionist courts for their rebel sympathies. In western Missouri, on the border with Kansas, a former county sheriff, who would have served as an officer of such courts before the war, had become the captain of a 70-man "Bushwhacking party." A Union soldier who captured him judged the 30-year-old guerrilla chief to be "a man of great ability."[18]

Having struck it rich in the California gold rush, Peter Mankins was the richest man in the White River valley of Arkansas when the war started, but that did not stop the nearly 50-year-old farmer from becoming the oldest guerrilla chief in the state. While Arkansas's best-known guerrilla chief, William Martin "Buck" Brown, led a remarkably young band of followers, mostly in their late teens, he was in his mid-forties when the war started, the owner of a grist mill and several acres of land. One of the most renowned rebel guerrillas in Kentucky was M.J. Clarke, better known as "Sue Mundy." He came from a prominent family in Simpson County. His father was a former postmaster and leader of the state militia. An uncle had been a congressman and diplomat, and Clark was related by marriage to Virginia's most famous partisan chief, John S. Mosby, who himself came from a slaveholding family of the middling gentry.[19]

Later in the war, a Florida irregular waxed eloquent, if in somewhat florid style, about the devotion of his state's guerrilla fighters, regardless of age. "The grandfather vies with his offspring in deeds of valor, and the silver-haired patriarch, bowed with the weight of years, stands firmly by the side of his fair-haired boys in forming that solid phalanx, contending for all that is near and dear to them, and against which the combined forces of the enemy can not successfully combat," he exulted. Though "suddenly and hastily assembled," this "citizen soldiery" exhibited a patriotic spirit "never excelled in the annals of warfare."[20]

Beyond individual traits, group identity could influence a man's decision to take to the bush. For instance, given the important role guerrillas played in protecting their communities, it was only natural that kinship and family ties bound together both rebel and Unionist bands. "Kindred will be divided by the sword. Ancient friendships changed to bloody feuds," predicted a Virginian, and it was so. Peter Rightor, then, depended on both his own family and the Curry clan to form an effective band. The Williams clan, led by Thomas Jefferson Williams, formed the heart of an "independent" Union band in central Arkansas. On the other side of the Arkansas war, Union soldiers learned that when tracking bushwhackers, a likely place to capture them would be homes "allied to the clan."[21]

Guerrillas also prided themselves on being uniquely qualified for their work. They were all crack shots, it was said, whether with pistol or rifle. As experienced woodsmen, they could handle knives and hatchets, too. They were fit and rugged, "stout and active," accustomed to a hardy life. They considered themselves elite fighters, more skilled and daring than the average soldier, ready to perform "the most desperate service."[22]

A few women also joined the guerrilla war, and they did so openly, unlike those who disguised their sex in order to enlist in the armies. Some women took to the bush because a husband or lover had chosen that path. Sixteen-year-old Nancy Hart rode with the Moccasin Rangers in western Virginia because her boyfriend, 24-year-old Perry Connolly, led the band. Sarah "Kate" King, claiming to be the wife of one of the war's most notorious guerrillas, William Clarke Quantrill, did the same thing. Eighteen-year-old Sarah Jane Smith left her Arkansas home to join two male cousins in cutting Union telegraph lines. Many of these women and girls, like their male counterparts, often had romantic notions of what it meant to be a guerrilla, but that made them no less dangerous. Other women, choosing not to tout a pistol or prowl the countryside, sheltered and fed guerrillas, activities for which they, too, could be punished by the Federals.[23]

Service in a guerrilla company also appealed to men who bristled against the regimentation and discipline of conventional armies. The excitement and unfettered freedom of guerrilla operations contrasted sharply with the drill and routine of camp life. Most rebel guerrillas, observed one man, "preferred the free but more hazardous life of an independent soldier or scout, to the more irksome duties of the regularly organized forces of the Confederate Army." A band of Louisiana rangers expressed their desire to be unconnected to any formal military unit. An Arkansan spoke for them all when he said of the conventional army, "That kind of warfare did not suit me. I wanted to get out where I could have it more lively; where I could fight if I wanted to, or run if I so desired; I wanted to be my own general." A Virginian declared, "The life of a guerrilla is a dangerous one, but it has its charms. Its independence and freedom from restraint, and, above all, the opportunity for bold and daring actions, which carry with them personal renown, makes this life far preferable to a position in the regular army, where men stand up like posts to be shot at, and where there is little or no opportunity for the display of personal courage."[24]

Time and again, rebel guerrillas expressed their desire to remain independent, subject to the orders of no one "save the Genl in Chief." They called it fighting "on their own hook," and it was the most common refrain to be heard among them. As another man expressed the attitude in his band, "[W]e agreed to try our own generalship." A Texan insisted on "fiting the Skermishing fite in my own way." "Give us our mountain Rifles and our own mode of fight," claimed another man, "and we are secure." Another band rebelled openly when the local Confederate commander tried to force them into a conventional cavalry regiment, to be assigned where the government saw fit to place them. "This created a great deal of dissatisfaction amongst the boys," recalled one man; "for service in a local Partizan Regiment, for which they had enlisted, was very different from that in a regular corps."[25]

Then again, not a few men believed they had no choice but to serve their communities, if not their nation, as guerrillas. Once the Union army set up shop in their neighborhoods, perhaps restricting personal freedoms through martial law and exposing the population to unauthorized seizures of property, even men who wished to remain peaceably at home took action. Consider, for example, the 22-year-old Missouri soldier who, after being captured early in the war, took the Union oath of allegiance and returned to his farm. He fully intended, he later insisted, to honor that oath and to live as a "peaceable, law-abiding citizen." However, after being "constantly harassed, annoyed and threatened" by the Union authorities, even being required to post a $ 5,000 bond because he had been heard singing a pro-Confederate song, the man's patience wore thin. Finally, when the Federals threatened to arrest and incarcerate his female cousin if he did not enlist in a Unionist militia company, he broke his parole and joined a nearby guerrilla band. "I could not and I would not longer submit," he declared, "and I then resolved that if die I must, I would die fighting for my own people."[26]

So, Confederates everywhere, even in regions only threatened by the repercussions of war, saw the practical benefits of a guerrilla defense. It satisfied Southern instincts for survival, suited their heritage, complimented local traditions, and provided security for communities against a variety of foes—be they Yankee invaders, intransigent Unionists, or rebellious slaves. The only remaining questions were, how would the plan work in fact, and how would the Yankees respond?

TWO

GUERRILLAS AT WAR, 1861–1862

So, it was game on, as rebel guerrillas struck at both invaders and traitors. From one end of the border to the other, the irregular war commenced weeks before the first important conventional battles at Bull Run and Wilson's Creek. In some places, Unionists were the early targets. Elsewhere, the Union army was greeted by an elusive foe that would not stand and fight, but inflicted significant damage by hitting at its rear, its flanks, its supply lines, and its communications. By the end of 1862, military and political leaders on both sides found themselves entangled in a war they had not anticipated.

The gravest situation was in northwestern Virginia, where the Confederates risked losing control of their capital state. Having been defeated in a series of small, if fiercely fought, conventional battles, the rebel army retreated in July 1861. Confederate guerrillas gamely filled the breach against Unionist neighbors and the Union army. They also made it their business to undermine confidence in the U.S. government by disrupting the operation of local and state government. They attacked and destroyed post offices and county court houses, paying particular attention to public records in the latter places. Some bands waylaid sheriffs and tax collectors. Others threatened judges in hopes of bringing the entire legal system to its knees.

The onslaught demoralized many Union soldiers. They had not bargained on anything like this sort of fighting when enlisting to preserve the Union. Tangling with bushwhackers on their own ground was a damned "dangerous business." Any expedition against the rebels that escaped with only a half dozen killed or wounded considered itself lucky. A Pennsylvania soldier reported, "We have been learning our full share of the realities of this conflict rendered more terable in this section than any other from the savage and brutal mode in which it is waged by our enemies. . . . who carry on a war more barborous than any waged by the savages who once inhabited this same country."[1]

A future president of the United States, Maj. Rutherford B. Hayes, saw the guerrilla war at first hand in western Virginia. The road between his camp and the next closest one, some 100 miles away, was "so infested with 'bushwhackers'" that travel between the camps was considered "unsafe." Daily expeditions of 10–100 men tracked elusive bands for dozens of miles, but they could not end the persecution, robbery, and killings. Hayes believed the army needed "a regular system of scouring the country to get rid of these rascals."[2]

As the spring of 1862 approached, federal troops and Unionists in western Virginia worried that the large number of discharged and paroled Confederate soldiers rumored to be returning home could make matters worse. Unionists dreaded the prospect of these armed ex-soldiers swelling the ranks of local guerrilla bands. Should that happen, no one would be safe. Farmers feared being shot down at their plows. Communities petitioned politicians and army commanders to arrest and imprison discharged rebels for the duration of the war.

Even nature seemed to favor the guerrillas once spring arrived. As new foliage camouflaged their camps and concealed their movements, they could move freely against the Federals and serve the Confederate army more effectively as scouts and guides. One rebel soldier appreciated the advantage this gave "Bush-Whackers." "[T]here is quite a number . . . dressed in bark-dyed apparel with their long rifles and deer-skin pouches," he observed. "Well may the Yankees fear them for they rarely draw a bead and pull a trigger without bringing [down] a pigeon."[3]

A similar mixture of rebel guerrillas versus both Unionist guerrillas and Union soldiers characterized events in Kentucky and Tennessee. With neither the U.S. nor C.S. governments willing to let Kentucky remain neutral, both armies had marched in as liberators by September, and Kentucky's guerrilla war grew apace. Unionists were slow to react, but as independent bands of rebels sprung up to reinforce the Confederate forces, Kentuckians experienced the reality of civil war. Where Unionists did put up a fight, rebel bands responded promptly. "If the *tories* capture a patriot, he immediately takes one of the tories," an admirer said of one guerrilla captain. "If they take a patriot's property, he will take a like amount from a tory."[4]

The circumstances perfectly suited the most dangerous Confederate guerrilla in the Upper South, Champ Ferguson. The tall, slender, 40-year-old Kentucky farmer, owner of some 460 acres, had shot a county constable before the war, but that was nothing compared to the 53 men he would be accused of killing between 1861 and 1865. He and his men prowled as far north as the Ohio River, with occasional dashes into Alabama and Virginia. "[T]he mountains of Kentucky and Tennessee were filled with such men, who murdered every prisoner they took," observed one Confederate officer. Ferguson shot his first Unionist, a neighbor, in November 1861. He committed seven more murders over the next five months, although Champ always insisted that every man he shot, tortured, or dismembered had first threatened him.[5]

The border region of Kentucky, Tennessee, and western Virginia also bred a hybrid form of guerrilla warfare, as several men who began the war as guerrilla captains graduated, as it were, to become conventional cavalry commanders. Interestingly, most of them, having learned the value of guerrilla tactics, continued to use them, which often blurred the line between irregular and conventional warfare. Best-known of this group was Tennessee planter, slave trader, and businessman Nathan Bedford Forrest. Entering the war as the head of a battalion of guerrillas, he became one of the Confederacy's most successful conventional cavalry commanders. Alabama-born merchant John Hunt Morgan was even more of a chameleon. Having begun the war as captain of an independent company, he too entered the conventional army, but his destructive raids along the border earned him the sobriquets "Bandit Morgan" and the "Highwayman of Kentucky." Novels were written about his exploits, and admiring rebels anointed him "the Marion of the War."[6]

Albert G. Jenkins and Turner Ashby were other members of this club. Jenkins, a Harvard-educated, ex-congressman, had been captain of the Border Rangers before becoming colonel of the 8th Virginia Cavalry. He would conduct raids throughout western Virginia and into Ohio. Ashby, a failed merchant and small farmer in Virginia, led a company of partisans that became part of the 7th Virginia Cavalry, with him serving as the regiment's colonel. Even then, while operating mainly in the Shenandoah Valley, his regiment's weapon of choice remained the Bowie knife, not the cavalry saber.[7]

Meantime, rebel guerrillas kept Confederate hopes alive in Missouri when Sterling Price's army retreated into northwest Arkansas. Union soldiers and the tories in Missouri faced hundreds, perhaps thousands, of guerrillas—the numbers swollen, as in northwest Virginia, by men whose enlistments in the conventional army had expired. Expeditions sent to scatter them rarely succeeded, mainly because the elusive bands, generally no larger than a few dozen men, simply vanished. Being mostly local farmers, they returned home to pose as peaceful citizens. Union soldiers thought them cowardly.

That did not make the levels of violence and brutality in Missouri anything less than frightening. One captured rebel, accused of hanging a Unionist, justified his crime by saying he wanted "to see one union man shit his last dieing turd." A gang of men kidnapped a "d__d Black Republican" and left his dead body lying in the road near his home. When the man's wife found the corpse, the entire upper body had been riddled by bullets, "his head and face . . . all shot to pieces."[8]

Raids out of Kansas continued to breed chaos, too. One of the most destructive onslaughts, led by Charles Jennison, carved a swath through the western part of Missouri in late 1861 and early 1862. "Playing war is played out," Jennison declared, as his men confiscated or destroyed the property of known rebels. A single resident of Westport lost $10,000 in moveable property, including eight slaves.[9]

However, far from cowing rebel citizens along the border, these jayhawker raids, as well as attempts by Missouri militia units to force order, only convinced more men to join the irregular war. With their property and persons seemingly threatened on all sides, men who had hoped to sit out the war now saw the futility of that prospect. Either financial or physical destruction seemed certain if they did not lend a hand in their own defense.

William C. Quantrill, a 24-year-old drifter from Ohio who had lived in both Kansas and Missouri before the war, was determined to defend his new Missouri home. After fighting with conventional troops in Missouri, he joined a home guard in March 1862 to protect Confederate citizens on the Missouri border from jayhawker raids out of Kansas. By July, the charismatic killer led his own band of 200 men. They operated mostly in Missouri but struck several times at Unionist civilians and Union soldiers in Kansas. The Federals initially dismissed Quantrill as a mere outlaw, but the rebel communities he protected regarded him as a hero. "He is exemplifying what one desperate, fearless man can do," proclaimed one enamored woman.[10]

Many of Quantrill's band were restless youths, mostly in their teens, who saw the war as an adventure and guerrilla warfare as a form of blood sport. The slightly older George Todd, a 20-year-old Canadian-born stone mason who became Quantrill's chief lieutenant, was nonetheless "hot tempered" and "callously brutal." Twenty-two-year-old William Anderson, known as "Bloody Bill," decorated his horse's bridle and saddle with Yankee scalps. Yet, these men also understood the political ramifications of the war. Some of them had even opposed secession. They also understood the financial consequences if their communities spiraled downward into chaos as a result of the war. With most of them coming from prosperous, middle-class farming families, not a few owning slaves, they vowed to protect their property and maintain social order.[11]

Regardless of their financial stake in the war, most Missouri guerrillas appear to have been motivated by a desire for vengeance and a determination to be the paladins of their communities. The captain of an irregular band operating along the Platte River, north of Kansas City, publicly proclaimed his reasons for becoming a guerrilla in November 1861. "I am charged with being a Bandit and Robber," decried 26-year-old Silas Gordon. "Such is not my position. I am acting in defense of the certain and legitimate rights of myself and neighbors against wrongdoers, coming from whatever quarter they may. As far as I am able I will punish thieves and robbers. I do not propose interfering with the movement of Federal troops, legitimately made; but I will oppose armed forces passing through or being quartered in our County, for the purpose of molesting our citizens, or taking their property."[12]

Other Missouri rebels seemed less likely candidates for the guerrilla war. Born in Philadelphia 31 years before the war, Henry M. Cheavens was reared mostly in Illinois and Missouri. Following a classical secondary education in St. Louis and college in New England, he was working in Missouri as a school teacher in 1861. Enlisting with Sterling Price, he was severely wounded at the battle of Wilson's Creek in August 1861. When he recovered 10 months later, Missouri's Unionist government tried to conscript him. Cheavens promptly joined one of several rebel guerrilla bands near his home in Boone County.

His new companions, numbering about 100, had hoped to join Col. John C. Porter's mixed regiment of conventional troops and irregulars. However, when a regiment of Missouri cavalry, led by the Union "guerrilla-hunter" Col. Oden Guitar, forced Porter out of the region, the guerrillas temporarily disbanded. Each man found refuge with a loyal rebel family, to enjoy, briefly at least, a bit of easy living.

"We were most of the time in the woods and had a different encampment every day," Cheavens reported once the band reunited, "[s]leeping and eating during the day while the night was occupied by traveling from place to place." They paused long enough to elect a "brave but rash" young man named Purcell as their captain and proceeded to re-arm themselves. Two weeks later, hoping to release rebel sympathizers being held at Columbia, the band raced into town at mid-morning "with a whoop and a yell," broke open the jail, released the prisoners, captured a U.S. flag (later shredded to provide mementoes of the occasion), and dashed away with 100 horses. Only one shot was fired, and that by a fleeing detachment of Federals.

The band could not celebrate for long. With Guitar's cavalry in pursuit, the company again disbanded. Cheavens found harbor with several different families this time. Whenever U.S. patrols grew thick, he took to the bush so as not to implicate his protectors. The entire band remained quiet until October 1862, when, in trying once more to join Porter's command, they were spotted by a federal patrol. The guerrillas raced for the hills, dismounted, and positioned themselves to bushwhack their pursuers. A stiff gun battle ensued; the rebels fled. Stopping after some four or five miles, they counted their losses as one dead, three wounded, and several missing, including Captain Purcell. They disbanded once more, this time for a month, only to have their camp when they reassembled. Four guerrillas were killed and several others wounded. Cheavens escaped but was captured by Missouri militiamen four days later. He was eventually exchanged, but his career as a guerrilla had ended.[13]

Long before then, the guerrilla war had spread both southward and northward from Missouri. Looking to the south, Union troops had pursued the Confederate army into Arkansas and defeated it at the battle of Pea Ridge on March 7–8, 1862. Within weeks, the rebels, led by Gen. Earl Van Dorn, abandoned the state to operate in Mississippi. Rebel communities would have been defenseless were it not for scattered guerrilla bands and local militia companies, harassed the Union army mercilessly as it marched toward the state capital of Little Rock. Advancing through the mountainous and often densely wooded terrain, Union soldiers disappeared daily, and their often-mutilated bodies were later found lying in the woods or swamps.

As with Union soldiers elsewhere, these advancing Federals feared and loathed their new opponents. "We are going down to the Mo. and Arkansas line again," an Ohio cavalryman informed a family member. "I was shot at the last time and this time I may not be so lucky, for we think out here we would rather be in a big fight than to be shot at when we are going along the road." An Illinois soldier tried to reassure his wife that the guerrillas posed no threat, but he was well aware that some 20 men in his regiment had been bushwhacked in a matter of weeks, and he would "rather be killed in battle than to be shot from behind a tree by these marauding bands of desperadoes."[14]

Union officers confessed their inability to halt the onslaught. The colonel of an Illinois regiment, reporting that one of his men had been "murdered in cold blood" by lurking rebels, had no idea how to combat such a "bitter and malignant spirit." Seeking advice from his commanding officer, he said, "I wish to know what course to pursue with regard to the guerrillas in this country, and hope you will issue a proclamation telling the people hereabouts what they may expect in case they continue to commit murders as heretofore."[15]

However, the Union situation worsened in late May, when Gen. Thomas C. Hindman arrived in Arkansas to restore Confederate defenses. Wisely, he made the guerrillas part of his plan. Actively recruiting independent companies of 10 or more men, Hindman told his guerrillas that they would have to arm themselves, and they would receive pay and allowances only for subsistence and forage. However, once sanctioned, the men could "commence operations against the enemy" on their own terms.[16]

Hindman urged his irregulars to create as much chaos and inflict as much destruction as possible. They were to "cut off Federal pickets, scouts, foraging parties, and trains, and to kill pilots and others on gunboats and transports, attacking them day and night, and using the greatest vigor." They did all of that and more, even extending their operations into southern Missouri. "There has been more done and with fewer men than any other part [of the country]," one satisfied guerrilla informed his wife from northern Arkansas. "So it does not require many men to harass a considerable army. . . . It is very exciting to be in the enemy's country not knowing what moment we will be attacked." The Federals soon abandoned the march on Little Rock and settled for occupying Helena.[17]

Looking north from Missouri, parts of Iowa became engulfed by the guerrilla war. Rebel sympathizers, mostly people whose families had emigrated from the South, threatened violence to the families of departed Union soldiers, preached rebellion against the United States, and assisted rebel guerrillas who slipped across the border. Confirmed reports and wild rumors alike had rebel raiders stealing horses, robbing banks, and burning homes.

Iowans stood their ground. Their governor created a border guard, while hundreds of independent irregular bands headed for Missouri. Rather than awaiting the next invasion, they had decided to join forces with Unionists in Missouri and make a fight of it there, even if armed only with "knives, hatchets, and clubs."[18]

East of the Mississippi, the war spilled into other parts of the Midwest. Communities in Illinois, Indiana, and Ohio had worried this would happen, especially when the roof fell in on Kentucky. They now wasted no time posting home guards and militia companies along the Ohio River, ready to oppose "any surprise from . . . Kentucky." Indiana's governor appealed for protection to Washington. "They are in deadly fear that marauding parties from the other side of the river will plunder and burn their towns," he said of his people. With no means of defending themselves, they lived "in a state of intense alarm." Acknowledging the crisis, the War Department assigned gunboats to protect commercial shipping on the Ohio River and prevent river crossing. Soldiers were dispatched to one of the most volatile spots in the Midwest, that part of southern Illinois known as "Little Egypt," centered on Cairo. Even then, loyal people slept with rifles near at hand, still expecting to have their "property stolen, houses burned, & union men murdered."[19]

The worst fears of Midwesterners were nearly realized in July 1862, when John Morgan's brigade conducted a 27-day, 1,000-mile raid through Kentucky. Driving to within 50 miles of Cincinnati, they captured and paroled more than 1,200 Union soldiers, and the emergency forced a Union army in Tennessee to abandon its march toward Chattanooga. Ohioans, so near seeing their Queen City ravished, turned out in droves to resist the invasion.

Strange to say, then, that despite the apparent success of rebel guerrillas, the Confederate government expressed reservations about the irregular war. In the early months of fighting, guerrillas had been extremely useful in checking invading armies, distracting the Federals, disrupting Union strategies, injuring Northern morale, and forcing the reassignment of Union soldiers and resources to counter guerrilla threats to railroads and river traffic. It seemed an ideal solution for a nation about to be invaded by superior numbers; but by the end of 1861, Southern opposition to the scheme had begun to mount.

Many politicians and generals had never been comfortable with guerrilla warfare, particularly men who had graduated from West Point. Everything they knew about victorious generals, from Julius Caesar to Napoleon Bonaparte, reinforced the idea that wars were won by large conventional armies fighting grand, climatic battles. To continue to rely too heavily on irregular forces seemed like a waste of manpower and resources. Equally, there was the difficulty of controlling and coordinating an irregular war waged by independent bands.

These theoretical concerns had been validated for many of the same men by their experiences fighting Indians and Mexicans in the decades before the war. Here, the issue became one of civilized versus uncivilized warfare. Robert E. Lee dismissed Mexican "greasers" as thieves and cowards "who had not the courage to fight . . . lawfully." Jefferson Davis had learned the same lessons.

American conceptions of democracy helped to shape these impressions. Rebel leaders in both the government and the army were, at the very least, ambivalent about the benefits of an unregulated people's republic. John C. Calhoun's fears about the tyranny of the majority had long been a cornerstone of Southern political thought, and whatever the elitist inclinations among rebel leaders, the exigencies of war could only exaggerate them. They could see no greater danger to their own authority or to Southern ideals of honor and manhood than an uncontrollable irregular army of backwoodsmen and crackers. If nothing else, the practical necessity of maintaining military discipline throughout the army meant that men such as Lee and Davis were unlikely to put much faith in a guerrilla war.[20]

There was also the image of the Confederate nation to be considered. What would countries such as England, which the Confederacy hoped to woo as an ally, think of them if they waged war in this fashion? It could only remind them of the "rabble in arms" that had broken with the empire four score years earlier. A sizeable portion of the British public still looked askance at American democracy. When British journalist William Howard Russell requested of Davis a passport that would protect him should he "fall in with some guerilla leader" as he traveled northward from Montgomery, Alabama, the president complied but told Russell that he exaggerated the danger. "[S]ir," the president reminded him, "you are among civilised, intelligent people who understand your position, and appreciate your character."[21]

All of this led the rebel government to limit the scope and intensity of the guerrilla war. At first, it tried to discourage the formation of guerrilla bands in the Deep South, where the need for them seemed slight. As early as May 1861, the secretary of war rejected applications for service by several companies of rangers. In June, Jefferson Davis told a hopeful company of Alabamians that they could not be accepted "if the term guerrilla implies independent operations." That same month, the secretary of war told an applicant, "The Department will not be likely to have any immediate use for mounted men organized at remote points from the scene of military operations." By July, General Lee informed his subordinates that the recruitment of more guerrillas was "not deemed advisable by the President."[22]

The government was even reluctant to accept men for irregular service on the border. The War Department rejected companies that did not have at least 64 men, could not provide their own weapons, or were unwilling to enlist for at least 12 months. Just as importantly, it rarely granted volunteers the independent status they sought. All men must serve where needed, President Davis insisted. The War Department informed one enthusiastic group that it would be "attached to a command deemed proper by the Government. . . . an Independent Company [being] altogether inadmissible."[23]

The government drove home its message through the remainder of 1861, but by that time, things had gone too far, The guerrilla war was in full swing, and the politicians and generals, whatever their desire, could not simply forbid it. The best they could do was contain the guerrilla conflict and control their overly-enthusiastic guerrilla warriors. Toward that end, Henry C. Burnett of Kentucky urged the Confederate Senate in April 1862 to pass a bill that would "facilitate the raising of guerrilla companies." The Committee on Military Affairs considered several proposals, but finally settled on one submitted by John Scott, a former editor of *Richmond Whig*. His plan, probably solicited by Sen. William B. Preston of Virginia, who opposed the use of irregulars but who would have seen Scott's measure as a way to limit their use, called for a system of strictly-controlled, government-sanctioned guerrillas, to be "mustered into the regular service" and used for "detached service."[24]

The resulting Partisan Ranger Act, passed after a week-long debate, gave President Davis exclusive authority to commission officers and authorize partisan units. Additionally, these irregular troops would be "subject to the same regulations as other soldiers." Chillingly, the original bill would have rewarded rangers with a "premium of five dollars per head on every one of the enemy killed." Instead, they would be allowed to retain any livestock and provisions acquired during their operations for their own use. Scott called it the "application of the prize principle of nautical warfare to land war."[25]

Politicians and newspaper editors across the South praised the new law, and ever more men rushed to enlist, though too often without appreciating the significance of the word "partisan." Harkening back to the days of the Revolution, the government hoped to instill the irregular war with a dignity and restraint it had hitherto lacked. Southerners understood the connotations, too, as many of the earliest volunteers for irregular service, back in the spring and summer of 1861, had sought permission to raise companies, battalions, and regiments of "partisans" and "rangers."

However, in responding to the new rush of volunteers, the War Department stressed the strict limits of the legislation. Even though authorized by Richmond, partisan ranger companies must ultimately be approved by district commanders, who would also decide where, when, and to what extent they would be used. "The object of this rule," generals were reassured, "is both to restrict the number of such Corps within the actual wants of the service, and to ensure the selection of suitable persons for such commissions." Similarly, Secretary of War George W. Randolph told a Virginia colonel, "The Partizan service is considered as subordinate to the general service.... To have two independent armies, conducting two independent systems of warfare in the same field, would lead to inevitable confusion and disaster."[26]

The confusion came anyway. Hundreds of soldiers tried to resign from the army in order to join the partisan corps, which was not at all what the government intended. Similarly, Congress erred by passing the Partisan Ranger Act at the same time it established national conscription. Many men mistakenly thought this gave them a choice between service in the conventional army and the ranger. The government had also intended for all guerrillas to operate under the new legislation, but the vast majority of existing bands had no intention of sacrificing their independent status.

Worst of all, as far as any hope of regulating the guerrilla war was concerned, untold numbers of regular soldiers, whether or not enlisting as partisan rangers, began leaving the army to join the irregular war. Their reasoning were irrefutable. When Arkansans fighting in Tennessee or Mississippians fighting in Virginia received letters from home or read newspaper accounts describing the plight of their communities under Union occupation, they decided that their first loyalty was to family, friends, and neighbors. Even men who remained with the army were sorely tempted to desert, and understood the reasoning of comrades who did head for home. "Uncle Dick gives a gloomy account of things & your family in New Madrid," a Missourian told his father from Mississippi. He found it hard to believe that the Federals would "punish innocent persons," as was told him, simply because he had joined the rebel army, but it made him consider his options. "For our family's Sake," he said, "I would prefer going in a Gurrilla Company—what do you think of it—all we want now is a clear field & plenty of Jack Morgans."[27]

It took a few months for the Richmond government to grasp these problems, most especially the imaginative interpretations of the conscription act. Not until the end of July did the War Department plug several large loopholes. Thereafter, men eligible for conscription or serving in the army were barred from the rangers. Additionally, the minimum age for ranger service became 35 years. Congress, following another intense debate over the value of irregulars in August and September, agreed that rangers should not be organized in districts that had not filed their quotas for the volunteer army. The changes should have reassured Confederate leaders that the situation was under control, but questions continued to arise among both politicians and generals about how to wage a mixed conventional and guerrilla war.

Though passed to help regulate the guerrilla war in the Upper South, the Partisan Ranger Act was also born just in time to help newly-endangered regions of the nascent nation. By mid-1862, the need for a disciplined, efficient irregular war in North Carolina, Alabama, Mississippi, and Louisiana had become clear.

The Union army had only a tenuous hold in North Carolina, confined largely to coastal towns, but a sizeable Unionist population required surveillance by the state government and local communities. Some 4,000 Unionists (plus 5,000 blacks) joined the Union army in North Carolina, but at least that many more men stayed home to fight an irregular war. The state formed six regiments of partisan rangers and twice that number of companies and battalions. In addition, numerous independent companies remained in the field. So, while Confederate troops were left to handle their Union counterparts, rebel irregulars tried to hold the Unionists in check.

Quite apart from the Union army, the eastern part of North Carolina held large pockets of "Buffaloes," as the state's Unionists were known. The first bands formed in August 1862 in Hertford County, where a hard-drinking Confederate deserter named John A. "Jack" Fairless organized a disparate crowd of deserters, fugitive slaves, draft dodgers, and "lawless white men" to resist the rebel government. Fairless's brutality and drunken behavior soon alienated even this tough crowd, with one of the band killing him in October 1862, but the Buffaloes posed an ongoing threat to life and limb among rebel citizens.[28]

The clash was even more severe in the central and western parts of the state, where hills and mountains provided ideal terrain for guerrilla warfare. The western counties experienced the most travail, largely because Unionists and deserters there could join forces with like-minded men in East Tennessee to establish their own domain. Confederate militias, county sheriffs, and conscript officers were warned to stay clear. "[I]f yo ever hunt for us a gin I will put lead in you god dam your hell fired soll," three fugitives warned a conscript officer. "[Y]o have give the people orders to shoot us down when they find us and if yo dont take your orders back i will shoot yo. . . . [W]e have never done yo any harms for yo to hunt for us [but] we will give yo something to hunt us for here after."[29]

As Union troops gained a foothold in the northern parts of Alabama and Mississippi, Unionists were emboldened to act as couriers and guides for the Federals. Men and women provided information about local roads and terrain, or informed provost marshals about the loyalties of their neighbors. Over 2,500 Alabamians eventually joined the Union army, despite the danger of retaliation against themselves or their families. Other Unionists followed the pattern of the Upper South by forming local companies to protect families and communities against rebel guerrillas.

Rebels in Mississippi responded more decidedly than in Alabama to Union occupation. "Now is the time for bushwhacking and the black flag," declared one newspaper. Among the first to respond was William C. Falkner, great-grandfather of the 20th-century novelist. The colorful Falkner had been a politician, planter, and lawyer, served in the Mexican War, and twice been acquitted of murder. When the war came, he commanded a volunteer infantry regiment until it reformed in April 1862. He then recruited 600 partisans, most of them from his home of Tippah County, who vowed to fight invaders "to the death." So too Capt. Isham J. Warren and his company of Mississippi Partisan Rangers, which became especially adept at capturing Union wagon trains.[30]

Louisiana Confederates found themselves in the toughest fix. Following the fall of New Orleans and Baton Rouge, in April–May 1862, Gen. Mansfield Lovell, Confederate commander in the state, had no option but to supplement his small army with partisan rangers. It was the only way he could "contain the enemy in New Orleans and protect the state from his ravages." Governor Thomas O. Moore endorsed the plan and appealed to loyal rebels to help defend the state. "Let every citizen be an armed sentinel to give warning of any approach of the insolent foe," he urged. "Let all our river-banks swarm with armed patriots to teach the hated invader that the rifle will be his only welcome on his errands of plunder and destruction." When, in late May, Lovell and his conventional troops were ordered to Mississippi, partisan rangers and independent guerrillas became the state's only defense.[31]

So, the guerrilla war had reached a critical point across nearly the entire South by the end of 1862. Partly from desperation, partly from a recognition of its value, the Confederate government had committed itself to at least a limited partisan war. The U.S. government was more coy. While tolerating the activities of jayhawkers out of Kansas, and allowing the formation of local defense companies in the lower Midwest, its War Department had declined to sanction an irregular campaign. Not only that, but it began to protest the rebels' guerrilla war in no uncertain terms.

THREE

BEING A GUERRILLA

If the motivation for becoming a guerrilla differed from the reasons men enlisted in the conventional army, it was also true that guerrillas and soldiers experienced the war in very different ways. Not only were guerrillas less formal in their organization and less disciplined in their behavior, but they also dressed differently from regular soldiers, used different weapons, fought differently, even ate and slept differently. In other words, they were irregular in every conceivable way.

Not that it is easy to piece together the details of everyday life in a guerrilla band. Independent guerrilla captains seldom kept the type of official written records, such as muster rolls or equipment requisitions, required in the conventional army—what might be called the *paper* army. They did not even submit after-action or casualty reports to explain exactly who, when, and where they were fighting. The paper trail is somewhat better for partisan rangers, who, as explained, were more firmly tethered to the regular forces. Yet, even then, few diaries and little private correspondence written by guerrillas have survived, as they have done by the wagonload for conventional soldiers.

Several circumstances explain the lack of correspondence, if not of diaries. First, and most essentially, because guerrillas generally operated near their own communities, they were in frequent contact with friends and families members. They simply had no need to write letters. Second, in the case of rebel guerrillas, which will be the focus here, the Confederate postal service was abysmal. When a man did serve far from home, the most reliable way of getting a letter across the country was through the army mail, but independent guerrillas were seldom in touch with the armies. Third, guerrillas were constantly on the move, far more so than conventional soldiers, who had comparatively more leisure time to write. This may also explain the scarcity of guerrilla diaries. The families of guerrillas, that is, the potential recipients of their letters, were also more likely to be on the move. As will be seen, they were more often the targets of Union retaliation than were the families of conventional soldiers. Many had their homes burned; others were forced into exile. Even if letters had been sent to them, the likelihood of their receiving the correspondence would be dicey.

Nonetheless, the point to be stressed here is that, despite the paucity of wartime observations of rebel guerrilla life, the available sources provide quite a vivid picture. For instance, the Union provost marshal reports and the military commission transcripts of trials for captured guerrillas provide testimony from both the guerrillas and their enemies concerning the activities of guerrilla bands and the attitudes of individual guerrillas toward the war and their roles in it. Similarly, if paradoxically, the letters and diaries of Union soldiers and sailors who found themselves pitted against rebel guerrillas provide valuable information concerning irregular operations. Newspapers are helpful for their descriptions of guerrilla actions, debates concerning the value of guerrilla warfare, and occasionally, published letters or statements by the guerrillas themselves.

Nor are the postwar reminiscences and memoirs of the guerrillas themselves to be ignored. Clearly, accounts of guerrilla life written decades after the war, like any wartime recollection, may be self-serving and less accurate than observations made at the time. As will be shown in the Epilogue of this book, rebel guerrillas often used their postwar writings to justify the irregular war. It is also true that two very particular groups of Confederate irregulars produced the bulk of the published memoirs—partisan rangers serving under John S. Mosby and the independent guerrillas of William C. Quantrill. Placed against the tens of thousands of participants in the irregular war, the combined number of men in these two commands represented a fraction of the whole. In Missouri alone, there were at least another dozen guerrilla bands besides the one led by Quantrill. Yet, if used judiciously, these reminiscences can fill many of the gaps left by other historical sources, and so, tell us something of guerrilla life throughout the South.[1]

All that said, the life of a rebel irregular depended to some extent on whether he was an independent guerrilla, government-sanctioned partisan ranger, or lone bushwhacker. For instance, in the matter of dress, the outstanding distinction between rangers and other irregulars was that they were expected to wear "something gray," if not regulation Confederate uniforms. Bushwhackers and guerrillas had no sartorial code. It may be assumed that lone bushwhackers, about whom we know the least, appeared for all the world like ordinary farmers, which is what they wanted Union authorities to think. "I do not remember ever to have seen a bushwhacker wearing a Confederate uniform," declared one of Quantrill's men. Rather, he said, they all wore "plain citizen's clothes." Yet, given the length of the war, and the wear and tear on their clothing, it was more often true that men wore a patch-work of whatever garments came to hand, "dressed partly in soldier and partly in citizen garb."[2]

One exception to the plain garb of some Missouri guerrillas, chiefly among Quantrill's men, was the "guerrilla shirt." Generally made by wives or sweethearts, these garments were as meaningful to their wearers as was a "tartan . . . to the [Scottish] Highlander." Some shirts were brightly colored or elaborately embroidered, others made of somber, subdued tones or "homespun butternut." Although they do not appear to have been adopted outside Missouri, the shirts provided an extra layer of warmth during the cooler seasons. Some men were also partial to checkered pants, although these were probably exhibited more often when sitting for a photographer than when fighting in the bush. Indeed, surviving photographs of Missouri guerrillas compound the difficulty of generalizing, as the men posed in a variety of fancy wear, including their Sunday best.[3]

If not as fancy, other distinctive pieces of guerrilla garb worn in winter or against the elements were dusters and long, close-fitting overcoats. Some Union militiamen, having captured a guerrilla possessed of the latter, prized it as much as the pistols, pocket watches, and cash they also took from their prisoners. One such lucky fellow suggested that this "surtout" be "sent to the cabinet of curiosities and preserved as a 'rare specimen' for the benefit of after ages."[4]

Members of Mosby's command, being restricted in their dress by regulations, revealed their inner dandy by adding gold braid, buff trimmings, and gilt buttons to their uniform coats. Nonetheless, surviving photographs of these and other partisan rangers seldom betray striking affectations. They are nearly always dressed in some variation of the regulation Confederate uniform. Mosby set the standard, his only reported variation from the prescribed uniform being an occasional preference for blue pants with a yellow or gold cord along the outer seam to accompany a double-breasted grey frock coat.[5]

Cavalry boots and spurs—prerequisites for all men who operated on horseback—completed the uniform, although a slouch hat usually complemented the ensemble. Many men, both guerrillas and rangers, crowned their hats with one or more fancy feathers or plumes, with ostrich feathers being a favorite. One of Mosby's rangers claimed that his leader sported a foot-and-half-long black plume. A member of Quantrill's band recalled specifically the preference for black felt hats, while the trademark of another group of Missourians was "a badge of red around the hat crown." Small wonder guerrillas described themselves as "gayly dressed."[6]

Hair styles often distinguished government-sanctioned rangers from independent guerrillas. Whether by design or circumstance, the latter could be shockingly shabby in appearance, their long hair and scruffy beards adding to their image as wild, untamed creatures. The "hair of each man was allowed to grow six to eight inches in length," reported one of Quantrill's men, "being brushed straight back from the forehead, the ends reaching the top of the shoulders." Of course, that would hardly have been an unusual style among Civil War soldiers, including such generals as George A. Custer and George E. Pickett, and while partisan rangers may have been held to higher standards of grooming than the bushwhackers, a young recruit in Mosby's battalion recalled with chagrin that his close cropped hair "added nothing" to his "favor."[7]

Facial hair, grown or trimmed at will, was also used by some prominent guerrillas to disguise themselves, although a more notorious subterfuge was the wearing of Union uniforms to deceive the enemy. Partisan rangers took exception to the suggestion that they would stoop so low as to don the enemy's clothes. One man did admit to resorting to using heavy Union overcoats, captured from enemy cavalry, in winter, but only because the Confederate government was unable to provide such comfort. In fact, there were cases where partisan rangers, especially in the West, used Union uniforms as readily as any independent guerrilla to get the drop on the Federals. Generally, though, government partisans "never masqueraded," as one of Mosby's men put it, in federal uniforms. Besides which, they were well aware that any rebel caught wearing Union blue in the enemy's country would surely be shot as a spy.[8]

On the contrary, Mosby's men claimed to despise Union soldiers who came in search of them dressed in Confederate gray. The most notorious such unit was Jessee's Scouts, a band of antiguerrilla hunters (more about them later) first organized by John C. Frémont for service in Missouri (and named for his high-spirited wife), but later employed by him as well in western Virginia. A rebel sympathizer who detested the tactics of Jessie's Scouts said they used the disguise to take prisoners and learn the political sentiments of people in her neighborhood. She was delighted, then, to report an occasion when a larger Union cavalry detachment, not recognizing them for friends, fired on the Scouts. "This created a panic," laughed the woman, "wounded two and they were severely reproached by the Major of the larger force for being dressed in gray."[9]

Other rebel irregulars were not as fastidious. Again, using Quantrill's band as typical, they routinely wore captured Union attire in order to lure unsuspecting Federals into an ambush or trap. Approaching one of their patrols on horseback, the rebels would canter up as they waved and smiled, only to whip out their revolvers and mow down or demand the surrender of the unsuspecting troopers. They might also dress in blue to enter a Union-occupied town or simply to pass through the countryside of an occupied region. Quantrill and two of his men reportedly entered the town of Hannibal dressed as Union officers in order to purchase ammunition. Playing a similar game, two Arkansans found it relatively easy to fool the Federals. Dressed in "the blue clothes" they used for such missions, "[We] conducted ourselves in such a careless way we were never suspected of being Confederates." John Hunt Morgan's men, who often operated as irregular cavalry, also wore blue uniforms to pass through Union territory. Another man insisted that so many guerrilla bands resorted to this disguise that "they were compelled to have some way by which they could know each other when they met." Otherwise, "they would have had many fights among themselves."[10]

Whatever the cut or color of his uniform, the guerrilla wore a revolver strapped to his waist—the weapon of choice for independent guerrillas and partisan rangers. Most men carried at least two pistols, the general preference being either the .44 caliber Army or .36 caliber Navy Colt. Both weapons were prized for being rugged and reliable in all weather. Some men carried as many as four six-shooters, two on their belt and another pair in saddle holsters. Despite the fact that virtually all irregulars were horsemen, few of them carried sabers. They nearly all carried knives, often monstrous Bowie knives, but sabers, to be used effectively, required close instruction and much practice, and as one partisan ranger remarked, "[W]e had no knowledge of the first principles of cavalry drill, and could not have formed in a straight line had there ever been any need for our doing so." Besides, most men considered swords to be obsolete, and that life could best be preserved in the close combat that marked nearly all irregular warfare by quick, accurate shooting.[11]

One of John Mosby's men claimed that after one fight with Union cavalry, the rangers kept the pistols they had so captured, but threw away the sabers and carbines, discounting them as "weapons we had no use for." Mosby himself wrote at length about the combat value of revolvers in his memoirs, and attributed much of his success to the weapon. When engaging Union cavalry, Mosby always tried to take the tactical initiative, and he believed that his men "reached the highest point of efficiency as cavalry because they were well armed with six-shooters and their charges combined the effect of fire and shock." He went on to say, "I think we did more than any other body of men to give the Colt pistol its great reputation."[12]

Gun-slinging western guerrillas likely would have taken exception to Mosby's boast, but it is true that most guerrillas preferred revolvers to rifles and carbines. "We often had occasion to conceal our weapons," explained a Missouri guerrilla, "and pass as noncombatants so that in due time all implements of war, save pistols and knives, were put aside." And, again, because so much of their combat occurred on horseback, shoulder weapons were simply impractical. This ultimate reliance on revolvers also measures the evolution of the image of the guerrilla. Early in the war, as the first guerrilla bands were being formed, many men assumed that they *would* be touting rifles. They often spoke of being mounted riflemen, armed with light large bored rifles that allowed them to fight as skirmishers or dragoons. The reality of service changed their tactics.[13]

"Every guerrilla carried two revolvers, most of them carried four, and many carried six, some even eight," noted an early student of Quantrill's band. "They could fire from a revolver in each hand at the same time. The aim was never by sighting along the pistol-barrel, but by intuition, judgment. The pistol was brought to the mark and fired instantly, apparently without care, at random."[14]

Still, there were no hard and fast rules, and depending on circumstances, rifles could come in handy if a unit was vastly outnumbered, hampered by terrain, or finding it necessary to deliver an initial fusillade. Some of Quantrill's men carried shotguns, and if heavy artillery were needed in an attack, they would hear the order, "Shotguns to the front." "There were six of these," recalled one man, "and behind them came those with revolvers only." Another Quantrill man reported, "We did not carry any long range guns. We could not handle them on horseback, nor could we afford to stand up and make a long-range fight." Nonetheless, he also recalled carrying "short six-shooting rifles" slung over their shoulders. Even one of Mosby's rangers confessed to using shotguns occasionally when dismounted.[15]

An example of the damage shotguns could do came early in the war for an Arkansas "spy company," as some irregulars called them initially. When four of the men were caught off-guard—and on foot—by a dozen Union cavalrymen, their captain wheeled and leveled his shotgun with the attackers within 40 feet of him. "I shot him with sixteen buckshot, and he fell directly in front of the squad," the rebel recalled. "With the other barrel I almost punched the gun against another, lifting him clear out of his saddle. I then shot three others with a navy pistol, almost touching each one with the muzzle."[16]

Lone bushwhackers or small isolated bands looking to get off a few shots before retreating into the hills, underbrush, or swamps would inevitably chose long-range weapons. The possible types ran the gamut, from old flintlocks and squirrel guns to exquisitely crafted rifles, but they were all deadly in the hands of the sharp-shooting backwoodsmen who wielded them. A band of 60 guerrillas in southwest Virginia stood no chance against a column of 4,000 Union soldiers who passed through their region, but they evened the odds by scattering in the woods on either side of the federal column. "We fired at the Yanks and they fired back at us," recalled one of the men. "The bullets flew awful thick and glanced off the rocks and made the dirt fly all around us."[17]

Rifles and muskets proved just as effective in the hands of Unionist guerrillas. Sidney Jackman, later a Confederate general, began the war by leading what the Federals described as a "band of robbers and desperadoes" on the Missouri–Kansas border. Taking on a raiding party of heavily-armed Kansas jayhawkers, he and his men made do with what they had. "My command, except one man, was armed with shot guns and squirrel rifles," Jackman recounted, "and not more than two pistols in the company." The jayhawkers carried both Sharps rifles and revolvers. "It would seem that, with the great disparity in numbers and quality of arms," Jackson admitted in all sincerity, "that our victory was purely providential."[18]

A member of John Hunt Morgan's command recalled being "considerably annoyed by Bush-whackers" in Kentucky. "[W]e were continually fired at by parties from the hillsides and some of the men and horses were wounded," he reported. "The people had all fled to the sides of the Mountains and in groups poured a terrible volley at us every few hundred yards. It was utterly impossible for us to catch them for they disappeared . . . as soon as our details were sent after them." A Georgia newspaper reported, "The Tories with their squirrel rifles pick off our men from behind rocks and trees and all manner of hiding places. In this way they have killed six or eight of our soldiers."[19]

Nearly as important as the weapons a guerrilla carried was the horse he rode. Quite simply, a good horse was indispensable. "[W]e paid particular attention to . . . the training of our horses," one of Quantrill's men declared, "so that they would not fail us in an emergency. On coming in possession of a new animal, the first thing a bushwhacker would do was to break him to leaping fences, logs and gulleys, and traversing rough ground." Guerrillas spent nearly as much time trying to obtain suitable mounts as they did confronting the enemy. Indeed, the sole purpose of some raids was to secure fresh mounts, with any horses taken divided by lot among the captors. "Each man kept his horses at the farm-house where he made his home," explained one of Mosby's command, "and there was not a barn or corral owned by our friendly allies that did not contain one or more of Mosby's cavalry horses, waiting to be saddled for a long, hard ride."[20]

Guerrillas relied on their horses for yet other reasons. Most importantly, they discovered that horses made excellent sentinels. "A slight snort, uneasy movements or a listening attitude called always for investigation," said an Arkansas guerrilla. His band seldom found it necessary to post a guard at night. All they need do was keep their horses tied nearby. This same man also noted that because Union cavalry mounts were generally larger than the average guerrilla's horse, it was easy to see when a federal patrol had been in the area. The larger hoof marks and the fact that federal horses shoes had eight, as opposed to six, nails, gave them away. Small wonder, this guerrilla insisted, "To feed and groom our horses was our first great care. . . . That we became very much attached to our horses under the circumstances, was natural. Had it been necessary, we would have cheerfully gone hungry to feed them."[21]

Union soldiers, recognizing how essential horses were to guerrilla operations, rejoiced nearly as much when capturing their mounts as when cornering the men themselves. A Wisconsin cavalrymen who spent much of the war battling with these "Knights of the brush" in Missouri and Arkansas, kept a careful record in his diary of the number of both men and horses killed or captured. On one scout, his squadron had a fire-fight with 10 guerrillas. All but two rebels escaped (those two being killed), but among the spoils captured by the Federals were six horses. A fortnight later, they attacked a camp of sleeping guerrillas. Again, all but two men escaped, but they sacrificed nine horses. A month later, the trooper learned that another patrol had let four other guerrillas slip through its fingers, "but our boys succeeded in capturing one of their horses," as though acquiring the single mount made their patrol a success.[22]

Union soldiers also understood the advantage enjoyed by enemy horsemen operating in familiar terrain. A Union colonel reported of the guerrillas in northwest Arkansas, "They are well mounted. I have tried in vain to force them to an engagement. They will not fight, and never intend to." But while mobile guerrillas frustrated the plans of federal officers, they simply wore out Union troopers. "The Secesh dashed into the brush as usual," reported an Iowa cavalryman, "and of course we followed through chaparral, brush, bogs, mud, sloughs, gulches and creeks, and over hills, logs, ravines and rocks. and about four miles, they firing as they ran, and we replying with revolvers whenever they permitted us to get within range." In this instance, the troopers eventually ran some of the rebels to ground, but only because the guerrillas had been unable to force their exhausted mounts up a "steep and miry" river bank. "They were well mounted and were familiar with the crossings of the creeks," the Union soldier continued, "so they had a decided advantage over us, and it was only our best mounted men who were able to keep up with our chivalric but nomadic foes."[23]

A supportive civilian population was crucial to their survival and the success of irregular operations. Evident in all parts of the South, this civilian network, as it were, was a natural outgrowth of the guerrilla's main mission of local defense. Besides sheltering horses, Confederate citizens provided guerrillas with safe houses and dependable sources of supplies. "[Our] men had no camps nor fixed quarters, and never slept in tents," insisted one of Mosby's men. They did not prepare their own food either. "When we wanted to eat," explained this same man, "we stopped at a friendly farm house, or went into some little town and bought what we wanted. Every man in the Command had some special farm that he could call home." A young woman living under their protection in Mosby's Confederacy suggested the closeness of these relationships in her diary. "The Bushwhackers," as she fondly called them, "rested beneath the shelter of the trees in the yard nearly all night. I gave them a scold in the morning for not coming in the house."[24]

Independent guerrillas were more likely than partisan rangers to rough it, but they, too, enjoyed the help and hospitality of the people they protected. Not only did this essential network of collaborators provide them with places to sleep, corral their horses, and obtain food, but it also provided timely information about the presence of Union troops passing through a community. "Jim Yonger and my Self walk to the Mure house," reported one of Quantrill's men, "and had a talk with the old man Muer and he told us the fedrels was campe at the Hutchings farme that was a bot to miles from us. The fambley fix a Basket of grub fors [for us], then we went back to camp and reported what we had learn."[25]

Of course, members of this guerrilla network had to be careful, lest they aroused the suspicions of Unionist neighbors and come under the scrutiny of Union authorities. A Missouri Unionist reported of a suspected secesh neighbor, "Mrs. Buford & her daughters have a very good support in whole or in part but whether . . . the Bushwhackers (who visit her house frequently) contribute to her support & also of her daughters I cannot positively state. I only know that the two families, Warren and Bufords, are very intimate with the Bushwhackers."[26]

The men recognized and appreciated the sacrifices these friends were willing to endure on their behalf. "Being inside the federal lines, we were often reduced to great straits," observed an Arkansas guerrilla. "It seemed strange that an army of three hundred could be maintained in this way, but the people of the country, although reduced to dire extremities themselves, having been overrun, were in full sympathy with us." The ladies, especially, young and old, willingly met them in the woods with provisions "at any hour of the day of night." Their "heroism, self-denial, and trust . . . in those dark days," he said, was unswerving.[27]

The homes of known supporters could also provide a refuge from the war, a place to relax, perhaps even frolic. Dances, sing-a-longs, and sumptuous dinners, especially during holidays, eased the rigors and dangers of campaigning. Mosby's greatest joy, a simple pleasure to be sure, was to find a home that could offer him *real* coffee, not an easy article to find in the wartime South. So potent was his addiction that it was said he had a sack of the genuine article smuggled through the lines so that he could distribute it strategically to selected families while still reserving "a small portion for emergencies."[28]

A Missouri band enjoyed the hospitality of an entire town, Knob Noster, to such an extent that it was described to the region's Union provost marshal as their headquarters. Gathering evidence against the men, the outraged provost marshal concluded, "[T]he band considered itself at home when in town. . . . among his friends and with his family enjoying his booty." Their captain, John Maddox, owned the local grocery store, which became the "usual place in the town for the band to meet." The men, "dissipated, noisy, insolent, and every way on the rowdy, reckless order," walked the streets of town openly, so confident were they of their security in Knob Noster.[29]

Of course, soldiers on both sides took advantage of such opportunities whenever they were offered, but guerrillas, given the nature of their operations and relationship with the civilian population, had far more access to private homes and comforts. A Louisiana ranger mentioned frequent visits to the homes of friends and young ladies, even, on occasion, when he should have been on duty. One evening, he and a companion attended a dance at a home near Baton Rouge. He had an especially "fine time" visiting with one young lady. "I fooled with her nearly all night," he recorded. "I kissed her as much as I wanted & she is a right sweet little thing. I stayed all night." However, a visit with two other members of his company to another home, "away out in the woods," where they intended to "sleep . . . with three young ladyes," nearly proved costly. The men awoke early in the morning to find the house surrounded by Federals. Quickly dressing and strapping on their pistols, they secreted themselves in the house, the diarist climbing up the chimney, until the soldiers had left, about a half hour later. A "most myrculous escape," he conceded.[30]

Even so, there were times when irregulars knew it was not possible to enjoy the comforts of home without endangering their hosts. Often, there were simply too many enemy troops in a neighborhood to risk being discovered, as the Louisiana partisan had nearly done. On those occasions, Mosby's men slept in the woods, orchards, or even open fields. If the weather required, or they knew they would have to conceal themselves for an extended time, they constructed shebangs of mud and brush. "Some few continued to sleep indoors," recalled one ranger, "but nearly all had hiding places, entered by trap doors or secret panels, in which they could find refuge in case the enemy came."[31]

Unhappily for their own comfort, winter was another time, given the length of the season, when it might prove fatal to guerrillas and hosts, alike, if they stayed in private homes. It was a dangerous time for guerrillas to be out and about in any case, once the forests had lost their foliage. With the conventional war at a standstill in most instances, the Federals also had an abundance of available men and plenty of time to send patrols and raiding parties into guerrilla-infested neighborhoods. Some men took the chance of staying with their families for at least part of the winter, sometimes from necessity, of providing for their comfort during the coming year. This was especially true in neighborhoods subject to Union raids, where homes may have been damaged or destroyed, but it was always a risky business.

Consequently, many irregulars sought secluded spots to erect winter quarters. Shebangs were again erected, although a snugger home could be made by three or four men constructing a dugout in the side of a hill or ridge. "We covered the dugout with a pitch roof, made of boards taken from my farm," explained a Missouri guerrilla, "and entered it by steps, like a cellar. There was a fireplace at one end, and all in all, our quarters were very comfortable." A group of Arkansas guerrillas were informed by a sympathetic citizen of a large cave they might use, and where, according to one of the men, "we could . . . whip all the yankees that came there; that the cave was up on a mountain and was big enough to take in all our horses." Other men simply moved from place to place to avoid detection, perhaps even carrying on with their scouting duties during the day. Another Arkansas guerrilla grew adept at selecting a secluded ravine to spend each night, where he and his companions could build a campfire without being spotted. Even so, he explained, "When morning came, we would usually go to some nearby farmhouse for breakfast, and always felt sure of welcome."[32]

Limited military operations, mostly scouting and raiding, could be carried on during the winter. One of Mosby's men, for instance, recalled that there was no idle time for their command. Mosby himself insisted that his men "never went into winter quarters, but kept up a desultory warfare on outposts, supply trains, and detachments." However, the war recommenced in earnest when spring came, and most irregulars, both the independent bands and the ranger companies, prepared themselves in similar ways.[33]

Any large-scale operation, whether defensive or offensive, began with a rendezvous. With bands of men and individuals widely scattered when not active, couriers were dispatched to inform Mosby's men where and when to meet, although they generally met at a blacksmith's shop, where horses could be inspected while orders and assignments were discussed. Quite often, a local guide or scout rode with the men, especially as the scope of Mosby's operations widened, and he became less familiar with the terrain and political sympathies of the citizenry.

Mosby's men did not receive orders to engage the enemy unless Mosby himself was to lead them. On most other occasions, they were asked only to observe the enemy, try to discern federal intentions, collect information from the citizenry, or investigate the possibilities for gathering supplies and horses in a particular neighborhood. If more men assembled for these missions than were needed, they would be dismissed or given secondary assignments. When they did attack, generally using a force of under 100 men, Mosby preferred to strike at night, which he believed magnified the confusion and terror of the enemy. The mission accomplished, the men scattered until again summoned. For the Union army, observed one Ranger, catching Mosby's men was "like chasing a Will-o'-the-Wisp."[34]

Mosby also tried to strike where his men would meet minimal resistance. Sutler trains, for instance, were a favorite target, not only because they were lightly guarded, but also because of the rich spoils to be gained. Other easy yet vital targets were Union-controlled railroads and telegraph lines. Mosby's men became expert at ripping up miles of track in a very short time and derailing trains. They knew that their purpose was not to defeat large armies, but to vex and harass them, and make them commit forces to stopping them that would have been better used trying to defeat Robert E. Lee. "It was necessary for the federal troops to guard every wagon train, railroad bridge and camp . . . to prevent Mosby from . . . one of his destructive rushes at any hour of the night or day," boasted one of the men. "Thousands of soldiers were kept from service at the front because of Mosby's activities." The partisan chief himself, reported to his superior, Gen. James E. B. Stuart, "The military value of the species of warfare I have waged is not measured by the number of prisoners and material of war captured from the enemy, but by the heavy detail it has compelled him to make . . . in order to guard his communications and to that extent diminishing his aggressive strength."[35]

Independent guerrillas operated in much the same way and with much the same purpose. "After leaving town upon a scout into the country they very often scattered out into very small squads—some times went one or no more than two or three," said a witness of the Knob Noster band. "It was rare that as many as ten could be seen together ten miles from town."[36]

If there was a difference, it lay in the larger role that revenge played in the lives of independent guerrillas. In most instances, though certainly not all, partisan rangers functioned as part of the army. Consequently, their assignments had at least some military value, even if, like all irregulars, they benefitted from the spoils collected. Guerrillas and bushwhackers were more interested in intimidating Unionist civilians. Their war was far more personal, and it more often involved theft, arson, and murder. As was said of one of Quantrill's chief lieutenants, "Revenge and revenge alone, permeated and took possession of every fibre of Bill Anderson's body. He had come to the place at last where an eye had to be rendered for an eye and a tooth for a tooth." A lesser known Arkansas guerrilla recalled that the entire partisan war was a "struggle for supremacy and revenge." Of the Knob Noster guerrillas, it was reported, "On a full understanding of all these dark proceedings it appears that here were men detailed from the band to commit the deeds of murder—detailed rather by personal revenge and hellish passion than by [their leader] Capt. Maddox."[37]

Consequently, it was generally thought that the independent bands, and certainly the ones on the western border and in the Upper South, were especially desperate fighters. One man recalled, "It was a common thing for us to fight two or three times a week, and very often two or three times a day." They were admittedly ill-disciplined. "Every man went and came at his own sweet will," although they "all obeyed with promptness the order of their chosen officer while on duty." While partisan rangers often took livestock and food from Unionist civilians, independent guerrillas made Unionists their favorite targets, and the thefts often served no military purpose. "Horses and cattle were booty mostly sought," claimed an Arkansas guerrilla, "but household goods, such as clothing, bed clothing, and, in fact, anything of value that could be carried off. As a result of these raids, many men were killed on both sides, among them quite a number of non-combatants, old men and boys in their teens."[38]

One of Quantrill's men recalled a typical fight by their band. They had been prowling the Missouri–Kansas border, "hunting for a fight," when Quantrill sent out scouts to "locate any band of Federals that might be in the neighborhood." Finally spotting a column of some 160 men, the guerrillas used their knowledge of the terrain to allow the troopers to ride into an ambush. "They got within forty steps of us when the order was given to charge," the guerrilla reported. "With a yell, every man tried to see who should be the first to mix it up with them. Of course they could not form a line of battle so they tried to get out of the way. We followed on their heels and slaughtered them by the dozen." As though to confirm the typical pattern of these short, desperate fights, he said of another attack on Union troops, "[N]o body of men on earth can stand before another body of men in that way; they must break away and run, and when they would start to run we would follow up and put it to them in the back. We always killed more of them by shooting them in the back than we did face to face."[39]

Still, even in the roughest patches of guerrilla territory, the war was not a relentless pursuit of either enemy soldiers or citizens. Having dispersed in small groups to decrease the chances of detection, they passed the time until next summoned to rendezvous in "rest and sport," including "squirrel shooting, leapfrog, race running, wrestling, swimming and story telling," although those would have been among their more innocent pastimes. The Louisiana partisan who liked to frolic with the ladies spent much of his time in camp playing gambling at cards and drinking.[40]

Men might also tend to their families, perhaps even take time off to live as honest farmers until they put in a crop. That is what the bushwhackers in an Arkansas community did one spring, although always with an eye open for Union patrols and with a thought toward the resumption of their raids. Finally, with their families secure for the coming year, the men made preparations for another campaign season. "We had all got into such a good humor while busily engaged in farming," recalled one man, "that we were nearly two days recounting our grievances before we were mad enough to think of snatching our enemies into eternity." Then, with revenge still the fire that motivated them, the gang headed for Missouri.[41]

The haphazard organization of so many independent bands led Union soldiers to think them merely duplicitous, but their irregular membership also said something important about how the men viewed their roles of the war. Many thought of themselves as only part-time guerrillas, or did not consider themselves to be guerrillas at all, at least not as the rest of the world defined that term. In other words, there could be a difference between being a guerrilla and performing guerrilla acts. A Virginian confessed to having operated as a guerrilla for a year, even to firing into a body of Union cavalry and "doing them much damage"; but he had then gone home, with no intention of re-entering the war. Another Virginian, this one a "mere youth," was known to shoot at passing steamboats, and "was with," though apparently not a member of, a guerrilla band when captured. Still, reported the local provost marshal, there could be "no doubt" of the boy's "sympathy with rebel scouts, 'bushwhackers' and horse-thieves."[42]

Henry Simpson, of Alexandria, Virginia, could boast of one of the more varied careers in the war. He entered the war at age 21 by aiding local rebels, enough to get himself arrested and placed in the Old Capitol Prison. The Federals released him in the summer of 1862 because his mother promised to keep her son at home and out of trouble, but within days, he had enlisted in the Confederate army. Taken prisoner a second time and exchanged, he ignored his oath of allegiance to spend part of his time bushwhacking. Captured a third time, this "dangerous, energetic, reckless young man" occupied a Union prison cell for the remainder of the war.[43]

Any number of captured men swore to having been conscripted or otherwise forced into guerrilla service. A 17-year-old Tennessean who floated in and out of an independent company near his farm, observed how the unit's captain maintained his ranks in just that way. "At the time of his capture," he said of him, "he had about 18 or 20 men. Of these a few were volunteers." The captain designated one squad to "go round conscripting that was the main business, pressing horses was the next object, they also pressed arms." They "never had any regular camp," observed the boy, but would rendezvous at a particular farm house at 8:00 a.m. or 10:00 a.m. "They would be together sometimes three or four days and then go home" for one or two days. "When at home they would engage in their usual occupations. . . . During the time I knew them I did not know of their engaging in any military enterprise at all." Here was irregular warfare in the most literal sense.[44]

FOUR

UNION REACTION, 1861–1862

Guerrillas cost the Federals dearly in lives and equipment during the first two years of the war. If allowed to continue, the obvious military problems caused by rebel raids, ambushes, and sabotage could translate into serious political problems for the Lincoln government. National and state officials worried about how to protect the lives and maintain the allegiance of frightened Midwesterners and demoralized Unionists in the border states. Fear and war weariness could cause disenchantment, and so make the war on the home front a test of wills. An escalation of the guerrilla war in occupied Union territory might even force the United States to abandon important territorial gains.

Faced with fighting what amounted to a second and separate war, the U.S. government looked for ways to strike back. It settled on a dual approach. First, the Union army would have to deal more effectively with their guerrilla foes. In addition, though, the government would challenge the legality of the guerrilla war and insist that the rebels adhere to the "rules of civilized warfare." Any Union soldier who had faced the guerrillas could endorse that plan. "We have been learning our full share of the realities of this conflict," came a typical response, "rendered more terable in this section than any other from the savage and brutal mode in which it is waged by our enemies. . . . who carry on a war more barbarous than any waged by the savages who once inhabited this same country."[1]

The first protests, accompanied by retaliatory measures, came in Virginia and Missouri. As early as the summer of 1861, generals George B. McClellan and William S. Rosecrans, while commanding troops in northwestern Virginia, assigned several thousand men to protect vulnerable railroads and telegraph lines against guerrilla attacks. The additional guards did their job, but that left fewer soldiers to protect Unionists communities. Unionists complained that the army had abandoned them. McClellan had not foreseen this dual role for the army, fighting the enemy while simultaneously protecting civilians, but he understood the problem at once.

On June 23, McClellan announced that if the rebels continued "to carry on a system of hostilities prohibited by the laws of war," their "marauding parties" would be treated according to the "severest rules" of military justice. Rosecrans, upon replacing McClellan, took even stronger action against this "species of warfare." Citizens must take "prompt and vigorous measures to put a stop to neighborhood and private wars," he insisted, and so, "prevent the country from being desolated by plunder and violence, whether committed in the name of secessionism or Unionism." Neighborhoods failing to suppress the violence would be treated "as accessaries to the crime."[2]

Neither McClellan nor Rosecrans, both of whom believed in a conciliatory approach to the rebels, appears to have followed through with these threats, but things were different in Missouri. In July 1862, Gen. John Pope, a hard-nosed West Point graduate from Kentucky and Mexican War veteran, took immediate steps to crush guerrilla resistance in his district. His brashness and conceit prevented Pope from being especially popular among fellow officers, but he knew better than McClellan or Rosecrans how to deal with rebels.

With his supply line, the North Missouri Railroad, under constant attack, Pope ordered residents within a five-mile radius to pay for the "wanton destruction" of its bridges, culverts, and tracks. When the outrages continued, he held citizens responsible for the "peace and quietude" of their own communities and the safety of their own property. If a community failed to keep the peace, federal troops would be quartered and provisioned there at the expense of the inhabitants. That, at least, he said, would compensate his demoralized men for the constant labor of hunting "lawless marauders."[3]

Pope's over-zealous subordinates soon abused the policy by making suspected guerrilla supporters "individually responsible, both in persons and property, for any outrage . . . committed on Union men." Soldiers arrested people "without cause," complained outraged citizens, and ransacked homes "for no good reason."[4]

As the new spirit of retaliation spread, similarly indiscreet measures occurred beyond Pope's district. Federals in southeastern Missouri punished the family of a captain of "marauders" by destroying or confiscating much of their property and threatening to hang them if the captain's men did not cease operations. Confederate political leaders in the state said they would hang federal prisoners in return. "I am content," Lieutenant Governor Reynolds declared, "that impartial men should judge who is morally responsible for their melancholy fate."[5]

The danger of an unchecked escalation of violence seemed obvious, but few people on either side were willing to back down. "[M]any are in favor of 'making a clean sweep' (as they express it) of secession," observed a Northern journalist in Missouri, "which means, I suppose, *taking no more prisoners.*" Pope, not wishing to alienate honest citizens unnecessarily, reminded his men to arrest only the people engaged in "open acts of hostility" or "stimulating others to such acts." McClellan and Rosecrans had cautioned their men to treat civilians with respect. However, junior officers and soldiers faced with the reality of combating deadly guerrillas and their devious supporters paid increasingly less attention to such warnings. While the generals spoke of occupying "the country of friends, not of enemies," their men "vowed vengeance" and scoffed at "talk of winning these people over with kindness." A solider in West Virginia declared, "[W]e are fully able to cope with them at their own game. No more prisoners is the watch word."[6]

While few Union commanders would have said so publicly, more of them had begun to think that retaliation might be the only means of crushing guerrilla resistance. A new Union commander in Missouri, John C. Frémont, finding that "bands of murderers and marauders" infested nearly every county and committed "crimes and outrages" almost daily, went beyond even what Pope had dared to do. The famous explorer, soldier, and first Republican presidential candidate put the state under martial law in August. Anyone taking up arms against the United States would shot, their property confiscated, and their slaves freed. Saboteurs of federal property and people "fomenting tumults" would "suffer the extreme penalty of the law."[7]

The orders won broad approval from soldiers and politicians, alike. "They should be *summarily shot by thousands,*" declared a son of Edward Bates. "They have well earned the fate, and the example made of them may be of great value elsewhere in deterring . . . robbers, spies, and assassins." Soldiers said they were tired of being shot by supposedly peaceful farmers and exhausted by fruitless marches against phantom foes. It was not the danger oftentimes as much as the wear and tear of campaigning that frayed men's nerves and lowered the threshold of what they would tolerate.[8]

Worn out by a 60-mile tramp in search of guerrillas, one infantryman admitted that his regiment was fed up. "I suppose the boys burnt one mill down after they ground what we wanted," he told his wife, "&busted into Stores & houses & took what they wanted & Sat some houses on fire & cut up verry bad. [O]ur Colonel tried to kep our Soldiers from distroying them but could not." An Ohio soldier confessed to a friend at home, "As I go through this traitor country . . . two impulses are struggling in my heart, one to lay waste as we go—like destroying angels, to kill & burn and make the way of the transgressors hard—the other is to wage a civilized warfare."

Thus far, the civilized impulse had won out, but if the rebels continued their "atrocities," he and all his comrades were determined to "make the land desolate."[9]

While many Northern politicians were also calling for blood, the majority tried to keep a lid on things. That included President Lincoln, who had hoped to end the war relatively quickly by showing his desire to treat the seceded states leniently if they would return to the Union. As he said in his inaugural address, "The government will not assail *you*. You can have no conflict, without being yourselves the aggressors." Consequently, he wanted his armies to respect both the person and property of noncombatants, especially in the Union slave states. He believed that kindness and magnanimity would create a groundswell of Unionist sentiment and generate a political backlash against the rebel government. Guerrilla resistance dashed that hope. True, Frémont, unlike Pope, had targeted mostly people who took up arms against the government, but the spirit of the orders struck the wrong note by mentioning the confiscation of slaves. Whatever Lincoln's feelings on that controversial subject in late 1861, he knew it was politically impossible to address it and keep Missouri, Kentucky, and Maryland in the Union.

The prospect of executing captured guerrillas also seemed counterproductive to the president. The rebels would surely retaliate, he said, which would compel the United States to respond in kind. However, when Frémont insisted that he acted "entirely according to the usages of civilized warfare," and that he deserved the traditional freedom allowed commanders in the field to deal with the enemy as he saw fit, Lincoln let the order stand. The irregular war, he believed, would soon sputter and die. "Doubtless local uprisings will for some time continue to occur," he decided, "but these can be met by detachments and local forces of our men, and will ere long tire out of themselves." Nonetheless, by letting the general have his way on reprisals, Lincoln created a crucial precedent for the Union's antiguerrilla policy.[10]

The president had been right about the probable rebel response to Frémont's measures. Jeff Thompson proclaimed that for every Confederate soldier put to death by Frémont, he would "'*hang, draw,* and quarter' a minion" of Lincoln's army. "While I am anxious that this unfortunate war shall be conducted, if possible, upon the most liberal principles of civilized warfare," the rebel partisan pledged, "I intend to exceed General Frémont in his excesses, and I will make all tories that come within my reach rue the day that a different policy was adopted by their leader."[11]

The response only convinced David Hunter, who, for a variety of military and political reasons, replaced Frémont as department commander in November, and Henry W. Halleck, who soon replaced Hunter, that stringent antiguerrilla measures were essential to end the rebellion. It was Hunter who, during his brief tenure in Missouri, ordered the Great Jayhawking Expedition led by Jennison in November 1861. Even when relieved by Halleck, and given command of the Department of Kansas, his reach could still extend into Missouri. Taking exception to the "depredations and outrages" perpetrated by Silas Gordon, he sent an ultimatum to the rebel citizens who shielded and supported Gordon. "I give you notice," he declared bluntly, "that unless you seize and deliver the said Gordon to me at these Head Quarters [at Leavenworth, Kansas] within ten days from this date, or drive him out of the country, I shall send a force to your city [Platte City] with orders to *reduce it to ashes, and to burn the house of every Secessionist in your county, and to carry away every negro.*" Perhaps even more terrifying, Hunter added, "Col. Jennison's regiment will be entrusted with the execution of this order." Whether or not in response to Hunter's threat, Gordon and his men did leave the region soon thereafter to fight, at least for a while, with General Price's army.[12]

More importantly, though, was how Henry Halleck handled the chaos he had inherited from Hunter and Frémont in Missouri. After seeing the damage being done to the morale of both his army and Unionist civilians, he retaliated against the guerrillas, rather than selected rebel communities. Guerrillas suspected of murder, robbery, or pillaging, he announced in early December, would be tried as common criminals. If found guilty, they would be shot. A few weeks later, as guerrillas continued to burn bridges, destroy railroads, and cut telegraph lines, despite the fact that he had assigned 10,000 troops to protect them, Halleck dispensed with the niceties of arrests and trials. "These men are guilty of the highest crime known to the code of war. . . . Any one caught in the act will be immediately shot."[13]

Finally, seeing the seriousness of the Union protest, and that Frémont was not an apparition, Confederate leaders protested the new policy. Sterling Price complained to Halleck in January 1862 that men labeled outlaws by the Federals had been "specially appointed and instructed" by him to destroy enemy railroads and bridges in accordance with "the laws of warfare." Going further, the rebel commander insisted, "It is necessary that we understand each other and have some guiding knowledge of that character of warfare which is to be waged by our respective governments." Seizing this opportunity to expose the enormity of the guerrilla war, Halleck replied, that "special appointment and instructions" could not disguise the purpose or status of Price's men. "You must be aware, general," he elaborated, "that . . . [y]ou cannot give immunity to crime."[14]

Halleck restated his refusal to accept the legitimacy of the guerrilla war with an additional order in March, and some district commanders, citing his authority, issued even more strongly worded directives. While he allowed officers "to adopt such measures as may be necessary to . . . punish all violations of the laws of war," Gen. James Totten, commanding central Missouri, wanted "the outlaws infesting the district exterminated." Totten was especially appalled by a widespread ruse employed by rebel guerrillas that spring—disguising themselves in Union uniforms to ambush troops and appropriate the property of civilians.[15]

The violence in the field and war of words with Confederate authorities followed wherever the Federals encountered guerrilla resistance. In Arkansas that summer, the drama played itself out during Samuel Curtis's march toward Little Rock, which, as shown, he eventually abandoned. Curtis himself responded to bushwhackers with a policy of no quarter, and one of his subordinates, Col. Graham N. Fitch, challenged the legal standing of Thomas Hindman's independent companies. Fitch's 46th Indiana Infantry formed part of a joint army–navy relief expedition up the White River to resupply Curtis. When the navy's gunboats and transports were forced to turn back by a combination of low water, rebel obstructions in the river, and heavy fire from Confederate troops and guerrillas on shore, Fitch blamed the failure mostly on the guerrillas.

Hindman responded immediately to this Yankee arrogance. In a refrain that became common among Confederates, he asked Fitch what right the Federals had to decide how the war should be fought. As Price had done Halleck, so Hindman insisted that the men firing on his column acted under his orders and were recognized as Confederate troops. He then added bitingly, "I assert as indisputable the right to dispose and use those troops along the banks of the White River, or wherever else I may deem proper, even should it prove annoying to you in your operations." To the local inhabitants, Hindman urged, "Attack him day and night, kill his scouts and pickets, kill his pilots and his troops on transports, cut off his wagon trains, . . . shot his mounted officers."[16]

The Union military forces also relied on repressive measures to exterminate guerrillas and intimidate civilians in Louisiana, where Gen. Benjamin Butler ordered his senior field commander, Gen. Thomas Williams, to "punish with the last severity every guerrilla attack and burn the property of every guerrilla found murdering your soldiers." The following month, Butler sent out patrols to capture noted desperadoes and offered a bounty of $1,000 "for every guerrilla's head." Any slave who brought in a head would earn his freedom.[17]

The navy, too, acted with alacrity on the lower Mississippi. Guerrillas concealed on the river banks fired into their warships and into transports that carried soldiers upriver. They captured slow-moving and lightly-defended coal barges and ambushed small parties that went ashore to acquire supplies or inspect the countryside. An exasperated Adm. David G. Farragut told the secretary of the navy, "The elements of destruction to the Navy in this river are beyond anything I ever encountered, and if the same destruction continues the whole Navy will be destroyed in twelve months." He ordered his gunboats to shell river banks where guerrillas had fired on his men, regardless of civilian communities.[18]

In Mississippi, Union commanders had reached the same conclusion. Gen. Gordon Granger summed up the situation there in the summer of 1862—"[T]his most infernal guerrilla system . . . is bound to waste our entire army away. . . . We must push every man, woman, and child before us or put every man to death found in our line." The war, Granger judged, must ultimately become "a war of subjugation, and the sooner the better."[19]

In the middle border region of Kentucky and Tennessee, Col. Joseph W. Keifer, a graduate of Antioch College and confirmed abolitionist, was among the first officers to recognize the trend. He had fought rebel guerrillas in Virginia before being transferred with his Ohio regiment to Tennessee, but it was only then that he called for blood vengeance against bushwhackers. "When in W. Va I had great sympathy for the Rebels who remained at their homes," he explained to his wife. "I thought they were ignorant, and more objects of pity than of punishment." His compassion dissolved in Tennessee. Guerrillas and their supporters stood "ready at all times to stab us in the back," he declared, and should be treated "in a more *severe* and *summary manner.*"[20]

As the Union's retaliatory policy took shape, local guerrillas joined Confederate commanders to insist on the right to defend their land by any means. "You call us guerrillas," an enraged partisan wrote to Gen. Ulysses S. Grant, who agreed with the shift toward punitive measures, "which you know is false. We are recognized by our government." If Grant executed or harmed Southern civilians in retaliation for guerrilla raids, this chieftain vowed to execute an equal number of Union prisoners. "You shall conduct this war upon proper principles," he declared, in reversing the usual roles in such dialogues. "We intend to force you to do it. If you intend to make this a war of extermination, you will please inform us at the earliest convenience. We are ready, and more than willing, to raise the 'black flag.' "[21]

Nonetheless, by this time, in mid-1862, some Northern politicians were also advocating retaliatory policies, one of the first being the new military governor of Tennessee, Andrew Johnson. Appointed to the post in March 1862, Johnson had been on the job barely a week when he received reports of Ferguson's marauding and a rumor that the guerrilla chief had been offered $1,000 to kill him. Johnson had earlier endorsed conciliation, but, as the East Tennessee native saw the guerrilla threat at first hand, he resolved to go toe-to-toe with Ferguson and his ilk. There would be a "terrible accountability," he warned, if rebel guerrillas did not cease their "depredations."[22]

Johnson also became one of the first Union officials to authorize Unionist guerrilla bands to deal with the rebels. The new governor turned to David Beaty, known as "Tinker Dave," a local man who led one of the deadliest guerrilla bands in the Upper South. Beaty formed his command in early 1862 in response to the "conscripting, killing, and shooting at Union men" by Ferguson and other rebel guerrillas. Thereafter, he and Champ became bitter rivals. A Union officer said of Beaty, "He is a whole souled fellow. If he had a Regiment, instead of a company, he would do wonders." Ferguson reportedly claimed that armed Unionists such as Beaty were his only enemies in the war. "I haven't got no feeling agin these Yankee soldiers," he said, "except that they are wrong, and oughtn't to come down here and fight our people. I won't tech them; but when I catches any one of them hounds I've got good cause to kill, I'm goin' to kill em."[23]

Johnson's practice of encouraging Unionist guerrillas grew popular. In western Virginia, the Snake Hunters were given authority to arrest their rebel counterparts. When that part of Virginia joined the Union in 1863 as the state of West Virginia, its government also sanctioned several counterguerrilla companies to operate as state troops, a practice also followed in Missouri. Taking the field mostly at night to avoid being ambushed themselves, they succeeded in capturing many "thoroughbred guerilla secessionists."[24]

Following the same thinking, the Union army assigned volunteer regiments of infantry and cavalry from the border states to track and destroy guerrillas in their home counties. Like Unionist guerrilla bands, they were familiar with the terrain and the haunts and identities of their foes, and they often had old scores to settle. No matter how much Northern troops despised the guerrillas, these homegrown guerrilla fighters had even more incentive to drive them out. "[T]hey have most of them been robbed by the 'Brushwhackers,'" explained an officer in one Missouri outfit. "Many of them have had fathers and brothers taken out and shot in cold blood by the rebels. A majority of them have had wives, mothers and sisters abused and insulted, and in many instances stripped of their jewelry and clothing by these scoundrels." It had become "next to impossible," this man concluded, for his men to "deal leniantly with 'brushwhackers.'"[25]

It was not hard to understand the psychology of the situation. As the colonel of one unionist regiment observed, "[T]he *Rebels* in Tennessee can only be quelled by Tennesseans." Troops in the 5th Tennessee Cavalry were so ruthless that rebel citizens called them Bushwhackers. Andrew Johnson begged President Lincoln to reassign East Tennessee troops serving in Virginia to their home regions. "[T]hey are willing & more than anxious," he assured the president, "to restore the government & at the same time protect their wives & children against insult robbery murder & inhumane oppression."[26]

But as the Confederate authorities had discovered, unbridled enthusiasm could lead to abuses, an issue that soon worried Union officials too. Robbery, vandalism, and murder became the hallmarks of a regiment of Tennessee unionists deployed as mounted infantry. "[N]umerous complaints . . . of outrages committed by both officers and men" soon betrayed a total lack of discipline. Having already killed a loyal Unionist whom they suspected of aiding rebel guerrillas in north Georgia, the regiment's colonel received strict instructions when sent to arrest the wife of a prominent local guerrilla. "[N]o depredations of any kind [will be] committed . . . by your officers or men," he was told. "For any acts of violence or depredations . . . the general Commanding will hold you strictly responsible."[27]

Nor was it long before entire rebel communities, not just individuals, became targets of the new spirit. Villages or towns suspected of harboring guerrillas were fined, pillaged, or simply leveled, a sobering step beyond what McClellan or even Pope had envisioned. When, in September 1862, guerrillas almost captured a packet boat on the Mississippi River near Randolph, Tennessee, Gen. William T. Sherman sent a regiment to destroy the town. He justified his action by saying, "It is no use tolerating such acts as firing on steamboats. Punishments must be speedy, sure, and exemplary." When local rebels ignored his warning, he leveled other guerrilla haunts and expelled families from communities where Union shipping was endangered. He called it "collective punishment."[28]

"[W]e are not going to chase through the canebrakes and swamps the individuals who did the deeds," he told a rebel woman who protested Sherman's harsh policies, "but will visit punishments upon the adherents of that cause which employs such agents." To another woman, he asserted, "In war it is impossible to hunt up the actual perpetrators of a crime. Those who are banded together in any cause are held responsible for all the acts of their associates." His measures thus far had been mild, he assured her, but make no mistake. If necessary, he would not hesitate to order the "absolute destruction of Memphis, New Orleans, and every other city, town, and hamlet of the South."[29]

Similarly, Adm. David D. Porter, who admired the antiguerrilla policies of both Sherman and Grant, arrested known guerrillas and their sympathizers, assessed collaborators at 10 times the value of plundered or destroyed Union property, and burned whole communities. "This is the only way of putting a stop to guerrilla warfare," he assured Secretary of the Navy Gideon Welles, "and though the method is stringent, officers are instructed to put it down at all hazards."[30]

Indeed, by the autumn of 1862, large parts of the South, not just a few burned settlements, resembled the wilderness from which it once been hewn. Of course, ruined farm lands and denuded forests were the natural result of large armies tramping across a landscape for an extended time. The insatiable need for wood alone ensured that result, and in that sense, Confederate armies were as much to blame for the vanishing forests as the Federals. However, Union armies had also made destruction of the natural South part of their strategic plan by this time, a conscious decision, as one historian has put it, to make war upon the land as well as the people of the South. The destruction was not always associated with retaliation against rebel guerrillas, as witnessed by the bombardment of Fredericksburg, Virginia, in December 1862, but no small part of it clearly resulted from Union efforts to quash the guerrilla war.[31]

Not surprisingly, neither Sherman nor Porter succeeded in eliminating the rebel attacks, a point worth pursuing. Safe navigation of the Mississippi and other rivers was the most urgent and complex logistical problem faced by Union soldiers and sailors in the West. Unsecured rivers adversely affected two separate theaters of operations—the Western and Trans-Mississippi—all the way from the Ohio River to the Gulf of Mexico. In the border region east of the Mississippi, armies could not possibly depend on the ridiculously vulnerable railroads. They needed boats of every size, shape, and function—from gunboats to coal barges—to operate.

Soldiers and sailors responsible either for defending shipping or responding to attacks were as frustrated as their officers by all this. One soldier, while embarrassed by the thievery that often passed for retaliation against civilians, had no qualms about using deadly force against river bushwhackers. When guerrillas wounded three soldiers in his river convoy, he watched with satisfaction as an escorting gunboat "threw a few shells into the woods." The following morning, when troops went ashore to burn houses where the ambush had occurred, he voiced no complaint.[32]

Lt. Le Roy Fitch, assigned to patrol the Ohio, Cumberland, and Tennessee rivers, was typical of Union naval officers ordered to meet the challenge. Fitch shelled guerrilla haunts and disembarked troops to pursue them without significantly reducing rebel operations. Frustrated by his elusive prey, he resorted to punishing the citizenry. Having burned the town of Palmyra, Tennessee, on the Cumberland, he reported to Admiral Porter, "[N]ot one house left. A very bad hole, best to get rid of it and teach the rebels a lesson." The town of Caseyville, Kentucky, got off lightly by comparison. When the citizens were slow to pay the $35,000 Fitch demanded for the damage done to a passing steamer, he confiscated the amount in kind, including over 1,000 bags of wheat, 40 barrels of whiskey, and 10–15 kegs of lard.[33]

Back on land, Union field commanders were carrying punitive measures into northern portions of the Deep South by the summer of 1862. When Gen. Ormsby M. Mitchel's division of the Army of the Ohio encountered guerrilla resistance in Alabama, he allowed his men to burn, plunder, and destroy enormous amounts of rebel property. The entire town of Paint Rock went up in flames, and Athens was sacked. An unprecedented number of personal crimes, including robbery, murder, and rape, accompanied the occupation. While not approving the crimes, one of Mitchel's officers rejoiced at the general's uncompromising treatment of rebels. "It is the inauguration of the true policy, and the only one that will preserve us from constant annoyance," he insisted. He told the citizens of Paint Rock, "If they wanted to fight they should enter the army, meet us like honorable men, and not, assassin-like, fire at us from the woods and run." Secretary of War Stanton liked the results of the expedition, too. He assured Mitchel, "Your spirited operations afford great satisfaction to the President."[34]

Indeed, Lincoln, finally understanding the extent of the guerrilla menace, was now prepared to initiate a shift in national military policy. With the war entering its second year and no end in sight, he had been feeling the political pressure to prosecute the war more vigorously, not just against guerrillas, but in every possible way. It was time to end the "kid-glove warfare," said politicians and the press, who were especially concerned by the seemingly futile military operations in the East, aimed at capturing Richmond. With midterm elections due that autumn, Lincoln simply had to alter public perceptions, and an effective counter-guerrilla strategy became part of the plan.

Abandoning his conciliatory approach, Lincoln endorsed the punitive measures already employed by local commanders against guerrilla-infested communities. He also approved the Second Confiscation Act, which gave his armies the legal power to appropriate the property of traitors, including slaves. That measure was only a step away from emancipation, which the president also considered more seriously. Even more strikingly, he decided to rely on veteran Union guerrilla fighters to take charge of the war. He resurrected John Frémont's career by telling him to end the guerrilla problem in western Virginia. There was no disagreement over policy this time.[35]

Next, Lincoln brought John Pope from the Western Theater to command a new Union army in Virginia. Through Secretary of War Stanton, he also approved Pope's plan, even stricter than the one applied in Missouri, to crush the guerrilla threat. Aimed not only at guerrillas, but also at the "evil-disposed persons" who assisted them, Pope's instructions allowed executions, financial assessments, and the destruction and confiscation of property. When Andrew Johnson asked permission to apply Pope's orders in Tennessee, Lincoln gave it. By then, as well, Lincoln had promoted Pope's old department commander in Missouri, Henry Halleck, to commanding general of all Union armies.[36]

Of course, Lincoln was not asking for wholesale slaughter. Indeed, some politicians and soldiers complained that the kind hearted president commuted or reduced the death sentences of far too many convicted guerrillas. Still, despite his own occasional references to tempering justice with mercy, the guerrilla conflict had caused Lincoln to view the war differently. Explaining the new rules to Gen. John S. Phelps, the military governor of Louisiana and Arkansas, he wrote, "I am a patient man—always willing to forgive on the Christian terms of repentance. . . . Still, I must save the government if possible. . . . [And] it may as well be understood, once for all, that I shall not surrender this game leaving any available card unplayed."[37]

Army commanders who did not fall in line with the new rules suffered the consequences. Don Carlos Buell, a vocal opponent of retaliatory policies, had expressed his disgust with events in Alabama, which fell under his jurisdiction. Partly in consequence, he lost command of his military department and became the target of a six-month long investigation into his direction of it. Buell had not kept up with the steadily hardening mood of the government, the public, or his own army. A senior officer called his conciliatory policy that of an "amiable idiot."[38]

Learning of these events, Jefferson Davis felt more trapped than ever by the unforeseen complications of the guerrilla war, with the entire conflict grown more brutish than he could have imagined. "We find ourselves driven by our enemies by steady progress towards a practice we abhor and which we are vainly struggling to avoid," he told Robert E. Lee on the last day of July 1862. The United States seemed willing to shatter all concepts of armed conflict between "civilized men in modern times," but if they persisted, the president said, the Confederacy would be compelled as a "last resort" to wage war "on the terms chosen by our foe."[39]

FIVE

TURNING POINT, 1863

The year 1863 is often mentioned as a turning point in the American Civil War. The usual reasoning is that those 12 months witnessed some of the Confederacy's most decisive battlefield defeats. Gettysburg and Vicksburg, alone, cost the rebels nearly 60,000 men and completely upset their strategic plans. But 1863 also saw dramatic turns in the guerrilla war, and considering their long-term consequences, they were every bit as important in determining the course and outcome of the wider contest.

The year began with the guerrilla war posing problems for both sides, and in curiously similar ways. The Federals had to find a way to defeat the rebel guerrillas militarily and challenge the legality of irregular warfare. The Confederates had to find a proper strategic role for its partisans and justify that role to the world. The winner of the military matchup would be decided in the mountains, forests, and swamps of the South. The political and legal tussle over the legitimacy of the irregular war was more far reaching, and nothing better illustrated the nature of that game than the reaction to events at Palmyra, Missouri, in December 1862.

When some Northern newspapers criticized Gen. John McNeil for executing 15 rebel guerrillas after a perfunctory trial, the general's provost marshal at Palmyra vigorously defended him. "Had one half the severity practiced by rebels on the Union men of Tennessee, Arkansas, and Missouri been meted out in return to them," he said, "every trace of treason would ere this have been abolished from our land." The rebels had been caught "with arms in their hands, murder in their hearts, and the oath of allegiance to the United States Government in their pockets." Scores of defenseless Unionists had been terrorized or murdered by just such ruffians, he went on, and "thousands upon thousands" of scoundrels, whose "long list of crimes . . . would make even fiends in hell shudder," still roamed the land.[1]

The provost marshal's insistence that guerrillas were no better than murderers remained the crux of the matter, and one not to be ignored by Gen. Theophilus Holmes. Having replaced Thomas Hindman as commander of the Confederate Trans-Mississippi Department, the 58-year-old "Granny" Holmes was as determined as his former West Point classmate Robert E. Lee to wage war according to civilized and Christian principles, but Union soldiers, he charged, no less than Confederate guerrillas, had bullied noncombatants in this war. Holmes, in fact, had "repressed the patriotic ardor" of Arkansas Confederates who wished to expand the guerrilla war. Yet, the Federals must understand, he stressed, that should irregular warfare prove the only means of winning independence, the rebellious population "would rise as individuals and each man take upon himself the task of expelling the invaders." Holmes informed one Union officer, "[W]e hate you with a cordial hatred."[2]

Complicating matters, both sides recognized by 1863 that a different type of guerrilla had entered the war. "There is a new class of men here," reported Col. Basil F. Lazear, whose 1st Missouri Cavalry (U.S.) were famed guerrilla hunters, "that are keeping up more disturbance than the rebels. They are thieves and murderers, and claim to be Union men." Actually, they might just as often claim to be good Confederates, although, in truth, they were loyal to neither side. The "new" men were often outlaws, deserters, and other misfits who saw opportunities to exploit the chaos of war for personal gain. Scattered complaints about such miscreants had been heard as early as 1861. Two years later, they seemed to be everywhere, and some hitherto legitimate bands had followed their path to the dark side. As Colonel Lazear observed further, "There is a terible state of affairs here the more I see of it the more complicated it seems."[3]

The changes gave the United States another claim to the moral high ground in the ongoing debate over the legitimacy of guerrilla warfare. In August 1862, Henry Halleck contacted the German-born Dr. Francis Lieber, a professor of history and political philosophy at Columbia College, in New York, whom he knew to feel deeply about the evils of slavery, secession, and the broadening guerrilla war. "The rebel authorities claim the right to send men, in the garb of peaceful citizens, to waylay and attack our troops," Halleck told him, "to burn bridges and houses, and to destroy property and persons within our lines. They demand that such persons be treated as ordinary belligerents, . . . [with] the same rights as other prisoners of war." He asked Lieber if the rebel position was legally valid [see Appendix A].[4]

Absolutely not, the professor replied, and proceeded to prove his point in an essay entitled "Guerrilla Parties Considered with Reference to the Laws and Usages of War." Having studied the role of irregular forces in previous military conflicts, most notably the Napoleonic wars, Lieber defined 10 distinct types of irregular activity, namely, the freebooter, marauder, brigand, partisan, free corps, spy, rebel, conspirator, robber, and rising en masse, although he regarded few of them as lawful. His analysis was sometimes confusing, strewn with qualifications and contradictions, but in that, the essay simply reflected the confused and controversial nature of the subject [see Appendix B].[5]

Lieber stressed the following points. To the extent their war represented a "rising of the people to repel invasion," the Confederates were entitled to "the full benefit of the law of war." However, such uprisings must also be waged "openly," in "respectable numbers," and "in the yet uninvaded or unconquered portions of the hostile territory." The only possible exceptions to this rule were partisan and free corps organizations. The former, clearly the model used by the rebels for their partisan rangers, operated "detached from the main army" and chiefly against lines of communication, in the rear or on the flanks of the invading force. Captured partisans deserved protection under the rules of war as long as they did not transgress those laws. In contrast, a free corps had no official connection to the army, even though it was often sanctioned by the government and might consist of "high-minded patriots." These troops slid too easily into "pillage and other excesses" and were "generally in bad repute," Lieber warned, yet there was "nothing inherently lawless or brigand-like in their character." They should be treated, he decided, "according to their deserts, on the principle of retaliation."

All other practitioners of irregular warfare fell into the general category of warrebel. This included the bushwhacker and guerrillaman, and they posed the greatest danger to an army in the field. While disapproving of the methods to suppress guerrillas used by someone such as John Pope, whom he called a "blowhard" and "irresponsible braggart," Lieber did endorse rough treatment for war-rebels. "[T]his renewer of war within an occupied territory," he explained, "has been universally treated with the utmost rigor of the military law. . . . Whether the war-rebel rises on his own account, or whether he has been secretly called upon by his former government to do so, would make no difference whatever." The army would be under no obligation to treat them as prisoners of war. Common sense dictated, he continued, that protection under the laws of war should not be extended to a man "simply because he says that he has taken up his gun in defense of his country, or because his government or his chief has issued a proclamation by which he calls upon the people to infest the bushes and commit homicides which every civilized nation will consider murders."

A delighted Halleck distributed the essay as a guide for the army, although his officers and men surely thought it a curious document, unlike any order they had ever received. It read like a legal treatise, filled with references to historical precedent, and often assuming that readers would be familiar with the activities of the Spanish *guerrilleros*, Prussian princes, and Austrian peasant uprisings that he relied on to illustrate his terms. Commanding officers might even wonder what possible value these supposed guidelines could have when Lieber himself admitted toward the end, "Indeed, the importance of writing on this subject is much diminished by the fact that the soldier generally decides these cases for himself. The most disciplined soldiers will execute on the spot an armed and murderous prowler found where he could have no business as a peaceful citizen."[6]

Recognizing the incomplete nature of his work, Lieber cautioned Halleck that a broader set of rules for the conduct of Union soldiers would not be amiss. "Ever since the beginning of our present war, it has appeared clearer and clearer to me," he explained, "that the president ought to issue a set of rules, and definitions providing for the most urgent cases, occurring under the law and usages of war, and on which our Articles of War are silent." Going further, Lieber admitted, "I do not know that any such thing . . . exists in any other country, but in all other countries the law of war is much more reduced to naked Force & Might, than we are willing to do it."[7]

Given permission by the commanding general to proceed, the professor produced, in concert with a panel of four army officers that included two lawyers, what has come to be known as the Lieber Code. Issued to the army as General Orders No. 100 in April 1863, it has been hailed as the first ethical guidelines for the conduct of war by a democratic state.

Yet, it is impossible to mistake the personal and immediate tone of the code. Gone are esoteric references to historical events and centuries-old precedents. Lieber refers frequently in the new document to the "American army" and to the enemies of the "United States." His abolitionist principles also played an important role in his desire to clarify the powers and responsibilities of an occupying army. Consequently, in a section headed "Public and private property of the enemy," Lieber made clear, in an important endorsement of the Emancipation Proclamation, that any fugitive slave under the protection of the Union army was "immediately entitled to the rights and privileges of a freeman." Still, his larger goal was to maximize the Union army's ability to crush rebel resistance without resorting to barbarity. "Military necessity" was the code's central principle, and while Lieber was careful to emphasize the need for soldiers to act with compassionate regard for both combatants and noncombatants, he defined the current war as a contest between a "legitimate government" and a collection of "disloyal citizens."[8]

The code deplored retaliation, which formed the essence of the guerrilla war, but it also explained why the general war had deteriorated so badly. As Lieber emphasized, "Unjust or inconsiderate retaliation" could only produce "the internecine wars of savages." Yet, he did not rule out retaliation under certain circumstances. Modern wars, he proposed, were waged "to obtain great ends of state, or to consist in defense against wrong." Nations waging war in a "noble cause" must base their actions on "principles of justice, faith, and honor," although Lieber also believed that "the more vigorously wars are pursued the better it is for humanity."

The section dealing with guerrillas was very much condensed, simplified, and clarified [See Appendix C]. The part dealing with partisans, prowlers, and war rebels, was only a page long, with other varieties of irregular activity addressed in a separate portion of the code. To this second part, Lieber added a new category, the war-traitor. Doubtless added to deal with the many citizens who aided rebel guerrillas without joining them in the field, the war-traitor was defined as a "person in a place ort district under martial law who, unauthorized by the military commander, gives information of any kind to the enemy, or holds intercourse with him."[9]

Lieber also used this broader code to mention at least two issues he regretted not mentioning in his initial treatise on guerrillas. "In the new edition the distinction between defending and attacking bands must be more insisted upon," he wrote in a memorandum. "It is very important." Lieber filled that legal loophole by stressing that any type of irregular activity, be it "fighting, or inroads for destruction or plunder, or by raids of any kind, without commission," was contrary to the laws of war.[10]

Similarly, he noted that any new edition should address the issue of paroles. Lack of clarification on this point, he explained "creates a new difficulty in the guerrilla baseness. How can small and unauthorized bands be paroled and afterwards watched whether they keep the parole, without any authority to resort to in ace the paroles are broken?" Lieber added an entire section, titled "The parole" to deal with the problem. Not only must "accurate lists . . . of the paroled persons . . . be kept by the belligerents," but any person breaking his parole should be "punished by death" if recaptured.[11]

The complete document could be read in many ways. Lieber meant it to give Union armies wide discretion and broad authority in putting down rebellion. Indeed, when confronted by an insurrection such as the current one, he said, commanders in the field should be able to "throw the burden of the war . . . on the disloyal citizens, . . . subjecting them to a stricter police than the non-combatant enemies have to suffer in regular war." The Confederates accused him of giving Union troops legal protection for their "acts of atrocity and violence." Lieber's "laws and usages of war," the rebels said, were a "confused, unassorted and undiscriminating" mess, nothing but Yankee propaganda, a feeble attempt to "frame mischief into a code." Even politically conservative Union officers dismissed it as a "defense of radical abolition principles" and called Lieber as a "very learned" but dangerous "bookworm." His code, when combined with Lincoln's recently enacted emancipation program "only served to unite the people of the rebel states, and to give strength to the rebellion."[12]

In the Department of the Missouri, where so much of the guerrilla debate had originated, Samuel Curtis announced his own general order (No. 30) two days before

Halleck issued the Lieber Code. Curtis addressed the issues of spies, guerrillas, and the laws of war by combining existing articles of war and a much truncated (and simplified) version of Lieber's original guerrilla essay. Three weeks later, President Lincoln decided to relieve Curtis of his command. The general had been embroiled in army politics for some time prior to this, and Halleck had been urging his removal, but Curtis could not have helped his own cause by this preemptive strike, or by his decision to abide by his own, less rigorous guidelines. The timing of Lincoln's action also fit his pattern that summer of pursuing the entire war more vigorously. Sixty-five-year-old Gen. Ethan Allen Hitchcock, a veteran soldier and briefly, in 1862, de facto chief of staff of the Union army, knew what was at stake. Praising Lieber for his accomplishment, he assured the professor, "The more I see of this war, the more strongly I see that power alone can bring it to a close."[13]

In any event, Union soldiers remained convinced that rebel guerrillas were a dangerous foe. "[O]f all villains and ruffians, these whackers are the worst," an Ohio soldier decided in Arkansas. More fiercely, an Iowa infantryman declared, "I have no pity, no mercy for the cowardly Scoundrels. [I] would rather put a minnie Ball through the brain of one of them renegades than the . . . [conventional] rebel down here. I want nothing to do with them. [T]hey are my deadly enemys." A junior officer told his mother, "You seem to think it would be terrible to hang guerrillas. . . . Well it would be oweing to circumstances." If ever he and his men confronted "a black flag," he explained, "I would be in favor of hoisting one myself and . . . I would say boys dont take a prisoner."[14]

The average Union soldier also relished an opportunity to strike back legally at people they knew to be aiding or encouraging the guerrillas. Every citizen not in the rebel army seemed either to be a guerrilla or to be cooperating with them in some byzantine and clandestine operational network. One soldier attributed a series of guerrilla attacks on railroad trains to sneaking citizens who had relayed information about schedules and cargoes to them. The only way to "clean out every guerrilla," decided another soldier, was to arrest every citizen, "for they all belong[ed] to the gang." An Ohioan in Tennessee decided, "[P]ut a little chunk of fire to thare houses, that is the way that we serve houses that harbors rebals."[15]

Backed by Lieber's Code, and with their enemy clearly defined, pursuit of the guerrilla network became more systematic, more aggressive, and more effective in 1863. Guerrilla hunting became a full-time job for some Union soldiers, and they relished it. "There is no playing war here," a soldier warned from Tennessee. "[W]e have to be sharp." When a boastful guerrilla captain (and Methodist minister) undertook a campaign of robbery, murder, and "harsh treatment of unionists" in Kentucky, a Union general in the region took action. "They were finally wiped out of existence," he reported with satisfaction, "[and] many of them had been killed by troops under my command."[16]

This is not to say the crackdowns solved every problem. Most notably, the security of Union supply and communication lines remained in peril. Wagon trains providing food, forage, and other supplies required heavy guards, and railroads were still extraordinarily vulnerable. Permanent guards and defensive patrols became mandatory along railroad lines in Kentucky and Tennessee, with guards often protected by blockhouses and stockades. An engineer responsible for constructing blockhouses in the Department of the Cumberland estimated that over 150 were built along seven railroads (totaling more than 700 miles of track) between 1862 and 1864. The soldiers learned the value of the blockhouses when companies operating without them were "cut all to pieces" by swarming guerrillas.[17]

The same game continued on Southern rivers, especially the crucial Mississippi River and its tributaries. Besides firing into the vicinity of attackers or landing troops to give chase, as naval commanders such as Le Roy Fitch had been doing on the Ohio, Tennessee, and Cumberland, worming expeditions were used to probe the Mississippi's network of waterways and punish rebel communities. "Cotton gin after cotton gin was laid in ashes," reported one Union soldier. "Large, long cribs of corn shared the same fate, and thus the flames did their work faithfully, destroying all personal property that we could not bring with us." In addition, the men led away many hundreds of mules and horses, herds of cattle, and untold numbers of sheep, chickens, and geese.[18]

Retaliation of this sort was already standard procedure on the river when Admiral Porter raised the stakes. Seeking to encourage absolute ruthlessness in ridding the Mississippi valley of guerrillas, he told subordinates, "There is no impropriety in destroying houses supposed to be affording shelter to rebels. . . . Should innocent persons suffer, it will be their own fault, and teach others that it will be to their advantage to inform the Government authorities when guerrillas are about certain localities."[19]

The admiral gave teeth to his plan by creating a specialized unit of guerrilla hunters called the Mississippi Marine Brigade. The self-sufficient unit of 1,035 men included infantry, cavalry, and artillery and patrolled the river on light, steam-powered craft with ample space for men, horses, artillery. Taking to heart Porter's credo that caution was for cowards, they retaliated forcefully against suspected guerrilla supporters. Usually content to burn mills and confiscate cotton and livestock, the men burned at least three towns in 1863—Eastport and Austin, Mississippi, and Simmsport, Louisiana.[20]

The Confederates found irony in this new federal resolve to crush the guerrilla war, for they had already decided to reduce still further their reliance on irregulars. The target this time was the vaunted corps of partisan rangers, which was proving to be more trouble than it was worth. Scores of rangers had been court-martialed by mid-1863. Most of their crimes were relatively minor ones, such as absence without leave, but the large number of cases was troubling. Complaints about the rangers' behavior by citizens had also grown. A farmer in western Virginia complained about the liberties two ranger companies had taken in pasturing their horses on his land and seizing his stocks of hay. "[T]here must be a screw loose somewhere in the management of this Warr or otherwise private property would be respected," he told President Davis in an angry letter. Failure to curtail "this reckless sistem of destroying property," he predicted, would leave the Confederacy "a great desert of woful waste."[21]

Entire units sometimes lurched out of control. Colonel Robert V. Richardson's 1st Tennessee Partisan Rangers provided useful service in western Tennessee and northern Mississippi. No one doubted his effectiveness in bedeviling the Federals, or that he had the confidence of the rebel citizenry. One Union cavalry commander, typical of many who pursued Richardson, acknowledged the difficulties of capturing him. "Parties of his men, numbering from 5 to 20, had been seen within two or three days, but I could get not the least information from any one as to where any of Richardson's could be found," he despaired; "and i will here state that of all the men who have taken the oath of allegiance to the United states, and to whom protection papers have been given, I could find none to give me any information whatever."[22]

However, success apparently bred arrogance. Starting with only 50 men in November 1862, Richardson had over 1,000 rangers by March 1863. The regiment effectively attacked federal scouting parties, destroyed railroads, captured forage trains, burned cotton, and rounded up draft evaders, but they also bullied Unionists, extorted money, and confiscated cotton and livestock without authorization, often for their own financial benefit. Many of the men had joined Richardson to escape conscription, and they dressed and behaved more like guerrillas than rangers. That autumn, the government revoked Richardson's commission, converted his command to a cavalry regiment, and placed it under new authority.[23]

The handling of Richardson expressed the new thinking about partisan rangers in Richmond. By the summer of 1863, the Confederate Congress had reduced the number of ranger companies in favor of "volunteer companies for local defense." The latter received no pay or allowances, but each company was made part of the Provisional Army. As an extension of this system, most existing companies, battalions, and regiments of partisan rangers were sent into the conventional ranks, most notably to serve—like Richardson's regiment—as cavalry. Not all partisan units were disbanded, but the survivors had to demonstrate their usefulness and reliability. Most of the exceptions were in Virginia, where several companies survived the purge.[24]

The most famous survivor was John Singleton Mosby. The Gray Ghost, as he became known, had been trying since 1862 to secure a ranger commission. He had, in fact, been operating successfully as a partisan in all but name in Gen. James E. B. Stuart's cavalry. However, Mosby craved independent action, and finally got it in March 1863, when he was made a captain of partisan rangers. A week later, he was Major Mosby and commanded a battalion.

Aware of the storm brewing over partisan warfare, Mosby was extremely selective in recruiting his men. He interviewed most of them personally to ensure their good character. Eighty percent came from Virginia, and all of them were excellent horsemen. Nearly 40 had been cadets at the Virginia Military Institute. Mosby wanted a battalion of "gentlemen," although that did not stop the citizens of northern Virginia, where he mostly operated, from hailing the "gallant band" as "our Bushwhackers."[25]

Nor would Mosby be intimidated by Halleck or Lieber. Even with his rangers acknowledged to be a cut above ordinary guerrillamen, he fought according to his own rules. "The complaints against us did not recognize the fact that there are two parties of equal rights in war," he pointed out in his memoirs. "The error men make is in judging conduct in war by the standards of peace. I confess my theory of war was severely practical—one not acquired by reading the Waverly novels—but we observed the ethics of the code of war. Strategy is only another name for deception and can be practised by any commander." Then, displaying a knowledge of the history if not the laws of war, Mosby emphasized, "The enemy complained that we did not fight fair; the same complaint was made by the Austrians against Napoleon."[26]

It was also true that efforts to dissolve partisan bands worsened the situation in some places. In Mississippi, for example, several hundred rangers organized smaller, independent bands rather than be sucked into the conventional forces. A larger number insisted on being able to join the regiments of their choice. Until given that reassurance, they went home to tend to their farms, families, and businesses. Some older, independent bands, led by the likes of W. W. Lowry, Sol Street, White Wilson, and Funderburk Mooney, tried to fill the void, but their stubborn devotion to independent operations prevented effective coordination with Confederate commanders in the field. And not even the combined efforts of regular and irregular Confederate troops could halt the capture of Vicksburg on July 4.

Shortly after the Vicksburg disaster, the stakes got very much higher everywhere in the guerrilla war, with the image of all rebel guerrillas suffering a severe blow. The shift began in, of all places, the Midwest. As talk about resisting the coming federal draft grew shrill in the early summer of 1863, rebel activity picked up on both sides of the Ohio River. Illinois had the most to fear. Citizens reported sightings of rebel cavalry and guerrillas along both the Ohio and Mississippi rivers, and scouting parties were spotted dozens of miles inland. The state's adjutant general received additional cavalry companies to maintain permanent forces in river towns along the Mississippi, where Missouri guerrillas seemed the most likely to slip across and pillage isolated farms.

Colonel Lazear assured his wife, who spoke of leaving Missouri for a place of safety east of the river while he was away from home, "I am like you I wish I was stationed there but I suppose it cannot be and if you were in Illinois I am afraid there will be as much trouble there as in Mo. before long." A Union soldier posted in the southern tip of Illinois, across the river from Cape Girardeau, Missouri, marveled at the situation. "[I]t is something new bushwhacking in Ill.," he informed his brother. "The country is full of deserters and Secesh. We have arrested a good many of both kinds."[27]

Ohio communities begged to be reinforced by independent or special cavalry companies. People feared that the thousands of guerrillas who terrorized Kentucky, a supposedly secure Union state, would soon surge across the river to plunder and murder Buckeyes. A raid by Albert Jenkins, cutting across a 20-mile stretch of the state the previous year, was evidence enough of Ohio's vulnerability. Military authorities acknowledged that they could not intercept every band of guerrillas, robbers, or horse thieves. "The citizens living upon the border must aid in their own protection," declared one general. "All the troops in the Dept if scattered along the line of the Ohio from Cairo to Wheeling could not entirely guard against small thieving bands."[28]

Indiana seemed best prepared. Following a destructive raid by partisan chief Adam Johnson out of Kentucky in the summer of 1862, its comprehensive and systematic militia organization, the Indiana Legion, was ever vigilant, supplemented in some places by locally recruited Border Cavalry and independent companies. Citizens were also sensitive to the least rumbling of internal dissent. Private railroad companies hired men to guard bridges and trestles against potential saboteurs.[29]

Still, it was Indiana where John Hunt Morgan struck on the morning of July 8, having ferried 2,000 mounted raiders across the Ohio River. From Indiana, he planned to dash through Ohio, leaving behind in both states a line of wrecked railroads, ravaged towns, and demoralized citizens. It was an incredibly high-risk venture, and designed more for self-aggrandizement than to further the Confederate cause. It is tempting to think that he hoped to compensate for Lee's retreat from Gettysburg on July 4, but Morgan knew naught of what had happened in Pennsylvania when he began his march.

For two weeks, his men did as they pleased, fully embodying the Union image of rebel freebooters. "We intend to live off the Yanks," bragged one sergeant, "and let them feel (like the South has felt) some of the horrors of war." Citizens buried their valuables and fled their homes upon his approach. Panic seized Hoosiers when word spread that Morgan might strike at Indianapolis. Instead, his men crossed into Ohio, came within a few miles of Cincinnati, and plunged farther eastward.[30]

Every available militia company and home guard in Indiana and Ohio joined Union cavalrymen to turn him back. Le Roy Fitch's gunboats denied him any possible escape route across the river. Morgan's men kept moving until finally cornered at West Point, Ohio, very near the Pennsylvania border and less than 100 miles from Lake Erie, on July 26. Over half of the "vile horde," including Morgan, surrendered. Only about 400 men escaped death or capture.[31]

Morgan's rampage sobered people on both sides, who hoped the guerrilla war might soon wane, and sucked much of the joy out of Union victories at Gettysburg and Vicksburg. Violent protests against the draft in New York and other states, including Ohio, had continued unabated in the very midst of the raid. The Northern home front seemed likely to implode, and that was even before events in Lawrence, Kansas, on August 21, 1863.

That was the morning when William Quantrill's gang of 450 guerrillas virtually destroyed the "fairest city" on the Plains. Within hours, they had reduced much of Lawrence to ashes, looted or destroyed $2 million in property, and murdered 150 men and boys. It had been a matter of revenge, retaliation for two years of jayhawker raids into Missouri. Like Morgan's raid, it showed that despite Union battlefield triumphs that summer, rebel passions were far from subdued. Unlike Morgan's raid, which had at least some military value, the attack on Lawrence was the work of brigands. The guerrilla war had reached low ebb morally.

Quantrill's gang dragged defenseless men from their homes and shot them in their front yards, often with wives or daughters still clinging to their loved ones. "One saw the dead everywhere," reported a male survivor, a minister, "on the sidewalks, in the streets, among the weeds in the gardens." The charred remains of shops, homes, a school, even an ice cream parlor smoldered for days. "The fires were still glowing in the cellars," said the minister. "The brick and stone walls . . . standing bare and blackened. . . . Here and there among the embers could be seen the bones of those who had perished."[32]

If the Federals needed further justification for punishing anyone associated with the guerrilla war, Quantrill had handed it to them. Columns of Union cavalry descended on Lawrence from all directions to drive the guerrillas back into Missouri. Outraged Kansans called for retaliatory raids into Missouri. "The people themselves, acting upon the common principle of self-defense," Kansas governor Thomas Carney warned, "will take the matter in their own hands, and avenge their own wrongs." In Missouri itself, generals John Schofield and Thomas Ewing, Jr., the Union commanders responsible for the security of the Kansas–Missouri border, fashioned their own response.[33]

Already having trouble in the central border counties controlled by Quantrill, Ewing had issued General Orders No. 10 three days *before* the Lawrence raid to remove rebel families from the region and "colonize" them in Arkansas. "While the families are here the men will prowl about, & the country is so well adapted by nature for bushwhackers that it is next to impossible to kill the scoundrels," Ewing asserted. Following the raid, he took stronger measures. On August 25, he issued General Orders No. 11, which forced some 20,000 people, loyal as well as disloyal, out of four counties. It was the most repressive U.S. military measure of the war against civilians, and applied, almost incredibly, to the people of a loyal state.[34]

The Kansas troops that enforced the order relished the opportunity to burn the homes of the departing Missourians, then rob and bully as they wound their way to Arkansas. The so-called removal sparked angry outcries across the South, although the most famous protest came from a Union man. Missouri artist and one-time Union soldier George Caleb Bingham, already famous for his depictions of antebellum rural life, painted a dramatic rendering of the burning homesteads and weeping women, which captured the essence of the guerrilla war.

Quantrill's men kept out of sight in the weeks after the Lawrence raid, and with their civilian network expelled, and many old camps being watched, they decided to spend the winter in Texas. About 400 men were riding south when, passing through the southeast corner of Kansas on October 6, they spotted a column of about 100 Union troops under Gen. James G. Blunt in open country near Baxter Springs, Kansas. In the attack that followed, the rebels killed or grievously wounded 90 of the poorly-armed detail, many of the Federals being musicians in Blunt's band. Not content with this, the guerrillas stripped and mutilated most of the Federals, and many bodies were incinerated when the rebels burned the wagons in which most had been traveling.

"Oh, it is a horrible sight to look on, the mangled remains of the poor victims," stammered one stunned witness to the scene. "I can give you no idea of it, I remain impotent, perfectly impotent to describe it." Among the slain were a 12-year-old drummer and Maj. Henry Z. Curtis, son of Samuel Curtis. Blunt escaped with a handful of men, but the experience unnerved him. Some people blamed it for his eventual mental collapse 18 years after that deadly autumn day. "I cannot throw it from my mind," he moaned shortly before his death. "It haunts me night and day."[35]

Many Confederates were appalled by the slaughter at Baxter Springs and Quantrill's mode of warfare. Gen. Henry McCulloch, commanding Confederate troops in North Texas when Quantrill's men arrived, voiced his concern to Gen. Edmund Kirby Smith, head of the Trans-Mississippi Department. "I appreciate his services, and am anxious to have them," McCulloch said tactfully; "but certainly we cannot, as a Christian people, sanction a savage, inhuman warfare, in which men are shot down like dogs." He tried, at the suggestion of Smith, to use Quantrill's men that winter to capture deserters, but the guerrillas spent most of their time raising hell and terrifying loyal Confederates.[36]

However, as things turned out, the Texas sojourn, which lasted until April 1864, marked the beginning of the end for Quantrill's band. Many original members of his band, discouraged by the collapse of discipline in their ranks, questioned the purpose of the war and their role in it. They splintered, with "Bloody Bill" Anderson leading the largest group of dissidents. Thomas C. Reynolds, Missouri's new Confederate governor in exile, and an early supporter of guerrilla warfare, also had some choice words for Quantrill. "A man of your ability should look forward to a higher future," he told him. "You must see that guerrilla warfare, as an honorable pursuit, is pretty nearly 'played out.'" The time had come when the guerrilla chief of an "undisciplined" band must either fall become a "slave of his men" or be put down.[37]

Elsewhere in the South, Union crackdowns against guerrillas proliferated during the final months of 1863. One of the most striking examples came in North Carolina, where Gen. Edward R. Wild led a regiment of black troops into the state from his base at Norfolk, Virginia. A thorough-going abolitionist, he had recruited his African Brigade from the refugee camps at New Bern, North Carolina. His three-week raid, beginning in early December 1863, freed 2,500 bondsmen, destroyed four guerrilla camps, burned over a dozen homes, captured or killed a number of guerrillas, and took four hostages, three of them women. "I adopted a more rigorous style of warfare," he said of his methods, and given an opportunity, he vowed to end any remaining guerrilla threat with "two weeks of stern warfare."[38]

North Carolina's governor, Zebulon Vance condemned the raid. "Such men as this Wild are a disgrace to the manhood of the age," he informed the U.S. government, "not being able to capture soldiers they war upon defenceless women! Great God! What an outrage." However, Vance's constituents responded in more measured tones. Judge Thomas Ruffin lived far to the west of Wild's exploits, but he likely agreed with a Virginia relation who wrote to him just as Wild entered the state. The relative had become disillusioned with the conduct of the war and the leadership of Jefferson Davis. As he considered the South's predicament, the Virginian worried that victory, even if still possible, might only come through "a protracted guerrilla war," and such a victory, he told Ruffin, could only turn their country into "one vast Missouri."[39]

SIX

THE WHEELS OF JUSTICE

With Lieber's Code in the books, the rules of rebellion should have been fairly fixed, but both Federals and Confederates continued to struggle with the nebulous nature of the irregular war. Definitions and circumstances set down in the quiet of a professor's study generally bore little relation to the circumstances faced by commanders and soldiers in the field. Lieber himself admitted that, when faced with deadly bushwhackers, "the soldier generally decides these cases for himself." Continuing, he stated forthrightly, "The most disciplined soldiers will execute on the spot an armed and murderous prowler found where he could have no business as a peaceful citizen." With the survival of an entire nation at stake, little could be left to chance.[1]

Good examples of the hardening views on both sides could be found in an exchange between the Missouri guerrilla chief Benjamin F. Parker and Union general James G. Blunt. The exchange came in May 1863, barely a fortnight after Lieber's Code had been distributed to the army and five months before Blunt's fateful encounter with Quantrill at Baxter Springs, but the issues that divided Parker and Blunt had clearly not been resolved by the new code, nor would they be by the war's end.

Reportedly operating with a commission as a colonel of partisan rangers, Parker's domain was the same one manned by Quantrill, with whom he occasionally joined forces, on the western border of Missouri. In communicating with Blunt, he protested the "unholy, savage and inhuman" treatment by the Union army of both rebel non-combatants and the men under his command. "[O]ur soldiers and citizens have been arrested and executed without trial," he declared, the citizens being shot under the pretext that they "fed, harbored and gave encouragement to bushwhackers." Equally detestable, Parker continued, had been the arrest and banishment of many women "for vindicating the sacredness of their sex against the slanders and insults of the base and unmitigated scoundrels calling themselves U.S. soldiers." Add to all that, the ruthless appropriation and destruction of property, and it was hard to see how the United States could pretend to be waging a "civilized and honorable warfare."

Was it any wonder, Parker asked, that honorable men should resist such "savage cruelty" by taking to the bush? "Can these things be tolerated any longer?" he challenged. "Can men stand back and see their families insulted and their property carried off by armed mobs? No! Every impulse that warms the human heart calls upon our people to arms. . . . Can you expect our arms to be surrendered up and we return to our former allegiance? No! Fight is the watchword of our people, and fight we shall until the hordes that now infest our country are withdrawn and our rights acknowledged among the nations of the earth." And finally, the ultimatum—"If total annihilation is the intention of your Government, then we are ready. . . . The perversion of the war for the Union to a war of extermination forces upon us retaliation. And if another Confederate soldier or citizen is executed without due process of law, five Union soldiers or citizens shall with their lives pay the forfeit."[2]

Copies of Parker's emotional outburst went to both Blunt and General Curtis, the former in command at Leavenworth, the latter headquartered in St. Louis. Curtis did not bother to reply. He simply forwarded the message to the district commander in his department with orders to "look out for this champion of Southern rights and give him such justice as he merits." Blunt, a former jayhawker who knew all about war on the Kansas–Missouri border, issued a public response in the newspapers to Parker's lecture.

"[Y]ou and your motley crew are insurgents and assassins," he reprimanded, "and are engaged in murdering and plundering unarmed loyal citizens, thereby barring yourselves of all rights and considerations extended to prisoners of war." Parker might take whatever action he liked, Blunt told him defiantly, but "every rebel or rebel sympathizer who gives aid, directly or indirectly, shall be destroyed or expelled from the military District." Nor would he exempt women from those prescriptions. "Experience has taught that the bite of a she adder is as poisonous and productive of mischief as the bite of any venomous reptile," the general declared. "Therefore, all persons known to be in arms against the Federal authorities of this District will be summarily put to death when captured. . . . All those who are in sympathy with your cause, and whom the military authorities may not feel justified in putting to death, will be sent south of the Arkansas River."[3]

Harsh as it sounded, Blunt's response was supported by key provisions of Lieber's two directives, even if not necessarily reflecting their spirit. As concerned the treatment of women, General Orders No. 100 stated, "The law of war, like the criminal law regarding other offenses, makes no difference on account of the differences between the sexes, concerning the spy, the war-traitor, or the war-rebel." More broadly, that same order declared, "The commander will throw the burden of war, as much as lies within his power, on the disloyal citizens, of the revolted portion or province, subjecting them to a stricter police than the non-combatant enemies have to suffer in regular war." Consequently, field commanders could "expel, transfer, imprison, or fine revolted citizens who refuse to pledge themselves anew as citizens obedient to the law and loyal to the government."[4]

As for putting known guerrillas "summarily to death," Lieber could be read as sanctioning that action, too, something the professor knew to be a distinct possibility. Writing after the war, he regretted that his essay on guerrillas had been "universally misunderstood." In his broader code, he stated that armed men who act "without being part and portion of the organized hostile army" were "not entitled to the privileges of prisoners of war, but shall be treated summarily as highway robbers or pirates." But did "summarily" mean instant execution? It certainly might, and Blunt, assuming he bothered to read Lieber's directives, could choose to interpret the word in that way. Less ambiguous was the fate of war rebels in Lieber's code. "If captured, they may suffer death," General Orders No. 100 declared. "They are not prisoners of war."[5]

As things turned out, the impending showdown between Blunt and Parker never came, as the partisan chief was killed in a shootout with Missouri militia a few weeks later, but the tough language used by both men suggested that neither side was likely to feel restricted or restrained by Lieber. Certainly, for Union officers in the field, it was easy enough to label any irregular as a plain bushwhacker, guerrillaman, or war rebel. They were more cautious with prisoners who claimed to be partisan rangers, but that depended entirely on circumstances, and whether the prisoner had been caught while engaged in legitimate military duties or while committing a crime, such as arson or murder. Even so, rangers in many parts of the South, and particularly in Virginia, carried certificates, signed by their commanding officer, that vouched for their status as government rangers. As one of John Mosby's men explained, the certificates became "a necessity, because men wearing Confederate uniforms, many of them deserters or absent from their commands without leave, were roaming about the country representing themselves as belonging to Mosby's command."[6]

In relatively stable areas of occupation, the Union army's provost marshal provided some check on summary punishments. In Arkansas, for example, after the capture of Little Rock, in September 1863, the Federals had nominal control of the northern half of the state. With the region divided into four districts, the provost marshals, besides maintaining discipline in the army, tracking down deserters, and administering the loyalty oath to civilians, gathered intelligence about local guerrillas and other "disloyal and dangerous persons." Spies, or simply unionist scouts who knew the neighborhoods and the sympathies of the people, were sometimes employed. One of those men compiled an annotated list of over 450 suspected bushwhackers and guerrillas operating in an eight-county region of north-central Arkansas in 1863–1864. The annotations described the alleged crimes perpetrated by each guerrilla and the relative danger each posed to the community. Some were described as bad men, others as vicious. The worst of the lot were rounded up. "[T]hey have brought in a good many Guerrillas and bushwhackers," observed an Iowa infantryman of Unionist scouts near Little Rock. "[T]he Penitentiary is nearly full of rascals of that character, and they will . . . leave there only for the *grave*."[7]

How many captured guerrillas actually went to the grave depended on circumstances, including who apprehended them and the evidence against them. If arrested by a provost marshal, the chances for leniency were good. In early 1864, a scouting expedition near Hot Springs, Arkansas, found itself constantly bushwhacked for three days before finally capturing one of their tormentors, armed with a revolver and shotgun. They then arrested a second man, reputed to be part of a local Independent Guerrilla Company. Hidden in his house, they found five saddle bags and portions of several Union army uniforms, including a pair of staff officer's trousers. Nonetheless, after being jailed for a few days, the provost marshal released both men, his reason being that no proof of treasonous activity had been found against them. The decision created "considerable dissatisfaction among the officers and men" who had captured the pair.[8]

Even men whose cases were heard by a military commission and who were found guilty of being guerrillas sometimes escaped death. Military commissions had operated virtually from the start of the war as the legal mechanism for trying disloyal citizens, including guerrillas, spies, saboteurs, or anyone materially assisting the rebellion. Defendants were entitled to legal counsel, but, as in a court-martial—the judicial forum in which Union soldiers were tried for their transgressions—cases were heard and sentences passed by a board of army officers, not a civilian jury. Thousands of military tribunals were held during the war, one estimate being as high as 5,460, although this number also included Northerners charged with treasonous activity. Jury or no jury, the main problem was the lack of uniformity in passing judgments. Some board members had little or no training legal training, even to the point of denying the accused his or her right to counsel. Other boards were either opposed to the death penalty or, at the other extreme, wanted to execute every rebel possible. Sometimes the witnesses, bearing a grudge against the accused, would say whatever was necessary to obtain a conviction. It was certainly true that some convictions were based on fairly flimsy evidence.

The nature and number of charges could also determine a person's fate, and there was nearly always more than one charge. For instance, a man might escape the worst punishments if found guilty only of operating as a guerrilla, but if he was also guilty of an additional criminal charge, such as murder, rape, or violating the Union oath of allegiance, severity was more likely. Then again, much depended on who passed sentence, as was the case when the politically conservative Gen. Frederick Steele commanded the army in Arkansas. The 45-year-old West Point graduate, known for returning fugitive slaves to their masters even after the Emancipation Proclamation had been issued, reviewed the decisions of all military commissions in the state, and he was as likely to commute a death sentence to hard labor as to hang or shoot a man.

Even when generals in the field approved a sentence, it might still be overturned when the case was reviewed in Washington, D.C., as provided for in army regulations. Two men enjoyed that sort of luck in December 1863, when their convictions by a military commission was partially approved by Steele but overturned by the judge-advocate general, Joseph Holt. Elbridge M. Ball and Benjamin R. Fortenberry, found guilty of violating the laws of war, robbery, and violation of an earlier oath of Union allegiance, testified that they had been forced to join a roaming guerrilla band in a string of robberies. The gang released them a few days later, but they were subsequently arrested at their homes and brought to trial.

Steele found the pair guilty only of the robberies, but Holt exonerated them completely, and for two reasons. First of all, it seemed clear to the judge advocate that not only had Ball and Fortenberry been pressed into service, but that they were also demonstratively loyal Union men who, though never mustered into service, had enlisted in a company that became part of the 4th Arkansas (U.S.) Mounted Infantry. Second, and more tellingly, Holt decided that "the witnesses for the prosecution were men of strong disloyal sentiments, had been in arms against the government, and had feelings of enmity against the prisoner[s]." In a revealing statement about Union policy, Holt concluded by stating, "In view of the well- established usage of this office to allow little weight to the evidence of witnesses of known disloyalty, when it puts in peril the lives and liberties of Union men, it is recommended that prisoner[s] be set at large."[9]

Union soldiers caught in the middle of the bushwhacker war derived a sense of relief and satisfaction from every confirmed sentence. When two guerrillas were publicly hanged at the Little Rock Penitentiary in Match 1864, at least one Union soldier looked on approvingly. It had been "positively proved," he reported, that one of the men, the band's captain, "was accessory to the hanging of twenty three Union men in and around this city. Some since we came here was hung by him but a few miles from town. Several more will be hung if justice is done them, and it is probable that justice will be done. There are hundreds of men in this that deserve hanging as much."[10]

Still, soldiers in the field could be exasperated by the leniency shown to men they considered dangers to themselves and the Unionist population. Having lost confidence in the judicial system, they, like General Blunt, took summary executions literally. "All is quiet around here except an occasional *Brush* with the *Bushwhackers,*" admitted a soldier at Little Rock in November 1864, "which dont amount to much neither way–only the *Hanging of a rascal when caught.* [Y]ou don't often see an account in the newspapers of the punishment of Bushwhackers, *but that is no sign that it is not done.*" Union soldiers patrolling the countryside near Joe Scott's home told his mother that if they ever caught him, they would hang him "to the first limb they came to." The Union officer who captured Ratcliff Chandler turned him over to the provost marshal, but also specifically requested that the prisoner be "brought to summary punishment." Describing Chandler as a "desperate character," he explained how the rebel had "committed several acts of barbarity on the families" of the very soldiers who had captured him. Their forbearance in not conducting a drumhead court martial, he implied, should not be forgotten.[11]

Provost marshals could also be frustrated, to such an extent that they looked for ways to avoid enforcing the strict letter of the law. Arkansas's provost marshal general decided that, while it might not be appropriate to order Union soldiers to execute guerrillas, the army's independent scouts might well be charged with that duty. Addressing the captain of one independent company in September 1864, he instructed, "[D]estroy all Guerilla bands you may encounter, as effectively as possible." The men might also confiscate from the local population any "contraband of war" that might otherwise assist the guerrillas, as well as all necessary "subsistence" for themselves.[12]

All of these incidents occurred in Arkansas, but identical situations of justice done or undone could be found in every part of the South, with pure chance and circumstances again being the difference between life and death. J. K. Blair thought he had escaped execution when the local judge-advocate challenged the findings of a military commission at Nashville that had sentenced him to be shot for "Being a guerrilla" and "Bushwhacking." "The evidence in the second charge and specifications being only the hearsay evidence of a witness of doubtful reputation," reasoned the judge-advocate, "is scarcely sufficient to sustain a finding of guilty." It was also the case that one witness described Blair as "a laboring man, works hard to make a living, peaceable man with his neighbors." Nonetheless, when the case was returned to the board for reconsideration, it reached the same verdict, and more than six months after the original trial, Blair was shot to death.[13]

Meantime, halfway across the state, at Memphis, Nelson Cook stood charged with "Being a guerrilla" and "Being a Brigand"—a curious dual identity, given Lieber's definitions. Several witnesses testified to Cook's misdeeds, including kidnapping, theft, and "acts of violence" as part of armed gang. He seemed to be at least as dangerous a character as Blair, although it was also true that he had not, in fact, shot anyone. It may have been that, then, that led the board to clear him of brigandage and sentence him to only six months at hard labor.[14]

The death of a Union solider or civilian often weighed heavily in a board's decision, as well as in appeals for clemency. James M. Fraley, sentenced to be hanged by a commission at Cedar Grove, Tennessee, probably could have escaped death for Highway Robbery and Engaging in a Guerrilla Warfare, but he could not dodge the third charge—a single count of Murder. It was the third charge that led Joseph Holt to uphold the commission's findings, emphasizing in his decision that Fraley had "brutally" slain a neighbor after robbing him of horses and arms. Compare his case to that of Hugh Lawson Bell, and the difference is clear. Lawson, also operating in Tennessee, was charged with murder, as well as belonging to a band of "horse thieves and robbers," being a guerrilla, and violating his oath of allegiance. However, having been presented with no clear evidence of the murder, the commission sentenced Bell to "hard labor for life." Joseph Holt, on the recommendation of the department commander, Gen. George H. Thomas, reduced even that sentence to hard labor for the "duration of the war."[15]

Though rare, plea bargains were not out of the question. For instance, many boards considered it sufficient punishment, if they thought a prisoner posed no further threat, to accept his oath of allegiance. Some men, as well, turned over the names of their accomplices. A 49-year-old Virginia farmer, accused of harboring guerrillas, was allowed to move to New Jersey after taking the oath. Several of John Mosby's men or civilian guides escaped prison in similar ways. One former ranger told investigators everything he knew about Mosby's operations and his whereabouts, ultimately volunteering to lead an expedition in pursuit of the Gray Ghost. Another man said he only joined Mosby to keep from being conscripted. "I had a crop of corn and joined . . . to save it," he testified, "so that my family would have something to eat during the winter." He deserted at the first opportunity, turned himself over to the Federals, and was prepared to take the oath.[16]

Escapes from either custody or prison were not unknown either. Most famously, John Hunt Morgan escaped from the state penitentiary at Columbus, Ohio. Captured at the conclusion of his destructive raid through Indiana and Ohio, he had been placed there for extra security by order of General Halleck. Four months later, Morgan and six of his men escaped through a tunnel they had dug under the prison walls. In Missouri, two of the war's most famous female guerrillas, Jennie and Sallie Mayfield, escaped from the St. Louis prison. Another Missouri guerrilla, sentenced to hard labor for the duration of the war, escaped from the military prison at Alton, Illinois, by simply walking away from the stone quarry where he had been breaking rocks.

The legal system also seemed to grow increasingly intolerant of people accused of aiding guerrillas, even when they had not themselves taken up arms. An extreme instance in Kentucky found one such man beaten to death while being interrogated by three Union soldiers, two of them officers. In Virginia, a man accused of carrying dispatches and provisions to John Mosby and of entertaining Mosby in his home avoided that fate, but only after languishing in prison for nearly eight months before his case even came to trial. When a military commission then sentenced him to a year of hard labor, friends petitioned the court for a reduced sentence, based on the lengthy time already spent in the Old Capitol Prison. Not only did the board reject the petition, but when the case was then appealed to Joseph Holt, the judge-advocate general agreed that the sentence should be "rigidly enforced." Moreover, Holt added, given the prisoner's close association with a band of men "engaged in robbing and murdering" Union soldiers and loyal citizens, "he might well have been punished with death."[17]

Female members of the guerrilla network—the "she adders," as General Blunt characterized them—were dealt with just as severely. Indeed, by 1864, there were far more female guerrillas than anyone could have anticipated. Not many of them were gun-toting brigands, but they often took to the field to guide local bands, deliver messages to them, smuggle goods to them, or cut telegraph lines. If caught and found guilty, they received the same prison terms and death sentences as the men. While not mentioning female rebels in his original essay on guerrillas, Lieber had seemingly become aware of their activities by the time he compiled his broader code. "The law of war, like the criminal law, regarding other offenses," he stated plainly, "makes no difference on account of the differences of sexes, concerning the spy, the war-traitor, or the war-rebel."[18]

More frequently, and in fact, rather commonly, women passed on information to local bands, fed them, or sheltered them at home. Armies in the field sometimes took responsibility for dealing with these she rebels, most notably by confiscating or destroying their property. Of course, this could be the swift and easy way to deal with secesh men as well, but it was regarded as especially appropriate for women who turned their homes into sanctuaries for brigands. The homes of two Missouri women were simply burned to the ground. "The feeling among the men was bitter against these two families," their commanding officer explained by way of justification. If arrested and found guilty of feeding, harboring, or otherwise aiding guerrillas, imprisonment or banishment were likely fates. This could be ordered by the local military commander or by a military commission, depending on how strong the evidence was against the women.[19]

On other occasions, the violence came not in direct response to the women's actions, but against the guerrillas they likely harbored. Too late to catch a band of guerrillas at their usual rendezvous, one federal expedition left a warning for both them and their women folk. "The Col. gave his men leave to pillage Capt. Brown's house and then ordered it burned," reported a member of the expedition. "He was a notorious leader of bushwhackers. There were so many women there it looked too bad but they were rank rebels." In another instance, some Federals mutilated the bodies of three dead guerrilla brothers before ruthlessly dumping them in their mother's yard.[20]

The extent of female involvement first impressed Colonel Lazear in the spring of 1863. Having prided himself on his ability to stay on good terms with the rebel women in his Missouri district, he suddenly faced the prospect of arresting large numbers of them. Ordered to detain 20 of them in one week, he lamented, "I expect they will give me the devil." He applauded General Ewing's General Orders No. 11 later that year for ridding the Missouri border of the most troublesome female rebels, but Lazear soon discovered that not even Ewing's drastic solution could solve the problem. A year later, in the summer of 1864, he complained, "This is the worst rebel country I was ever in. Nearly all are rebels of the worst kind. I have several women under arrest and will send them all out of the county." He spoke of a "reign of terror" in his district, and of how women in one town encouraged guerrillas "engaged in burning robing and Murdering" in the place.[21]

That said, some commissioners had become aware that not everyone associated with the guerrillas approved of the violence or assisted the rebels willingly. When George M. Elliott appeared before a commission in Louisville, charged with being a guerrilla, there was no doubt that he had ridden with at least one marauding band. However, Elliott insisted that he had served only as a guide, and that even then he had been "forced against his will" to assist the rebels and "threatened with death" if he refused. That he also had a better-than-average defense attorney, who challenged the charges in an extraordinarily long (5 pages) and detailed affidavit may have helped his case, but in any event, the commission found him not guilty.[22]

This same insight led other commissioners to discern degrees of guilt among the members of the same guerrilla bands. In a rare case, in which all 23 members of a notorious band of Tennessee guerrillas was captured and tried together, split verdicts were delivered on their guilt. They had been accused of being guerrillas and of murder, but they were all cleared of the murder charge, and the commission decided that only half of them were genuine guerrillas. That half was sentenced to hard labor for the duration of the war. The other men were released, most likely because the evidence showed that they had been conscripted by the leader of the band. "He went to their houses," said a witness, "took their names and ordered them to report to him at a certain place and said if they didn't he would take them and treat them as deserters."[23]

More ominously, as the gangs of marauding deserters and genuine brigands grew in number, rebel guerrillas were accused of being outlaws *and* guerrillas, the fine distinctions of the Lieber Code long forgotten. Some men even escaped conviction by military commissions as guerrillas only to be found guilty of civil crimes, such as murder. Others might still be convicted as guerrillas, but for reasons that had nothing to do with military operations. For instance, Gideon D. Bruce, an Arkansas blacksmith, had ridden with several guerrilla bands before turning horse thief and plunderer in 1863. His most violent crime occurred when he and a "very bad man" named Ben Guess tortured and extorted money from Wilford Baskett. Dressed in Union uniforms, they accused Baskett of being a "d__d old Secesh" and demanded $750 from him. When he denied possessing any such sum, they squeezed his neck between two fence rails while they "kicked and spurred" him. Finally, after frightening Baskett's wife to surrender what little money she had, $17.20, the villains twice hanged Baskett from the limb of a peach tree before releasing the pressure on his throat. The military commission that heard his case sentenced Bruce to hard labor for being a guerrilla.[24]

In instances where there was no hard proof of specific misdeeds, a man might be held on charges of being a guerrilla simply because he seemed a danger to society. Two Virginians, charged only with being dangerous characters, were imprisoned at Point Lookout, Maryland. Three guerrillas confined in the Old Capitol Prison were described as dangerous characters who "should be securely kept." The youngest of the men was a petty thief who "commenced his career by . . . stealing a revolver, clothes, etc." Another man, a citizen, was arrested because his brother was a guerrilla and the local provost marshal feared that he would become a guerrilla "if allowed to go at large."[25]

SEVEN

GUERRILLAS RAMPANT, 1864–1865

One vast Missouri or not, the Confederates were far from dead, and while the Federals had sunk their teeth deep into the guerrilla behemoth, tough times lay ahead for everyone. Winter saw most guerrillas go to ground. They might still harass defenseless civilians, but military operations became too dangerous without nature's veil of foliage and vegetation to disguise their movements, encampments, and rendezvous. However, come the spring of 1864, the resurgence began.

William Quantrill left Texas in April with about half his men but determined to reassert his authority in Missouri. There followed the most relentless and destructive period of guerrilla warfare the state had seen, and Quantrill was only part of it. Plenty of other ruthless characters shared the stage, and neither side expected anything like a civilized war. "No more forbearing" in this war lamented a St. Louis rebel. "People of every political opinion and all ages, fleeing from their homes," he observed that summer. "The guerrillas prowling into the country and the Federals ravaging towns. Murder, arson of daily occurrence. Fights rendered horrible by their ferocity. No quarter being given, no mercy shown. It is horrible."[1]

U.S. military authorities, no less than civilians, were taken aback by the onslaught. Missouri's provost-marshal general, called on Edward Bates for help. He warned that "massacres, private assassinations, burning, plundering and thieving" had surpassed all known limits. Thomas Ewing complained that the federal government assigned nothing like an adequate number of troops to his district. Rebel guerrillas, he said, could "rob and plunder over the whole state with comparative impunity."[2]

The boldest thrusts came in the western and northern parts of the state, where a general uprising seemed to be underway, but waves of veteran bushwhackers had infiltrated all parts of Missouri by this time. In the southeast, Sam Hildebrand began his savage odyssey of retaliation when a brother was lynched by Unionists, "I sought revenge and I found it," Hildebrand boasted; "the key of hell was not suffered to rust in the lock while I was on the war path."[3]

The actions of Bill Anderson, Quantrill's defecting lieutenant, produced the most outrage. He, too, had returned to Missouri with his part of the band, including Frank and Jesse James. He had come, he announced in a pair of Lexington, Missouri, newspapers, to protect the community from the "thieves and robbers" that now infested it. "[T]hey do not belong to any organized band," he declared; "they do not fight for principles; they are for self-interest. . . . I will help the citizens rid the country of them." However, should the citizenry turn on him, and assist the Union army in pursuing him, they would suffer for it. "I will kill you," he said quite plainly. "I will hunt you down like wolves and murder you. You cannot escape." He issued a similar warning to the Union troops in Missouri, and urged the young men of the state to join his patriotic band. "[L]eave your mothers and fight for your principles," he intoned. "Let the Federals know that Missouri's sons will not be trampled on."[4]

Both unionists and the Union troops in Missouri learned the truth of Anderson's words in September, when he and his command rode into the small railroad junction of Centralia. His 80 men were content at first to rob and terrorize the residents of the town, but then a train arrived at the depot. On board were about two dozen unarmed Union soldiers going home on furlough. The guerrillas ordered them off the train, stripped them, and executed all but one man, whom they left to tell the tale.[5]

A civilian witness to the raid left a riveting account of the vulnerability of defenseless civilians caught in the vortex of such violence. "Women and children cowered behind boxes or in the stores, crying, moaning, and wringing their hands," he reported. "The men stood around like statues, numb with horror and fearful of what might happen next. The guerrillas seemed transformed into fiends, half drunken with the whiskey they had stolen. They gave no heed to anyone, man, woman, of child, except to insult or terrorize them." Then, coming to the heart of the matter, he added, "Those who have never seen men unrestrained, can have no idea of how those guerrillas conducted themselves while they had full possession of the little village." It was this lack of restraint, the absence of any rules, that would be remembered by nearly every victim of the guerrilla war.[6]

That might have been the end and the worst of it had not a Union cavalry patrol happened on the scene shortly after Anderson's men rode out of town. The soldiers gave chase. Anderson, aware of his pursuers, joined forces with several other bands in the vicinity to increase his strength to 400 men. Nearly all 115 Federals were killed in the ensuing gun battle. Still not satisfied, the rebels mutilated most of the bodies and took about a dozen scalps.

If Missouri, as usual, seemed to represent extremes of barbarism, that is not to say that most other parts of the South escaped the resurgence. The Union commander at Little Rock, Arkansas, which the Federals had finally captured in September 1863, marveled at the inability of 230 troops, including 50 cavalry, to maintain order around Clarksville, located halfway to Fort Smith, on the state's western border. "I want those guerrillas captured, killed, or dispersed," he exclaimed in April 1864 to the commander at Clarksville. "Where do 300 or 400 guerillas come from? . . . You done well in capturing 23. You will do better by killing or capturing the rest."[7]

In the northwest corner of the state, death was never far away for troopers in the 1st Arkansas Cavalry (U.S.). Having discovered the bodies of two comrades who had been captured by local guerrillas, one of their officers, "carrying a black flag, . . . rode up and down the line calling for volunteers, men with backbone, good horses and plenty of ammunition, to follow him and take revenge on the murderers." Fifty men volunteered for the mission, though, as usual, they never found the culprits. "The only thing we saw to shoot," recalled one man, "was a big fat hog and we embraced that opportunity."[8]

Equally startling examples of Union frustration could be found in Mississippi. Following the capture of Jackson and the surrender of Vicksburg in 1863, Mississippi rebels would seem to have been on their heels. By 1864, the state's guerrilla population had been reduced by death, capture, and recent amendments to the Partisan Ranger Act. Surviving bands had been reduced in size, some to as few as a dozen men, and most of the state's most effective guerrilla chiefs were gone. A resurgence seemed unlikely.

Nonetheless, some Mississippi bands continued to cause trouble, the most lethal being Capt. William E. Montgomery's Herndon Rangers. Based in Bolivar County, midway between Vicksburg and Memphis, their principal tasks were to capture and burn river traffic and cotton, fire into troop transports, capture unescorted river craft, round up fugitive slaves, and arrest or punish troublesome Unionists. His success made Montgomery a target for retaliation. As early as November 1863, the Mississippi Marine Brigade burned his plantation and liberated his slaves. When an incensed Montgomery redoubled his efforts against them, the Federals threatened to take his family as hostages against his "good behavior." Undeterred, the partisan continued to operate until the end of the war.[9]

As suggested by Montgomery's activities, Unionists everywhere also suffered in the new onslaught, even more than before in some instances. As the Union army moved ever deeper into the South, emboldened Unionists posed an increasing, rather than decreasing, threat to rebel communities. Guerrilla leaders reacted accordingly, so that unionists who dared make trouble generally suffered. Targeting the family of a man who was away on business, Champ Ferguson's men assaulted his wife and 17-year-old daughter "with guns and pistols." They apparently did not rape the women but did strip them of their clothing and ransacked the house.[10]

The result was a surge in the number of Unionist as well as rebel refugees. Homeless people wandered everywhere, and the sight of so many widows and orphans led Union soldiers to give thanks that "the horrors of war" were confined to the South. "[T]he husband of one of the women," reported an Ohio soldier of a group of refugees, "was taken from his own house by a band of rebel guerrillas and hanged a few rods from the house . . . and left him hang[ing] in the presence of his wife and children. [Two] sons of another woman . . . were shot at the same time. [T]hey were robbed of everything." The soldier related this story to his own wife and daughter.[11]

In Louisiana, the situation unraveled following the failed Red River campaign of March–May 1864. Loyal Louisianians warned Gen. Nathaniel Banks, the state's Union commander, that the rebels meant to "burn all the cotton gins and sugar houses in Louisiana and along the Mississippi River," and that guerrilla warfare would be "organized on a large scale and encouraged in every possible way." The Federals placed bounties on the head of known guerrilla leaders, some as high as $10,000. The number of troops assigned to "get shet of Bush Whackers" increased throughout the state. The Marine Brigade worked overtime, and gunboat commanders patrolling the river punished citizens who harbored guerrillas. One squadron commander announced that he would "shoot a prisoner . . . for each person killed by rebels firing on transports."[12]

People were appalled by the randomness and gratuitous nature of the violence. There seemed to be heartless cruelty and intense bitterness after 1863, not only in the guerrilla war, but also in some conventional operations, such as the massacres of black Union soldiers at Fort Pillow (Tennessee) and Poison Spring (Arkansas) and of Indians by Union troops at Sand Creek (Colorado). Champ Ferguson participated in one of the most notorious of instances of racial retaliation, at Saltville, Virginia, in October 1864. Having helped to defend the vital saltworks against an unsuccessful attack by Union troops, including parts of two black regiments, his company stalked the battlefield to execute the wounded. Ferguson personally entered a hospital to kill two of the 46 blacks murdered that day.[13]

In Ferguson's case, though, race was only part of the equation. He also murdered a white officer wounded at Saltville, a relative through marriage as a matter of fact, named Elza Smith. As always, Ferguson justified the killing as self-defense. "Yes, I killed him," he would later admit, "but it was to save my own life; Smith had sworn to kill me, if he found me. He was wounded, and in the hospital. I knew he would get well, and my life wouldn't be safe, so I killed him."[14]

Another reason for the timing of the surge in anarchy was political. With a Northern presidential election to be held in November, not a few rebels believed that an escalation in violence might result in Abraham Lincoln being replaced with a Democrat willing to cede Confederate independence. Sterling Price chose the moment to invade Missouri, hoping at the very least to provoke the election of a pro-Confederate governor and legislature that would lead Missouri out of the Union. The timing of his raid, launched on September 17, also seemed fortuitous, coming, as it did, 17 days after William T. Sherman captured Atlanta. Sherman hoped that the fall of the pivotal railroad depot would ensure Lincoln's election. Success in Missouri could neutralize that advantage.

Price sent agents into Missouri to encourage guerrilla chiefs to create as much havoc as possible in the weeks before the raid. He hoped that a popular uprising would produce some 30,000 reinforcements for his 12,000-man Army of Missouri. He miscalculated. While many bushwhackers, including the splintered parts of Quantrill's command, grew active when Price entered the state, most of them failed to coordinate their movements with those of the general. Bill Anderson, for instance, indulged himself with the raid on Centralia during those weeks. Most guerrilla bands had never been very reliable when it came to cooperating with Confederate armies, their prized independent status being more important to them than the strategic goals of the Richmond government, but by 1864, they seemed to care even less about what might be best for the nation. Consequently, a combination of Union troops, state militia, and home guards forced Price out of the state by the end of October. Continuing their retreat through Indian Territory, he and approximately 6,000 survivors finally re-entered the extreme southwest corner of Arkansas in December.

Elsewhere on the border, Kentucky seemed a likely spot to disrupt the election and reverse rebel fortunes in another Union slave state. However, Federal commanders there, anticipating just such a stratagem, took preemptive measures. Most visible was Gen. Stephen G. Burbridge, who commanded the District of Kentucky from Lexington. General Halleck from Washington and General Sherman from Georgia, the latter needing a pacified Kentucky in order to maintain his supply lines, encouraged Burbridge as early as June to suppress rebel guerrillas in the state. "Any attempt at rebellion in Kentucky must be put down with a strong hand," Halleck directed, "and traitors must be punished without regard to their rank or sex." Burbridge, a native Kentuckian, understood. "I deem it of the utmost importance for Kentucky's future that the State should be carried for Mr. Lincoln," he informed the Washington government in October. "I have used every means in my power to accomplish this end." The means eventually used included the execution of guerrillas when and where captured, measures that earned him the nickname "Bloody" Burbridge.[15]

In West Virginia, by now a state in the Union, intense local wars continued unabated. What was more, and paradoxically, fewer Union soldiers remained to defend the state as the war rolled farther south. "The County has been in a state of Anarchy since the Federal Troops have been withdrawn," the citizens of one community protested to Gov. Arthur I. Boreman. "Guerrilla bands have been prowling through the country, greatly annoying the union Citizens, and we are now in a more defenseless condition than we were two years ago." One worried woman worried, "Unless it is stopped, I awfully fear another Lawrence massacre."[16]

Within the Confederacy, too, political considerations gained importance. Rebel guerrillas had intimidated local officials, disrupted elections, and destroyed court and tax records from day one. However, the stakes increased when Lincoln's government tried to establish Unionist state governments in the occupied South, most notably in Arkansas and Tennessee. In the former state, one man complained to Isaac Murphy, the newly-elected governor of a Unionist Arkansas government, that "bushwhackers and thieves" rode roughshod over defenseless people all across the supposedly secure northern half of the state. Since the capture of Little Rock, he explained, the rebels had instituted a "new system" of defense by "killing or driving out of the country" all Union people in order to disrupt the loyal government.[17]

Tennessee rebels frustrated Andrew Johnson's efforts to install a stable government in Nashville. One Tennessean had warned the military governor as early as October 1863 that it was "idle to talk about reorganizing the state Government—or reestablishing civil authority" until people could be protected from "the depredations of Guerilla bands." Nothing had changed by the summer of 1864, especially not when Johnson was named Abraham Lincoln's running mate. Fear of rebel reprisals became so widespread that local officials responsible for suppressing marauding bands during the election, resigned for fear of their lives.[18]

Strikes against Northern communities were the ultimate political statement, and Midwesterners were on high alert through the election season. The most serious disturbances came in Iowa and Illinois, and they were both related to the timing of Price's Missouri raid. On October 12, a dozen rebel guerrillas entered southeast Iowa from Missouri. Jim Jackson, a veteran of John Hunt Morgan's operations in Kentucky and Clifton Holtzclaw's guerrillas in Missouri, led them on a 12-hour spree of robbery, murder, and kidnapping. Smaller gangs as well as Confederate recruiters continued to come and go through the autumn, with a variety of crimes reported in their wake. Most of the culprits appear to have returned safely to Missouri, even though Iowa militia flooded the southern counties to arrest or disarm dozens of resident copperheads.

Illinois was hit even harder, most of the trouble, as with Iowa, coming from neighboring Missouri. The climax came that summer, when a shadowy character named Thomas L. Clingman terrorized the southcentral part of the state with a gang of 300 Missouri guerrillas and Illinois copperheads. Local home guards were useless against them. Not until some 150 Union soldiers joined the manhunt could Clingman's band be brought to heel. Smaller gangs continued to operate in Iowa and Illinois for the remainder of the year, but all appear to have scattered by the end of 1864. Not coincidentally, the worst fears of guerrilla raids out of the South receded with Price's retreat back into Arkansas.[19]

Indiana, still reeling from Morgan's raid, suffered mainly from expectations of what might happen. "We are experiencing serious apprehension of danger along our Southern border from the guerrilla operations," Indiana's adjutant general confessed fully a year later. Probably not all strangers suspected of being disloyal were guerrillas or Confederate agents, but there were enough instances of violence to demand vigilance. Bands of "butternuts and thieves," some numbering in the hundreds, were blamed for robberies and the murder of "respected citizens" as far north as Terre Haute.[20]

Finding that the usual counterinsurgency measures did little to weaken guerrilla strength, some local Union commanders in the South developed novel solutions to the problem. In northwest Arkansas, Col. Marcus LaRue Harrison and his 1st Arkansas (Union) Cavalry found it impossible to eliminate rebel threats to Union communications lines or to protect local Unionists. Having narrowly missed capturing Buck Brown, the region's most notorious guerrilla leader, commanding some 500 men, they vented their frustration by burning his home and several local mills, used by the guerrillas as rendezvous, but that had little effect on rebel operations.

Harrison insisted that Brown posed more danger to local Unionists than to the army. That was probably true, although it did not lessen the amount of vigilance required by the army to protect telegraph lines, forage parties, and supply trains against those desperadoes. After one two-hour long fight, Brown's men were "routed in confusion" with a loss of several killed and wounded, but the frequency of such encounters also sapped the energy of Harrison's soldiers and their horses. Brown and other roving bands, easily avoiding Harrison's patrols, to make life a misery for loyal Union citizens by causing them "great annoyance, constantly plundering and driving them from their homes, until the rebel rule in the surrounding country" had become "almost complete." In other words, Arkansas guerrillas posed serious political, if not military, problems.[21]

Consequently, in the summer and autumn of 1864, Harrison devised an entirely original defensive scheme by resettling Unionist farmers on abandoned or confiscated rebel lands. Seventeen settlements were authorized, although how many of them were established is uncertain. They were self-contained communities of roughly

50 families apiece, each one within range of the army's protection but with the settlers armed and prepared to defend their farm colonies as home guards. These armed farmers occasionally took the field, too, and became effective antiguerrilla forces.[22]

Meanwhile, literary forces in the North and the South shaped two contrary images of the guerrilla war, and of Confederate guerrillas in particular. The Northern image, it goes without saying, was not a flattering one, although it did reinforce the impression of rebel bushwhackers as dangerous and unscrupulous foes. With the guerrilla war very much on the minds of Northerners, Yankee pens produced a body of literature to satisfy their curiosity. The quintessential Northern stage play, produced in Washington in 1864, was *Beau Sickman; or, The Bushwhackers of the Potomac,* but novels became the favored literary form for dramatizing the guerrilla war. Many of them were set in either Missouri or West Virginia, thus showing the perils posed by rebel villains to loyal Union states. *The Border Spy; or the Beautiful Captive of the Rebel Cause,* published in 1863, was supposedly written by a member of John Frémont's staff. Indeed, Frémont's camp seemed to be alive with literary ambition, with his spunky wife, Jessie, penning her own novel, *The Story of the Guard: a Chronicle of the War,* published in 1863. Two other best sellers, *The Guerrillas of the Osage; or the Price of Loyalty on the Frontier* and *The Stars and Bars: or, the Reign of Terror in Missouri,* were published the same year.

A more positive impression came from the South. The occasional poems written early in the war to advocate partisan warfare had grown by 1864 to include plays, novels, and still more poems, all of them designed to romanticize, rather then debunk, the guerrilla's role in the war. The first original drama staged in Richmond, in late 1862, was *The Guerrillas,* and a slew of popular novels followed in its wake. Like northern novels, most of them were set in the border states, with stories about John Hunt Morgan being especially popular. But poetry had always been Southern literature's forte, and wartime poets such as William Gilmore Simms, Henry Timrod, and Paul Hamilton Hayne upheld that tradition. So did lesser-knowns, such as S. Teackle Wallis, who exhorted in "The Guerrillas: A Southern War-Song":

> By the graves where our fathers slumbered!
> By the shrines where our mothers prayed!
> By our homes, and hopes, and freedom!
> Let every man swear on his blade,
> That he will not sheath nor stay it,
> Till from point to hilt it will glow,
> With the flush of Almighty vengeance,
> In the blood of the felon foe.

The real world tended to reinforce the North's fictional image, for while the practical effect of the guerrilla resurgence was to frustrate the Federals and intimidate the Unionists, a very different side of the irregular war—its tendency toward outlawry—became more visible. Like the organized guerrilla war, what began as a military problem for the Federals became a social problem for the Southerners. The gangs became such a problem in some communities that Unionists and rebels joined together, momentarily at least, to combat them.

Kentuckians, despite the policies of Bloody Burbridge, complained that "organized bands of thieves" had thrown the countryside into a "most lawless state." Roving gangs, which most people took to be deserters, preyed equally on Confederates and Unionists. They were "mere marauders banded together, willing to rob and murder on either side." A petition from one community, seeking state protection, claimed, "*These gangs* are enemies of all mankind—have no principles, fight for no cause & they ought to be exterminated." Civilians could not fathom such violent acts being committed "so far removed from the seat of *public* war."[23]

A Missourian of German descent, trying desperately not to take sides in the war, reported that a band of robbers in his neighborhood simply walked into people's homes and demanded money. If the people objected or claimed to have no valuables, the gang abused them and took whatever they fancied. In Arkansas, a band of rebel deserters made "dayly and nightly" raids on settlements east of Fort Smith to steal anything of value, especially horses. "Men who were original secessionists, the first to volunteer in the Confederate service," one Arkansas marveled, "are now to be found in the ranks of the enemy, and prowling through robbing and occasionally murdering their neighbors."[24]

One of the most active bushwhackers in northeast Arkansas was a Union deserter known as Cairo Pete. Although Pete fired into federal expeditions along the Saint Francis River, everyone recognized that his principal occupations were murdering and stealing. Provost marshals, well acquainted with the troublemakers in their districts, described bandits such as Pete as "bad" men, "very bad" men, "mean" men, and "desperadoes." Their crimes had less and less to do with the war, and more and more to do with settling private scores, acquiring riches, or inflicting pain.[25]

Federal authorities treated these criminals as legitimate guerrillas, which says volumes about the continued Northern perception of rebel irregulars. Gen. Henry W. Slocum, responsible for protecting the Nashville & Chattanooga Railroad, and never one to mince words, summed up the attitude of most Union officers in the spring of 1864. "The outrages committed in this section of the state of Tennessee, during the past few months, by organized bands of outlaws, known as Guerrillas," he declared, "and the fact that the crimes of murder and robbery are still weekly occurrences, render the execution of those who are convicted of these crimes a matter of necessity, as it is the only course that can, in my opinion, be adopted, which will restore peace and order in this locality." His statement came as he endorsed the decision of a military commission to execute five members of a "band of marauders" for murder, robbery, and "numerous depredations."[26]

Ultimately, though, the biggest problem posed by these gangs was the widening circle of violence they spawned. They used violence or the threat of it to obtain food, horses, money, or whatever else they needed, and they bushwhacked or executed home guards, conscript officers, guerrillas, and soldiers sent after them. Lone conscript officers dared not enter places such as Winston County, Alabama, or Jones County, Mississippi, and companies of home guards who opposed them generally found themselves outnumbered.

One of the worst pest holes was North Carolina, where tories, deserters, and outlaws ruled large regions. "Deserters are thick and heavy," reported one conscript officer. "[T]hey have been holding meetings and planning for the winter Campaign." A state of anarchy existed in the western end of the state, an area covering some 13 counties. Deserters and Unionists had become "insolent & dangerous" and supported themselves as outlaws by pillage and plunder. "If something is not done for this country by the government," a man warned in November 1864, "our settlement will soon follow the sad fate of the French Rev[olution]. A man reported from the eastern part of the state that "acts of violence murder plunder & defiance" marked the degradation of society.[27]

Even portions of states supposedly occupied by the Federals had problems. No one was certain which side the suitably named William Dark supported in northern Arkansas, but he was a terror to the local people. He had been a convicted felon before the war, released from the state penitentiary in 1861 upon condition that he joined the Confederate army. He left the army two years later, but whether to ride roughshod as a Union jayhawker or as a loyal Confederate partisan is still disputed. In either case, Dark and his followers engaged in arson, murder, and theft, seemingly paying little attention to the loyalties of their victims. Conditions became so bad that both Unionists and Confederates in his neighborhood formed home guards that joined in bringing Dark to justice. Even so, his mantle was assumed by two other, equally dreaded brigands, a Captain Cochrane and Mark Cockram. They too fell in time, Cochrane and his band of 15 men being hanged by local regulators, with Cockram killed in a good battle with recognized Confederate partisan rangers.[28]

Louisiana offers several other examples. The central and northern parts of the state, the regions farthest from Yankee control, were "full of deserters and runaway conscripts." Gen. St. John Richardson Liddell's novel solution was to invite these men to escape punishment by joining his regiment. Assuming their main interest to be "legalized plunder, with the smallest possible amount of service or danger to themselves," he hoped to limit their excesses by keeping them in view.[29]

More typical were the blunt orders from Gen. Richard Taylor to the commander of a battalion of Louisiana cavalry, acting essentially as partisan rangers. "[M]ove with your command . . . for the purpose of scouring the parish of Rapides, north of the Red River, in quest of jayhawkers and deserters," came the instructions. "Two officers were killed by a party of these men last evening. . . . Such outrages must be punished with a strong hand, and . . . every man found with arms in his hands, against whom reasonable suspicion exists of a determination to resist the laws, will be shot be you on the spot. Such men must not be arrested." All other suspicious characters should be driven into the swamps. "[S]tarve them out," he was told, "if there is not other means of reaching them."[30]

Both Federals and Confederates denounced the gangs of southern Louisiana as threats to law and order. "We have been and still are much alarmed about the Jay-hawkers, who are very bad," a defenseless citizen declared. "They commit all kinds of outrages upon men, women and children, rob, murder and rape. Oh, it is dreadful!" This woman knew of 12 people in one town who had been killed.[31]

Ozème Carrière was the most dangerous and elusive outlaw in south Louisiana. A deserter from the Confederate army, he reportedly had a thousand men in his battalion, based in Saint Landry's Parish. "It is no longer the case of a few isolated desperadoes," the Confederate conscription officer in that area warned; "the entire community . . . is implicated in these organizations. . . . Carrière is daily becoming more and more popular with the masses, and that every day serves to increase his gang." Particularly worrisome to Confederate authorities was the large number of slaves seeking his protection. Before long, predicted the conscript officer, "[A]ll the good, loyal, and honest men in the western part of the parish will have to flee from their homes and abandon the country." Fortunately for the Confederates, Carrière's raiders, like most of their kind, soon terrified even their friends by turning to indiscriminate banditry, murder, and arson.[32]

Two states, Texas and Florida, could trace most of their problems to innate Unionist sentiments augmented by men who had abandoned the Confederate cause. In effect, their gangs showed at least a semblance of political motivation in that they were strongly anti-Confederate. The gravest concerns in Texas came in its northern tiers of counties, where the people had always tended toward Unionism. With the three largest gangs of brush men, as they were called, totaling as many as 900 men, they posed a serious military problem. Like Liddell in Louisiana, Henry McCulloch offered amnesty to deserters who rejoined the army. Hundreds of men took advantage of the deal, many of them also volunteering for a special 500-man Brush Battalion to break up the remaining gangs. Unfortunately, too many of these redeemed sinners were backsliders. When McCulloch disciplined them for plundering loyal Confederate citizens, they again deserted, and McCulloch abandoned the experiment.[33]

Florida had several Unionist enclaves, most notably along the Saint John's River, the Atlantic coast, and in the northern tiers of counties that bordered Georgia and Alabama. That is where deserters congregated, too. The three strongest bands, led by William W. Strickland, James Cocker, and William White, operated in northern

Florida. Taking more drastic action than did McCulloch, Col. Henry D. Capers, the rebel officer charged with breaking up Strickland's band, burned their homes and imprisoned 16 of their women and children. He would release the families and pardon the men, he said, if the deserters returned to the army. They refused to bend. "I ain't accountable for what they do now," Strickland warned Capers. "As for myself, I will do anything that any half white man ever done, only to go into the Confederate war any more." Governor John Milton, seeing the folly of Capers's action, ordered the women and children released.[34]

Interestingly, at the same time, Capt. John J. Dickison, Florida's best-known partisan ranger, even after his command was converted to conventional cavalry, was given permission to exploit the full limits of the rules of war when dealing with intransigent unionists. He was another of those partisans about whom legends were spun and poems penned. Columbus Drew, for one, praised him in "Camp Song of the St. Augustine":

'Twar night again at Waldo, and the men were all alert,
And Dickison was girding well his sword upon his shirt.
A rumor vague was passing, by none well understood
Save by their valiant leader, the pine grove Robin Hood.

Seeking advice from his district commander, Gen. Patton Anderson, on how to handle the arrest of a rebel sympathizer and her daughter, he was told by Anderson's adjutant-general, "If you capture an equal number of Yankee citizens, they will be held as hostages for Mrs. Thomas and daughter. The laws of war give the right to capture and hold any person who gives information." Three weeks later, Dickison and his men were officially praised for their soldierly qualities and held up as a model of "patriotic endurance and daring."[35]

Still, the lawlessness, whatever its source, was but a symptom of a larger evil. It had become an increasingly confusing war, more difficult to distinguish merciless thugs from legitimate guerrillas. People complained about increased levels of violence and retribution. They spoke of thieves and murderers, men of villainous character. Men like John Gatewood, who roamed freely through Alabama, Tennessee, and Georgia, shooting deserters and Unionists. In one instance, Gatewood executed a Unionist refugee even as the young man's mother begged for his life. Grabbing his victim by the hair, he reportedly "pulled him over with his face upwards, and placing his revolver near his lips, in spite of his mother's efforts, emptied the contents of it into her son's mouth mangling and blowing away his face in the most shocking manner conceivable."[36]

George M. Jessee, operating primarily against the Union army in Kentucky, never missed an opportunity to execute captured black soldiers. When the government threatened to exile his wife from the state, he vowed to retaliate by filling every sink hole in the county with union women. Obed C. Crossland murdered, hanged, and kidnapped Unionists in both Tennessee and Alabama. He claimed only to be protecting his neighborhood, but he became so notorious that when captured and sentenced to death by a military commission, Abraham Lincoln, known for his leniency on these occasions, signed the warrant.

The callousness showed itself, as well, in the actions of Unionist guerrillas and home guards who vowed eternal vengeance against former neighbors. A Captain Brixey led a "rough, blood thirsty set of desperadoes" in Tennessee. Once a scout for the Union army, he still cooperated with the Federals when it suited him, but he could be a volatile ally. "[T]hey never spared an enemy (or friend either, I should think, judging from their conduct)," one solider said of Brixey's band. Having stolen a pair of horses and two slave boys from an elderly judge, Brixey was ordered to return the horses. He complied, but the judge was found dead the next day in a ravine.[37]

So, despite the rebel guerrilla resurgence of 1864, the larger picture looked troubling. People who lived daily in its shadow and experienced the unbridled violence of the irregular war no longer saw it as a source of security. Indeed, there was another side to the events of 1864–1865 that caused loyal Confederates to abandon not only partisan warfare, but the entire movement for Southern independence.

Edmund Ruffin, an early advocate of the guerrilla war. (Library of Congress)

William Gilmore Simms, a rebel poet laureate of guerrilla warfare.
(Library of Congress)

John Hunt Morgan spread panic through the lower Midwest. (Library of Congress)

Thomas C. Hindman was the first person to organize a guerrilla war in the Trans-Mississippi. (Library of Congress)

John Pope, an early advocate of Union retaliation. (Library of Congress)

Henry W. Halleck set precedents for a punitive war. (Library of Congress)

William T. Sherman understood the dangers and weaknesses of a guerrilla war. (Library of Congress)

David Dixon Porter combated rebel guerrillas on land and water. (Library of Congress)

The Federals used Francis Lieber's "code" to claim the moral high ground. (Library of Congress.)

John Singleton Mosby, the model of a Partisan Ranger. (Library of Congress)

The raid on Lawrence, Kansas was the war's most horrific act. (*Harper's Weekly*, September 5, 1863/Library of Congress)

Thomas Ewing Jr., author of the war's most repressive order against civilians. (Library of Congress)

EIGHT

FINAL RECKONING, 1864–1865

It is a commonplace that the Confederacy collapsed because, by 1865, its outnumbered and ill-equipped armies could no longer match the heavier battalions of the North. However, while less visible, the chaotic state of the Confederate home front was no less injurious to the rebel cause. The rules of war had undergone a sea change since the spring of 1861. The decided response of the Federals to irregular warfare, the faltering commitment of the Confederate government to its guerrillas, the escalating retaliation, and the addition of a genuine outlaw element to the mix had a devastating impact on Southern noncombatants. The war had been made a far deadlier affair than it ought to have been, certainly bloodier than the armies alone could have made it. It would be too much to claim that the guerrilla war was the deciding factor in Confederate defeat, but it was certainly *as* decisive as any other factor, including battlefield defeats.

If Union retaliation prior to 1864 had not convinced the rebels to abandon their guerrilla war, the extension of Union policies in 1864–1865 did the trick. The toughest new policies came on the middle border, in Kentucky and Tennessee. One would think that the region had been tamed long since, but as the Union marshaled its forces for the more immediate goal of conquering Mississippi, Alabama, and Georgia, rebel guerrillas in the rear of their advance still posed potential problems, both to Union troops and loyal Unionists.

The rebels had few conventional troops in Kentucky, but by 1864, the state lay so far behind the Union advance that guerrillas had complete possession of many communities—enough control certainly to pose a threat to Northern elections in 1864. General Burbridge dealt with that problem, but it should be emphasized that his repressive policies were encouraged, even dictated, by the highest-ranking military and civilian authorities in Washington as part of a comprehensive plan to shut down the guerrilla war. Halleck, as shown, was one of those people, but his orders came directly from Secretary of War Edwin Stanton and the president himself. When it appeared that his reelection might be in doubt, Lincoln gave Burbridge the power to suspend habeas corpus and impose martial law in Kentucky. Furthermore, Halleck informed his district commander, "The Secretary of War directs that under the authority conferred on you by the President, you arrest and send to Washington, under proper guards, all persons so inciting insurrection or aiding and abetting the enemy."[1]

Joseph Holt, one of Lincoln's chief political advisors as well as judge-advocate general, stuck in his oar as well. "[T]he recent orders of General Burbridge enforcing indemnity from rebel sympathizers for thefts and robberies of guerillas, and directing the execution of guerilla prisoners in retaliation for murders committed by these bands, cannot fail to produce the happiest effect in mitigating these atrocities," he assured Stanton at the end of July. "These executions have inspired a most wholesome terror, and it is to be hoped that the stern but necessary policy thus inaugurated will be in nothing relaxed."[2]

William T. Sherman, who had been sending similar encouragement to Burbridge in the midst of his own Georgia campaign, encouraged all district commanders in Kentucky and Tennessee to follow the Kentuckian's lead. In Tennessee, Gen. Robert H. Milroy set the standard. Unlike Burbridge, who had never faced guerrillas before being assigned to Kentucky, Milroy had already battled them in Virginia, and so understood what had to be done. Having authorized the shooting of bushwhackers, confiscation of their property, and the burning of their homes, he turned enforcement over to a brigade of "wild, half civilized" Tennessee cavalry as his prime "guerrilla hunters." Nor did he shy away from punishing dangerous women. "Shoot if you can by accident," he instructed troops sent to apprehend one particularly "disloyal" woman. Of that same woman's daughter, he added, "[A]lmost as bad as her mother. Burn Everything."[3]

A day of reckoning had come for more than one Tennessee guerrilla. James M. Johnson had been known as a "pretty wild boy" until making "a profession of religion" shortly before the war. He became a preacher, and neighbors vouched for his "very pious and upright life." When brought before a military commission for bushwhacking a Union soldier, the evidence was largely circumstantial, but Johnson was so unrepentant that the Union officers hearing his case insisted that he be hanged. In upholding Johnson's sentence, Joseph Holt, staying true to the government's policy, approved hanging as "a fit punishment for a violation of the rules of civilized warfare and the commission of an inhuman murder." He also hoped that Johnson's fate would serve as "a terror to those who, like the prisoner, believe that they may rightly and with impunity turn guerrillas and 'bushwhackers,' and assassins and highwaymen."[4]

Yet, something more than Lincoln's reelection was at stake in the summer of 1864. Even if reelected, the president knew that Northern support for the war would not continue indefinitely. He must find a find to end it. Again looking to the West, as he done when bringing Henry Halleck to Washington in 1862, he called on Ulysses S. Grant to be his new general-in-chief and gave him leeway to create a new grand military strategy. Grant responded with a plan that has been characterized in many ways. It has been called total war, absolute war, destructive war, hard war, relentless war, and savage war, but by whatever name, it represented a coordinated strategy of exhaustion by Union armies in 1864–1865 that ultimately pushed the rebels to the point of surrender. Carried out most successfully in Georgia, the Carolinas, and Virginia, it signaled the physical and psychological destruction of the South, each part of the plan designed to stretch rebel armies and resources to the breaking point and crush civilian morale.

That much is well-known to students of the war. Less often appreciated are the roots of Grant's plan, which bore a striking resemblance to the strategy enacted since late 1861 to combat rebel guerrillas. Grant knew he could never annihilate the Confederate armies, just as he had come to realize that rebel guerrillas could never be totally suppressed. However, he and other Union commanders who had confronted guerrillas had seen popular support for irregular warfare weaken when noncombatants realized that they were to bear the brunt of it, as happened when rebel property was confiscated or destroyed. By 1864, Confederate civilians were also reaping the whirlwind of the outlawry and unbridled violence that had become inseparable from the guerrilla war. Rebel guerrillas continued to operate in every part of the South, but the Union army's two-pronged offensive, aimed first at their extermination and second at cowing their civilian network, had reduced their effectiveness. Grant believed that if the same two-pronged approach could be used to neutralize rebel armies while simultaneously demoralizing previously untouched portions of the Southern home front, the rebel government would be forced to surrender.

Grant had also seen the effectiveness of this approach outside the realm of the irregular war during his Vicksburg campaign. Having crossed the Mississippi River below the rebel city, he ordered his men to "live as far as possible off the country" through which it passed. Whatever his men could not consume was destroyed, including all food stuffs and whatever else the Confederacy might use "in prolonging the war." In May 1863, he declared, "Mules and horses can be taken to supply all our wants, and, where it does not cause too much delay, agricultural implements may be destroyed. In other words, cripple the rebellion in every way, without insulting women and children or taking their clothing, jewelry, &c."[5]

Having settled on his strategy in 1864, Grant also relied on other men experienced in the guerrilla war to conduct the necessary campaigns. Halleck stood at the top of the list. He would remain in Washington to coordinate the movements of the multiple armies involved, thus allowing Grant to stay in the field and oversee the destruction of Robert E. Lee's army. Playing more active roles would be David Hunter, Philip Sheridan, and, most especially, William Sherman. These officers had learned from experience that only the toughest rules of engagement could hope to quell the rebellion.

No one understood what Grant was trying to do, or the rationale behind his plan, better than Sherman. As early as 1862, while dealing with guerrillas in Tennessee, Sherman had witnessed the growing resentment by Confederate citizens against the hardships forced upon them by both the guerrillas and the Confederate government. He believed that many noncombatants must eventually see the futility of the guerrilla war and prefer the protection of the Union army to the chaos of banditry.

Now, two years on, that is exactly what had happened in many parts of the South. A man in southern Arkansas claimed that he felt more safe under federal than under rebel rule. In the northern half of that same state, a hitherto loyal Confederate woman almost welcomed Union occupation, "anything for Peace and established Laws again," she said. As the Federals burned rebel homes in central Tennessee in response to Champ Ferguson's raids, citizens saw that guerrilla chief as a danger to their own security. In Virginia, some people had long wished that John Mosby would cease operations if he could not prevent the Union army from retaliating against unprotected communities.[6]

In retrospect, the reactions were hardly surprising. After all, much of the logic of the guerrilla war had been based on the inability of Confederate armies to defend every community against the invading Union armies and internal rebellions by Unionists and slaves. But as guerrillas and partisans showed themselves unable to meet those challenges, rebel citizens became as frightened as the Unionists of the turmoil and social disintegration. More than that, as confidence in the guerrilla system faded, popular support for the Confederacy also eroded. Citizens felt trapped by the violence, and there seemed no way out but to end the war.

Some Confederate soldiers understood the predicament. "I believe that bushwhacking has been the main cause of all the killing and burning that has been done," an Arkansas soldier told his wife. He had nearly left the army himself in order to fight as a guerrilla near home, but then considered the consequences for both himself and his family. Another Arkansan agreed. "[T]he least a soldier is about his house the better his family comes off with the enemy," he declared. "They then have no excuse that he is bushwhacking or doing any mischief."[7]

The Confederate government had understood the situation for some time, and the politicians made one last desperate attempt to limit the damage in February 1864 by all but repealing the Partisan Ranger Act. Virginia's rangers, supposedly the best disciplined of all the partisan corps, had behaved no better than "thieves" that winter, "stealing, pillaging, plundering, and doing every manner of mischief and crime." One Confederate general called them "a terror to the citizens and an injury to the cause." Henceforth, they would operate as regular cavalry in the conventional army.[8]

The only exceptions to the law were the battalions of John Mosby and John McNeill. Robert E. Lee, who had always questioned the value of partisan rangers, recommended that those two units be spared the ax, even recommending Mosby for promotion to lieutenant colonel. "He is zealous, bold, and skillful," the commanding general told Secretary of War James A Seddon, who had framed the law, "and with very small resources has accomplished a great deal." General Stuart, Mosby's earliest and most consistent advocate, endorsed Lee's view. "His sleepless vigilance and un-ceasing activity have done the enemy great damage," Stuart said of the Gray Ghost. "His exploits are not surpassed in daring and enterprise by those of *petite guerre* in any age."[9]

Mosby's rangers proved their worth by playing an important role in resisting an important part of Grant's grand design, the campaign in Virginia. Virginia's guerrilla war came to a head in the autumn of 1864 with a destructive, often murderous, orgy of retaliation and counter-retaliation that had begun several months earlier, when Gen. Franz Sigel tried to sweep aside Jubal Early's smaller Confederate army in the Shenandoah Valley. Grant had assigned him the task of capturing the valley, the Confederacy's most abundant remaining source of grain and livestock. Sigel failed utterly, thanks in no small part to constant pressure by Mosby, McNeill, and former partisans-turned-cavalrymen John Imboden, Elihu V. White, and Harry Gilmor.

Gen. David Hunter, a veteran of the guerrilla wars in Missouri and South Caro-lina, replaced Sigel in May. He promptly ordered reprisals against local residents for any further guerrilla actions. Those reprisals ranged in severity from financial assess-ments of 500 percent to total destruction of property. When Mosby responded by burning 12 Union supply wagons, Hunter ordered a nearby town and every home for several miles around it destroyed. He eventually burned only three houses as a warning, but he made up the difference a few weeks later in Lexington, Virginia, by destroying the home of former governor John Letcher and part of the Virginia Military Institute.

But Hunter, too, was gone by the end of the summer, having been outfoxed by Jubal Early. Almost in desperation, Early had slipped around the Federals to launch a raid that threatened the outer defenses of Washington, D.C., and carried him into southern Pennsylvania. At Chambersburg, about 30 miles northwest of Gettysburg, his cavalry made similar demands and inflicted similar punishments to the ones doled out by Hunter. When the residents failed to fork over either $100,000 in gold or $500,000 in greenbacks, Early's men reduced the town to ashes. General Grant took notice. In replacing Hunter with Phil Sheridan, he gave his chief cavalryman the same orders that had been issued to his predecessors in the valley—confiscate or destroy all food, livestock, and property of military value. However, to avoid any misunderstanding about his expectations, Grant added, "[W]e want the Shenandoah Valley to remain a barren waste."[10]

To accomplish his mission, Sheridan understood that he would have to deal not only with Early, who had returned to the valley, but also with John Mosby. He ordered his army "to exterminate as many of Mosby's gang" as possible, and by whatever means. As a result, much of northern Virginia, not just the valley, became engulfed in a destructive campaign. Sheridan's men thought it entirely justified. What were a few burned homes or a little looting set beside the barbarism of the guerrillas, who slit men's throats "from ear to ear" and hung lifeless corpses upside down from trees? "I think you can hardly call us very bad names in view of the atrocities by these infernal traitors," one man told his wife.[11]

The violence peaked in November. Having routed Early's army the previous month in the battle of Cedar Creek, Sheridan turned to the destruction of Mosby's home turf in Loudoun County. "It was a terrible retribution on the country that had for three years supported and lodged the guerrilla bands and sent them out to plunder and murder," judged a Union officer as he surveyed the smoke from hundreds of burning buildings and a thousand haystacks. Sheridan's only restrictions on the troops were that no homes be burned and no civilians physically harmed. "The ultimate results of the guerrilla system of warfare is the total destruction of all private rights in the country occupied by such parties," he declared. Quite a few Unionists and neutrals also suffered. "The task was not a pleasant one," confessed a cavalry captain, "for many innocents were made to suffer with the guilty, but something was necessary to clear the country of those bands of Guerillas that were becoming so formidable."[12]

Many years later, in writing his memoirs, Sheridan acknowledged the harshness of the campaign, but he also understood its necessity. "I endorsed Grant's programme," he explained, "for I do not hold war to mean simply that lines of men shall engage each other in battle, and material interests be ignored." Fighting on the battlefield is but a "duel," he observed, "in which one combatant seeks the other's life." War, though, "means much more, and is far worse than this. Those who rest at home in peace and plenty see but little of the horrors attending such a duel, and even grow indifferent to them." Grant's plan and Sheridan's own operations were intended to wake complacent rebels to the reality of war, for "it is another matter," he continued, "when deprivation and suffering are brought to their own doors. Then the case appears much graver. . . . Death is popularly considered the maximum of punishment in war, but it is not; reduction to poverty brings prayers for peace more surely and more quickly than does the destruction of human life."[13]

That was Sherman's view of war, too, as he turned his hand to destroying Confederate will in Georgia. Grant had ordered him to "move against [Joseph E.] Johnston's army, to break it up, and to get into the interior of the enemy's country as far as you can, inflicting all the damage you can against their war resources." The phrase "war resources" had an ominous and ubiquitous sound to it. There were guerrillas in Georgia, too, although they proved less effective than did Mosby's men in Virginia. A combination of Confederate raiders and independent guerrilla bands tried to disrupt the fragile supply line between Chattanooga and Atlanta, but Sherman had assigned tens of thousands of men to protect supply depots and the railroad lines that would carry munitions, food, and equipment to his advancing army.[14]

He toughened the rules of engagement, too, by ordering all "suspicious persons and families" imprisoned, with "no mercy" shown to "guerrillas or persons" who threatened the railroad or telegraph. His soldiers, who had long subscribed to the "Jim Lane theory of pacification," knew what to do. They hanged men who "betrayed" Union soldiers "into the guerrillas' hands" and burned the homes of known bushwhackers and of the people who had harbored them. The entire town of Cassville was set ablaze "on account of its being a guerrilla haunt."[15]

Guerrilla resistance in Georgia did not end, but it was very much reduced by the time Atlanta fell in September, and in discussing his next move, the march eastward to Savannah, Sherman could not have been clearer about the purpose of his campaign. "This movement is not purely military or strategic," he emphasized, "but it will illustrate the vulnerability of the South." Southerners, he went on to say, must be made to feel that "war and individual ruin" were "synonymous terms." The "utter destruction of its roads, houses, and people will cripple their military resources." Regarding the army's labors at the end of its march, one of Sherman's men said, "Our work has been the next thing to annihilation."[16]

The operation pleased General Halleck. "Your mode of conducting war is just the thing we now want," he assured Sherman. "We have tried the kid-glove policy long enough." Understanding, like Sherman, the character of the war by 1864, Halleck believed the Union armies could do little that "the conduct of the enemy, and especially of non-combatants and women of the territory" did not justify. "I do not approve of General Hunter's course in burning private houses," he told Sherman, "or uselessly destroying private property," but it was equally clear that the "safety" of the army required "severe rules of war."[17]

South Carolina learned just how severe those rules could be when Sherman turned north from Savannah in February 1865. The descendants of Francis Marion and Thomas Sumter stood little chance against the onslaught. Not that they folded their tents. Rebel guerrillas managed to kill twice as many Federals as they had done in

Georgia, but that only increased the ire of Sherman's men. Although South Carolina towns and plantations had been targeted for rough treatment in any case, the punishment meted out fully conformed to the new character of the war.

Elsewhere in the Deep South, areas not targeted by Grant's grand plan also witnessed the winding down of the guerrilla war, usually as a result of harsh military suppression. Some people saw it coming a year earlier. "The war is now conducted against us with feelings of *personal hatred*," a resident of Greensboro, Alabama, emphasized in November 1863, "and with all the cruelty of savages. There is no honour, justice, right or *principle* claimed by our enemies. It is with them a matter of passion & might. They would exterminate our race if they could. They will make it a war to annihilation if they can." Even so, the situation was very much worse the following autumn, with every Union soldier seemingly acting as "a law unto himself" and whole communities "ravaged" by federal occupation.[18]

By this time, too, Alabama Confederates had the same love–hate relationship with their guerrillas that had developed elsewhere. On the one hand, guerrillas were often the only defenders to whom communities could turn. On the other hand, it was their very successes against the Federals that had brought retaliation upon the people, not to mention renegade guerrillas who preyed on the citizenry. Rebel guerrillas still tried to slow the Union advance by burning bridges and cutting telegraph lines, but their dwindling numbers betrayed them.

The worst part of Union occupation may have been the free rein it gave to Unionists and outlaw bands. In Alabama, this included the infiltration of outlaw gangs from Mississippi and Florida. "[S]tealing . . . horses, driving off cows & calves, robbing, burning & stealing whatever they find valuable," they roamed unimpeded through the countryside. "These are trashes . . . not soldiers," cried one woman. The situation may have been even worse in Mississippi. Federal raiding parties penetrated all parts of the state, and the gangs, whom few dared oppose, grew bolder. "They are abolitionists, spies, deserters, liars, thieves, murderers, and every thing foul & damnable," railed one rebel judge, enraged by his own inability to dispense justice. "[D]eserters . . . are daily increasing in number and outrages," he continued, "and constitute by far the greatest common & public nuisance in the land—hardly inferior to so many yankee troops in the country."[19]

The most unnerving thing was to find formerly loyal Confederates switching sides. In some places, these turncoats even assisted the deserters and bandits by identifying the families worth plundering. "You cant believe how bad the people have got to be," lamented a Mississippi woman. "[P]ersons that we thought were good and honest before the war have turned out to be the worst kind of men."[20]

This was the situation virtually everywhere in April 1865, when the defenses of Petersburg and Richmond fell. Lee's army escaped westward only to meet its destiny at Appomattox. Most of the political leaders, including Jefferson Davis, headed south.

But while Lee, seeing the futility of continued resistance, surrendered, Davis refused to concede defeat. The struggle for Southern independence had only entered a "new phase," he announced from Danville, Virginia. The loss of Richmond, he insisted, had merely freed Confederate armies from the necessity of "guarding cities and particular points." They could now move at will and "strike in detail the detachments and garrisons of the enemy."[21]

It almost sounded as though Davis was endorsing widespread guerrilla resistance, but that would have gone against his long campaign to limit the guerrilla war. At best, he had considered guerrillas and partisans temporary adjuncts to his armies, a position Lee endorsed yet again 11 days after surrendering his own men on April 9. Lee urged the president to end the war, despite the presence of other Confederate armies in the field. The nation was unable "morally or physically" to continue fighting, the general wrote. "A partisan war may be continued, and hostilities protracted," he admitted, but that could only cause further suffering and devastate the country. "I see no prospect by that means," the general concluded, "of achieving a separate independence."[22]

The president's cabinet endorsed that view when Davis polled his secretaries toward the end of April. John C. Breckinridge, the new secretary of war, said that a desperate guerrilla campaign would "lose entirely the dignity of regular warfare." Secretary of State Judah P. Benjamin, the president's longest-serving and most trusted cabinet member, reminded him, "[G]uerrilla or partisan warfare would entail far more suffering on our own people than it would cause damage to the enemy." Benjamin doubted, too, that very many people wished to continue fighting by any means.[23]

Naturally, a few diehard rebels remained. Some guerrillas and partisan rangers, refusing to surrender when the conventional armies laid down their arms, posed a danger to Union troops and Unionist citizens through the summer. Rumors swirled about the successes achieved by a few indomitable bands. Some Virginians insisted that John Mosby might yet salvage the situation. Informed that his battalion refused to surrender at Appomattox, a Virginia woman gushed of their leader, "God bless his *noble, brave unyielding Southern heart.*" Equally telling, a rumor that the Gray Ghost had been wounded and captured sparked rejoicing in Union ranks.[24]

The farther removed geographically men were from the surrenders in the east, the less willing they were to believe the cause was lost. In the Trans-Mississippi, some bands continued to burn or sack Unionist homes and leave the bodies of dead Unionists on the roadside. Indeed, as returning soldiers, homeless or desperate for food, joined them, their numbers could be formidable. When, in mid-June, remnants of Quantrill's gang appeared to be still on the prowl, the order went out from the local Union commander: "[T]he most immediate and vigorous pursuit [shall] be at once instituted for [Jim] Jackson and [Arch] Clement and their party. If they are found, kill them at once. Hold no further parley with them under any pretext, but destroy them wherever found."[25]

For the majority, though, as Benjamin surmised, the war had long since ended. The most notorious guerrillas, especially the ones that tended to live outside the law, were either dead or soon would be. Bill Anderson and George Todd, Quantrill's former lieutenants, had died in gun battles during Price's raid. Quantrill, having slipped into Kentucky to join forces with Marcellus Clarke and Henry Magruder, was mortally wounded in an ambush in May. He died a few weeks later in a military prison. John W. Mobberly, who claimed to be a partisan ranger long after the Confederate government had disbanded his unit, died in an ambush that spring in Virginia. In Arkansas, Buck Brown was killed in a minor skirmish with Union troops. Other men continued to be executed by order of military commissions. Clark went to the gallows shortly before Lee's surrender; Magruder met the same fate six months later. Captured in May, Champ Ferguson was hanged in October. Tinker Dave Beaty gave evidence against him at the trial.

Scores of guerrillas were serving prison terms when the war ended, often at hard labor. Men who had been sentenced for the duration of the war were automatically released. Others, who had been given set terms of two or more years, appealed their sentences, asking for immediate release. The failed appeal of a Tennessee lad offers a poignant example of the way in which many young Southern men were victimized by the guerrilla war. Oscar Scarborough had been condemned to die in February 1864, primarily for firing into steamboats, stealing horses, and wearing a Union uniform. The sentence was reduced to five years at hard labor. Everyone, even members of his military commission liked the "peaceable young man," whom none considered "blood thirsty." A campaign began in May 1865 to have him released. "[T]here is no doubt but my brave thoughtless Tennessee boy done some things he should not have done," wrote his mother, "but he never was guilty of Murder or robery, and never done a thing he did not believe to be his duty as a soldier." His had been "an error of the head and not of the heart." Judge-Advocate Holt, who denied the appeal in November 1865, did not agree.[26]

By that time, the vast majority of both Northerners and Southerners had seen, experienced, or heard all they wanted of war, especially the irregular kind. An Alabama clergymen who hoped people would put aside bushwhacking and organized guerrilla resistance spoke for many citizens when he said, "These are wrong in principle and practice, and whatever apology men may have for them during the war, there can be none now." An Alabama cavalryman said much the same thing. Discussing the recent surrender of Lee's army, he admitted to a Union general who had seen more than his share of rebel guerrillas, "Guerrilla or partisan would be the only warfare that we could resort to, and that would prove disastrous alike to friend and foe. However much may have been said heretofore of guerrilla warfare as a last resort, yet no good man, however patriotic he might be, would encourage, much less participate in, such a struggle."[27]

More strikingly, Gen. Nathan Bedford Forrest, who had entered the war as a partisan fighter and retained many of their tactics as one of the Confederacy's most formidable raiders, grew alarmed by the drain on public morale caused by the guerrillas. The provost-marshal general of the Army of the Cumberland reported in March 1865, following a discussion with Forrest concerning prisoner exchanges, "In relation to guerrillas, General Forrest remarked that he is as anxious to rid the country of them as was any officer in the U.S Army, and that he would esteem it a favor if General [George H.] Thomas would hang every one he caught."[28]

Even most guerrillas agreed. Like Davis's cabinet, they thought it "would not only be fruitless of any good, but be a source of serious injury to the people by inviting retaliatory measures." Men too angry or too frightened to surrender left the South. Many of them went west to Texas, Kansas, or as far as California. A few went to Mexico with Jo Shelby to serve as mercenaries for Emperor Maximilian. Most simply disappeared, sinking back into the anonymity from which they had sprung.[29]

EPILOGUE: LEGACY OF
THE GUERRILLA WAR

Ending the guerrilla war was one thing. Escaping its legacy, particularly the unchecked violence and outlawry it had spawned, was quite another. As Union troops continued to occupy the South through the 1860s, and as wartime Southern Unionists became formidable foes in the political battles of Reconstruction, former Confederates turned once again to guerrilla warfare. No longer called guerrillas, they adopted such romantic sounding names as the Ku Klux Klan and Knights of the White Camelia, but they remained just as deadly. The outlaws of the war also survived, quite literally in some cases, the James and Younger brothers of Missouri being the most notorious examples. Brutalized by four bloody years in a crucible of death and destruction, murder and robbery had become their way of life.

Aside from outlaws such as Jesse James, whom one biographer has christened the "last rebel of the Civil War," it is difficult to know how many members of these politically-motivated postwar paramilitary organizations had been wartime guerrillas. They also played distinctly different roles than during the war and appear to have been motivated by different purposes. No longer able to claim association with genuine armies, or to be fighting on behalf of a nascent nation, they were far more vulnerable to the charge of being terrorists. Able, like many Confederates, to insist that they had not fought the war to maintain slavery, this new war of "blood redemption," as one scholar has called it, had less to do with the protection of homes and property and more to do with was the suppression of African Americans.[1]

Only as the travail of the war and Reconstruction faded, and with it, this blurred distinction between wartime guerrillas and postwar night riders, did the memory of the South's guerrilla war begin to take shape. Historical memory and the role of memory in writing history have become popular themes in recent years. Yet, efforts to manipulate or obscure the historical record for the purpose of controlling our recollection of events have ancient roots. Some Egyptian pharaohs and Roman emperors, for instance, obliterated any record or image of their immediate predecessors, usually to disguise the circumstances of their own rise to power. In the modern era, the reminiscences and memoirs of public figures are intended to promote particular versions of the past. They are written to influence *our* memory. Sometimes, these attempts to shape the past are successful. Later generations believe them, even in the face of contradictory evidence. As the editor of the *Shinbone Star* famously proclaimed in *The Man Who Shot Liberty Valance,* "When the legend becomes the fact, print the legend."

Historians have only begun to investigate how successful Confederate guerrillas may have been in shaping modern impressions of their roles in the war, but their case is an interesting one, and a good example of the tricks one may play with historical memory. Tens of thousands of men waged war as guerrillas, and all had their own reasons for doing so. Some were more patriotic than others, some more compassionate than others, but all could be pretty tough customers. The Federals, as seen, had accused rebel guerrillas of ignoring the rules of civilized warfare, but even the majority of staunch Confederates had turned against their irregulars by the end of the war, so unpredictable had they become, and so indiscriminate the violence and suffering they produced. "Everybody is down on them," a Mississippian declared toward the end of the war.[2]

Naturally enough, men who had served as guerrillas saw things differently, and in the decades following the war, they tried to salvage their reputation. "From the mass of rubbish that has been written about the guerrilla there is little surprise that the popular conception of him should be a fiendish, bloodthirsty wretch," wrote one of the brotherhood in 1903. "Yet he was, in many cases, if not in most, a man who had been born to better things, and. . . . [w]hen the war ceased those of the guerrillas who were not hung or shot, or pursued by posses till they found the hand of man turned against them at every step, settled down to become good citizens in peaceful walks of life."[3]

Hoping to foster just such an image, other former guerrillas wrote their memoirs or reminiscences, or published articles in journals devoted to the Lost Cause, such as the *Confederate Veteran* and *Southern Historical Society Papers,* to justify their mode of warfare and their own actions. While they approached their task in a variety of ways, with some accounts being more reliable than others, they generally used one of the following four arguments to make their case.

Most often, they insisted that their style of irregular warfare had been forced upon them by circumstances. It was the only way, they maintained, to defend their homes and families against barbarous Unionist guerrillas, or fulfill the desire to avenge atrocities committed by the Union army. In other words, they blamed the uncivilized nature of the war on the enemy. If the rebels seemed to be "bad men," it was because of the "cruel treatment" they and their families had received from the Federals. Men who "went to the bush," explained an Arkansas guerrilla in 1897, "and fought through the balance of the war in a guerrilla warfare, . . . would have staid in the regular army if it had not been that their friends had been so cruelly treated as they had–that was the quickest way for them to get revenge." Another guerrilla, writing in 1905, gave a graphic description of the conditions in his community that sent him to the bush. "There were many acts of barbarous cruelty. Sick and wounded men were dragged out of their beds and brutally murdered in the presence of families. House burning was of almost daily occurrence. It was no unusual sight to see from some elevated point in the country smoke ascending from burning homes in widely separated localities."[4]

A more personal story came from an ex-guerrilla who left the conventional army in order to defend his family. I "felt aggrieved from the treatment they gave my stepfather," he explained in the 1890s. The Federals kept the 65-year-old man locked up for nearly a month, until the guerrilla's mother, herself quite feeble, walked 25 miles to plead for his release. "This kind of treatment to innocent people had a great deal to do with shaping the remainder of my life as a soldier," he confessed. Union soldiers "had possession of our homes and made heavy threats," he said, and "they continued to hunt me down until I decided to try to play an even game with them."[5]

The protests came so often as to become nearly a cliché. Sam Hildebrand entered the bush because of the abuse his family endured at the hands of Unionist neighbors and federal soldiers, including the murder of three brothers. Deprived of a "happy home and the joys of domestic peace and quietude," Hildebrand said he was forced to wage a "merciless war" in "self-defense." Considering the motives that propelled William T. Anderson, better known as Bloody Bill, into the brush, one of his men recalled, "Not until his aged father had been made to dig his own grave, forced to stand over it, falling therein when shot; and not until a sister had been killed by a house falling on her that had been purposely undermined by a band of Jennison's Jayhawkers who had murdered his father, did Bill Anderson take up arms against the government."[6]

A non-guerrilla, a man who had fought as a conventional cavalryman, confirmed this point for readers of the *Confederate Veteran* in 1921. "I was always strongly opposed to guerrilla warfare," he said, "believing it wrong and a poor way to settle anything; yet I want to give you a few facts as to the causes for guerrilla warfare. . . . [I]t was strictly a war of retaliation. . . . [against] the boasted . . . barbarity" of the Federals. He mentioned those hellish days reluctantly, he continued, being loath to reopen old wounds, "but it will be many years yet, if ever" he said plainly, "before the people of . . . the South forget these outrages of rapine, murder, and destruction of their homes and property."[7]

The unfair treatment meted out to captured guerrillas could also be used to justify the fierceness of their war. Once the Union army began to treat captured guerrillas as brigands and murders, subject to drumhead courts martial and swift executions, they had no choice but to respond in kind. "We tried to fight like soldiers," insisted a Missourian in 1915, "but were declared outlaws, hunted under a black flag and murdered like beasts." Only after the Federals changed the rules, claimed more than one rebel, did guerrillas execute Union prisoners in like fashion. Until then, insisted one man, irregular bands had vied with one another to see who could "be the most magnanimous toward prisoners."[8]

A second approach, if necessity would not suffice, shifted blame for their own supposed cruelty to bushwhackers. Although the Federals used the terms bushwhacker and guerrilla interchangeably, the former expression also became associated with genuine criminals who passed themselves off as legitimate, patriotic rebel guerrillas when, in truth, they only used the chaos of the war to steal and murder for private gain. It was they, said ex-Confederates, who shaped false wartime perceptions of all guerrillas. In 1930, one former rebel described just such a gang that operated on the Kentucky-Tennessee border. "They were the most hideous looking human beings in the form of men that we ever saw," he declared; "their long hair and beards, old flopped hats, ragged clothes, bare feet, filthy, savage appearance, all indicated the lowest type of humanity." He identified these particular men as the notorious Sizemore gang, "desperate characters [who] banded together in the mountains . . . [and] who left no living witnesses to testify to their atrocious crimes."[9]

Other commentators turned the tables by claiming that most of the bushwhacking, with its implications of cowardice and lone gunmen murdering foes from under cover, was done by the Federals. In 1909, a former officer testified to fighting a "a formidable force of Federal bushwhackers," by which he could have meant either Unionist guerrillas or U.S. soldiers, in West Tennessee. In 1928, a Kentuckian recalled sitting in camp playing a game of poker during the war when a bullet suddenly whizzed above his head. "Some one yelled," he said, 'Bushwhackers, Yanks.'" Gen. Basil W. Duke, who, as one of John Hunt Morgan's raiders, had seen much of the war in Kentucky, emphasized in 1906 that while both Union and Confederate bushwhackers prowled the state, "the former were more numerous." Another man, in retelling the exploits of his own regiment, the 11th Kentucky Cavalry, recalled doing battle with "a little army of [unionist] home guards and bushwhackers."[10]

The editors of the *Southern Historical Society Papers* reinforced this impression by reminding readers of just how treacherous those skulking Unionists had been. "Bush-whackers, native born white men of East Tennessee and Southern Kentucky, as savage and relentless, and nearly as ignorant, as any redskin of romance or of history," read an 1881 indictment, "infested the country, waylaid the roads, and from mountain side and behind rock or bush shot down the unfortunates who, journeying by themselves or in small parties, wore the Confederate gray, and dispatched the wounded, without mercy, in the name of patriotism and the Union."[11]

Union army units recruited from among Southern Unionists were especially vulnerable to charges of marauding and meanness, and were even more reviled. In northern Alabama, they became associated with the buggers, described in 1910 by a survivor of their deviltry as renegades who "joined together with the lowest of the po white trash . . . into gangs of outlaws" to murder, rob, torture, and burn out loyal Confederates. Among the worst offenders in Alabama was the Second Tennessee Mounted Infantry, U.S.A., which, while admittedly having some "good soldiers," also included "some of the worst wretches that ever disgraced the uniform of the U.S. Army or any other army."[12]

Having thus tarred the outlaws and the Federals as the real culprits in the guerrilla war, even the most murderous and least honorable rebel could be portrayed as noble by comparison. For example, Champ Ferguson became such a scourge to Unionists and Union soldiers that when captured toward the end of the war, he was executed for murder. Yet, a biographical sketch published by the *Confederate Veteran* in 1899, described him as just "a typical mountaineer" who had been reared with "that strict idea of right that belongs to the mountain character." He had fought nobly for a cause in which he believed, the article insisted, a sharp contrast to his most fierce Unionist rival, Tinker Dave Beaty. Quoting Basil Duke, who had fought alongside Champ and against Beaty, the article noted that Tinker Dave "possessed a cunning and subtlety which Ferguson, in a great manner, lacked." Even more to the point, "There was not related of Beaty so many stories illustrative of his personal courage as of Ferguson."[13]

Another man insisted that his guerrilla band was simply more humane than the Union soldiers with whom they dueled. "The Federals did not practice taking prisoners in this country," he explained in 1897. "Every man or nearly so that fell into their hands was almost sure to be killed." What great luck, then, when they managed to capture a Union officer infamous for his treatment of rebel guerrillas. "This man expected to pay the penalty of death," the rebel continued, "[and we] asked him what he thought we ought to do with a man that had told our mothers, wives and daughters he would hang us in our front yard if he ever got hold of us." Imagine the officer's astonishment when the guerrillas released him, though with a warning. "[W]e did not murder Federal soldiers when they fell into our hands," he was told, but hereafter, "if they should burn a house or turn a family out doors," they would "burn a federal on every corner of it."[14]

A third approach to rehabilitating the image of rebel guerrillas was to admit the presence of some loathsome characters in their ranks, but then to dissociate themselves from them and stress how relatively few bad men there were in their ranks. "Now I don't pretend to say that we had no men in the Southern army or among the guerrilla forces who did not commit any bad crimes," contended the Arkansan quoted earlier. "We had some men in our command who got to be almost as bad as the Kansas Jayhawkers. Some men are natural thieves anyway, and often crimes are committed by them contrary to the will of their commanding officers. . . . No good Southern people approved of this kind of conduct, [but]. . . . [t]hat class of men were found on both sides."[15]

A member of Bill Anderson's band agreed. An unbridled killer such as Bloody Bill was likely to attract some hard men, and one loyal follower acknowledged in 1913 that while most of the band had honorable reasons for waging a guerrilla war, "a few marauding members" may have "crept" in their ranks. "But every army has it sulkers and its traitors," he reasoned. "The many must not be held accountable for the acts of the few." Another of Quantrill's men acknowledged that some "bad men" calling themselves guerrillas "plundered the helpless, pillaged the friend and foe alike, assaulted non-combatants and murdered the unresisting and the innocent," but "[s]uch devils' work," he stressed, "was not Guerrilla work."[16]

This approach also allowed Lost Cause defenders to distance themselves from the most heinous acts committed by their guerrillas. For instance, few old Confederates wished to be associated with William Quantrill's raid on Lawrence, especially not the murder of defenseless men and boys. So, after publishing the reminiscences of one of Quantrill's men, who suggested that extenuating circumstances must be considered in judging the massacre, the editor of the *Confederate Veteran* felt compelled to add his comment at the end of the article. Whatever the provocation for Quantrill's men, the editor wanted the world to know that the Lawrence raid was abhorred by all honorable men.[17]

Not by chance, many commentators emphasized either the respectable, peaceable families from which the vast majority of guerrillas came or the noble personal qualities exhibited by the men themselves. A Missouri guerrilla described himself as a law-abiding American citizen, intent only on planting a spring crop until the oppression of Kansas jayhawkers and Union soldiers caused him to put down his hoe and pick up a revolver. Another man insisted that he and his friends had been drawn into the guerrilla war by a "luminous patriotism" that led them to "kill in the name of God and his country."[18]

Likewise, they were remembered fondly by friends. "He was a good soldier and a favorite among all his comrades," read the obituary of a Virginia irregular, "having won their high regard by his attention to duty, his sturdy honesty, and sterling worth." Of an Alabamian, it was said, "He became a Christian early in life, and . . . [h]is unfaltering faith and confidence in the promises of God were an inspiration to others throughout his life." A North Carolina guerrilla captain was described as being "unmistakably a gentleman, . . . a man of considerable culture, a lawyer by profession."[19]

A former Arkansas guerrilla went to great lengths to honor the memory of his former captain. In telling of one of the company's exploits for the *Confederate Veteran*, he insisted, "I never knew a nobler, braver, or truer gentleman. . . . I never heard a word escape his lips that might not have been uttered in the presence of ladies. He was modest and retiring in disposition, and always ready to give others credit who really were not as deserving as himself." Interestingly, too, never once did the narrator refer to himself or his leader as a guerrilla. Instead, they belonged to a "company of cavalry," attached to "Buck Brown's Battalion." He gave no hint that Buck brown was one of the most active and effective rebel guerrilla leaders in the state.[20]

Shedding the guerrilla label was important to other men. Former partisan rangers, especially, liked to emphasize that they had been the most disciplined and least vengeful of the Confederacy's irregulars. "Mosby's Guerrillas were not highwaymen, bushwhackers or ruffians," claimed one of their number, and . . . they did not war upon any element other than the commonly recognized as the enemy." Which is not to say this defense was exclusive preserve of the government's partisans. Even one of Quantrill's men insisted, "[We] were regular Confederate Soldiers."[21]

Ex-guerrillas also liked to emphasize how they had defended the persons and property of Confederate women during the war, in sharp contrast to the Union ruffians that had occupied their towns and pillaged their farms. "My little band not only fought for our country," insisted a guerrilla captain, "but we foraged among the enemy and the fruits of our labor went to gladden the hearts of starving women and children . . . whose husbands and fathers were at the front dying." One of Mosby's men reminded people in 1896 that "defenseless people would have been at the mercy of the roving bands of deserters," . . . horse thieves and desperadoes" had it not been for Virginia's partisans, who "performed the duties of police as well as soldiers."[22]

A Missouri woman adamantly confirmed this side of the guerrilla's nature in 1901 by insisting that the reputation of Quantrill as a bloodthirsty bandit bore no resemblance to the "modest, quiet, good-looking man . . . gentle of manner and courteous" that she had known. Her description might have been written by one of Quantrill's own men, who praised him in like language. One of them recalled, "He never sought notoriety, but on the contrary was very modest and retiring, especially in the company of ladies. I have heard him time and again say that he would shoot any man in the command who would insult or abuse women or children."[23]

Fourth, and ultimately, some former guerrillas simply made no excuses. Rather, they expressed pride in their service, and dared anyone to challenge their motives for joining the guerrilla war. "There is no period of my life that I am so proud of," insisted a Missourian. "It does me good to think over these times, and recall the deeds of those days. The only sad thought is that the flag for which we fought had to go down."[24]

A chief proponent of this line, despite the sensitivities of some of his men, was John Mosby, the most successful partisan ranger of the war. "We were called guerrillas and bushwhackers," Mosby declared in 1899. "Now, while bushwhacking is perfectly legitimate in war, and it is as fair to shoot from a bush as behind a stockade or an earthwork, no men in the Confederate army less deserve these epithets than mine, if by them is meant a body of men who fought under cover and practiced tactics and stratagems not permitted by the rules of regular war." What else, if not guerrillas, were the "embattled farmers" at Lexington and Concord? Later that same year, Mosby insisted, "I have often seen the term—Guerilla Chief—applied to me in Southern papers. I never regarded it as an insult."[25]

Mosby returned to this line of defense in his memoirs, published in 1917, at the same time corroborating his position with testimony from no less a Union hero than Philip H. Sheridan, his great antagonist in the summer and fall of 1864. Referring to Union general's memoirs, published in 1888, he pointed out, "Sheridan says that my battalion was 'the most redoutable' partisan body that he met. I certainly take no exception to that. He makes no charge of any act of inhumanity against us." Indeed, Mosby concluded, Sheridan rendered the "highest compliment ever paid to the efficiency of our command" in discussing their hit and run tactics.[26]

Another partisan ranger, Adam Rankin Johnson, did not dodge the name either. He even titled his memoirs, published in 1904, *The Partisan Rangers of the Confederate States*. In explaining why he wrote the book, Johnson said that his prime goal was "to pay tribute to the Kentucky boys, who, most of them gently born and nurtured, left home, family, friends, fortune behind them, and, enlisting in my command, fought for the Cause of the South." Also, like Mosby, he insisted, "The many epithets hurled at me individually by my foes did not disturb me in the least," and Johnson was pleased to recall that the name Partisan Rangers was "a title highly relished" by his men."[27]

This line of reasoning could easily complement other justifications for guerrilla service. For instance, a Missouri guerrilla explained how his band launched one of their raids against the Federals because his family had been banished from their home as a means of retaliating against him. "[E]vry body nose how our blud boiled," he recalled, "then evry Body in the bresh was mad." The raid, then, came as a "warning" to the Federals, "and i think," this guerrilla noted, "they did not banish any one after that time." Even more to the point, he insisted, "[W]e had nothing to regret in that we had dun[.] only wishied we had dun more. We was not made to wore with wimmen and children."[28]

Of course, in taking this approach, one could justify nearly anything. Champ Ferguson refused to concede that any of the dozens of men he killed had, in fact, been murdered. "I . . . will die a Rebel," he insisted after a military court had sentenced him to be hanged. "I believe I was Right in all I did." Nobody knows for certain how many Yankee soldiers and Unionists Sam Hildebrand killed in Missouri and Arkansas. Some estimates go as high as 200. But in dictating his wartime experiences in 1870, the illiterate guerrilla had no qualms about what he had done. He had fought only in self-defense. "War was the objective and war it was," read his published testament. "It is very difficult to carry on a war for four years without some one getting hurt. If I did kill over a hundred men during the war, it was only because I was in earnest and supposed that everybody else was."[29]

No one hammered at this theme more repeatedly than Hildebrand, who, in 1870, was one of the earliest guerrillas to publish his account of the war. "I make no apology to mankind for my acts of retaliation," he said. "I make no whining appeal to the world for sympathy. I sought revenge and i found it; the key of hell was not suffered to rust in the lock while I was on the war path." And again, "My enemies say that I am a 'Bushwhacker.' Very well, what is a 'Bushwhacker?' He is a man who shoots his enemies. What is a regular army but a conglomerate mass of Bushwhackers?"[30]

Frank James, along with his more famous younger brother Jesse, had ridden with Quantrill during the war. Afterwards, Frank recalled perhaps the second most notorious incident—after the Lawrence raid—in which some of the band participated, the raid and battle of Centralia. On that day, men led by Bloody Bill Anderson, nearly wiped out a detachment of Union cavalry, besides scalping or mutilating several of the Federals. James justified the action by insisting that the enemy had carried a black flag, into battle, meaning "no quarter." "We did not seek the fight," James went on. "[The Union officer] foolishly came out to hunt us and he found us. Then we killed him and his men. Wouldn't he have killed every one of us if he had the chance? What is war for if it isn't to kill people for a principle?"[31]

Note the word *principle*. That was James's way of saying that even Bloody Bill's notorious band refused to concede that they fought for any other reason. James also made this equally revealing statement concerning the willingness of at least some ex-rebels to overlook the grim reality of the guerrilla war. "Funny, isn't it?" he observed. "I've met or heard of thousands of men who claimed to be with Quantrill or his lieutenants during the war, when the truth is there were never more than three hundred or four hundred from the beginning to the end of the war."[32]

Another member of Quantrill's band, John McCorkle, described the events at Centralia as an ordinary skirmish in 1917, and that the slaughter had been caused by the arrogance of the Union cavalry commander. "[H]e was bragging how he was going to extinguish our entire command," McCorkle wrote, "showing his black flag and saying he would take no prisoners." The ex-guerrilla portrayed the annihilation of the

Federals, with no mention of the mutilations, as simply a contest in which the rebels had bested an "utterly demoralized" foe. McCorkle's interpretation of the fight was particularly striking, and probably intended to be, when compared to another episode earlier that day, in which Anderson's men had executed a dozen unarmed Union soldiers in Centralia itself. According to McCorkle, Captain George Todd "severely reprimanded" Anderson by telling him that "he did not endorse such actions."[33]

Even more defiantly, McCorkle and some others did what the editor of the *Confederate Veteran* dared not attempt—to justify the Lawrence massacre. It was widely known that one of the reasons Quantrill led the raid was in retaliation for the collapse of a prison in Kansas City that injured or killed several female relatives of men under his command. McCorkle called it "murder," and said it was the "direct cause" of the raid. Having thus offered a justification for all that followed, McCorkle concluded, "Quantrill and his command had come to Lawrence to be avenged and they were. In this raid, a few innocent men may have been killed but this was not intentional."[34]

Another of the raiders insisted, "The fact is there was one boy killed and one woman wounded, and that was all there was to it." Most of the people who died, he said, were Union soldiers in the town, although he greatly exaggerated their numbers. Instead, he emphasized the physical destruction of the town. "There has always been a great howl about the Lawrence raid. But. . . . [w]e had two objects in view in going to Lawrence. One was to seek revenge. . . . The other was to let Kansas know that fire would burn on the west side of the line." Cole Younger, who would ride with the James gang after the war, admitted that it was "a day of butchery," but he, too, mentioned only a fight with Union soldiers. He was most keen to stress that no women had been killed in the raid.[35]

A less famous guerrilla, operating in Arkansas and Missouri, took pride after the war in the restraint he and his friends had shown during those tumultuous times. As one notable example, he recalled a "retaliatory raid" against a "noted [unionist] raider and houseburner" named James Moore. Swooping down on Moore's farm in hopes of capturing him, he and his men found only the Unionist's wife and daughters. Making do with the situation, they escorted Mrs. Moore and the children to safety before burning the house and all the outbuildings. "Looking back . . . now," wrote the rebel, "after a lapse of over forty years, when all the bitterness engendered by the war is a thing of the past, I sincerely regret the burning of the Moore house; not through any sympathy or respect for him, but because women and children were the immediate sufferers. But that was war. . . . We could have burned many more homes had we chosen to do so, but we were content with the burning of the one."[36]

This unrepentant tone grew partly from a belief that, say what you will about their mode of warfare, rebel guerrillas believed they had made important contributions to their nation's war effort. Indeed, they were convinced, and not without reason, that the Union army had condemned them as outlaws mainly because their military operations against the Federals had been extremely effective, while their harassment of Southern Unionists had been a political embarrassment to the U.S. government. "We had . . . accomplished more than we had reasonably hoped with such limited means, opposed often and threatened by so much larger forces than our own," surmised Adam Johnson. He went on to give a long list of his regiment's accomplishments in Kentucky, and noted with some pride that "the mere mention of our name inspired fear in the hearts of the Federals."[37]

One of the most comprehensive postwar justifications for the guerrilla conflict came from a non-guerrilla, though someone who knew them well. Major John N. Edwards had served as adjutant to Gen. Joseph O. Shelby during the war. As such, he came in contact with some of Missouri's best known guerrillas, including members of Quantrill's band. After the war, he became an apologist for the outlaw exploits of Jesse and Frank James, but he also saw no reason for the James boys or any other rebel to apologize for their wartime careers. He created an elaborate picture of the guerrilla as noble, even romantic hero, a representation that incidentally mirrored his depiction of the postwar James boys. One student of the war says that by excusing even the worst bushwhacker excesses, Edwards hoped to create nothing less than an "irregular Lost Cause."[38]

Edwards's principal vehicle was an 1877 hagiographic volume entitled *Noted Guerrillas*. In explaining the war waged by men such as Quantrill and Bloody Bill Anderson, he utilized all four of the defenses mentioned above, but, like Sam Hildebrand and his own friend Frank James, Edwards ultimately saw no need to excuse their actions. "Civil war might well have made the Guerrilla," he said pointedly, "but only the excesses of civil war could have made him the untamable and unmerciful creature that history finds him. When he first went into the war he was somehow imbued with the old-fashioned belief that soldiering meant fighting and that fighting meant killing. He had his own ideas about soldiering, however, and desired nothing so much as to remain at home and meet its despoilers upon his own premises."[39]

It tells us something, I believe, that these ex-rebels constructed such elaborate justifications for their actions. One does not find this behavior with regular rebel soldiers. The fact was that former guerrillas knew that they were different from the average fighting man. They had fought a different kind of war, and they were viewed differently in the postwar years. Some knew, as well, that however justified *they* thought themselves to be, they would never convince the world of their honest intentions. Said one partisan commander toward the end of the 19th century, "The large majority of these who joined the guerrilla bands had deadly wrongs to avenge, and this gave to all their combats that sanguinary image which yet remains part of the guerrilla's legacy." Some men continued to bask in that legacy, but they also knew that however justified *they* thought themselves to have been, the rest of the world would have to be convinced of their noble intentions.[40]

In that context, it notable that ex-guerrillas boasted of the productive and peaceable postwar lives led by themselves and former comrades. Cole Younger rattled off the names of sheriffs, judges, state legislators, congressmen, and other professions taken up by Quantrill's men. Another Missourian wanted it known that his trusty old Colt revolver rested "sheathed and rusted in its well worn scabbard," and that his grandson would live to understand the "futility of strife, the horrors of war, and the beauties and blessings of 'Peace on earth, good will to men.' " An Arkansan, writing his memoirs at the request of his grandchildren, concluded, "If it serves to impress upon their minds even to a limited degree the horrors of war and the blessings of peace, I will be amply repaid for my time and labor."[41]

Nonetheless, few ex-Confederates who had served in the conventional army cared to be associated with that legacy. As other old soldiers, North and South, formed veterans' organizations, they rarely invited guerrillas to join them. Partisans and guerrillas tended to form their own, separate, groups and hold their own, separate reunions. As stone monuments were erected on Civil War battlefields to commemorate the brave deeds of conventional soldiers, few reminders of the guerrilla war stood among them. As John Edwards put it in his usual florid style, "[T]he Guerrilla had no graveyard. . . . No *cortege* followed the corpse; beneath the folds of the black flag there was no funeral. Neither prayer, nor plaint of priest, nor penitential pleading went up for the wild beast dead by his lair, hard hunted yet splendid at last in the hopeless equanimity of accepted death."[42]

One exception to this lack of commemoration was a 25-feet tall granite monument erected in Virginia in 1899 to honor Mosby's men. Yet, the event commemorated was a telling one. The monument was dedicated not to Mosby's command generally, nor to any victory it had achieved. Rather, the granite shaft marked the spot where six of Mosby's captured men had been executed by Union troops. That said it all. No one wished to celebrate the *deeds* of rebel partisans. Irregulars could only find sympathy as victims of war. Even Mosby, despite taking pride in being guerrilla chief, had no wish to dwell on how the conflict had been conducted. "The bloody part of the War," he wrote, "I like to keep in the background."[43]

And that is where matters rested for decades. Nearly a century after the war, in the mid-1950s, a popular historian of the American Civil War, Bruce Catton, described the guerrilla conflict as "a colorful, annoying, but largely unimportant side issue" of the war. Happily, that is no longer the case. The guerrilla war of 1861–65 has attracted increasing scholarly attention. Far from a side issue, we now know it to be a fascinating, complex labyrinth, and one of its most fascinating elements is the way in which the wartime record of events has been overlaid by the anxious concerns of men who wished to be judged well by future generations. In that sense, the story of the guerrilla war is an intriguing example of the convergence of memory and history, and of how memory may be used not so much to obscure the past as to illuminate it.[44]

APPENDIX A: LETTER FROM GENERAL HENRY W. HALLECK TO DR. FRANCIS LIEBER, AUGUST 6, 1862

On August 6, 1862, Gen. Henry W. Halleck, as general-in-chief of the Union army, wrote the following letter to Dr. Francis Lieber to solicit his opinion on the legality of the Confederacy's guerrilla war.

MY DEAR DOCTOR: Having heard that you have given much attention to the usages and customs of war as practiced in the present age, and especially to the matter of guerrilla war, I hope you may find it convenient to give to the public your views on that subject. The rebel authorities claim the right to send men, in the garb of peaceful citizens, to waylay and attack our troops, to burn bridges and houses, and to destroy property and persons within our lines. They demand that such persons be treated as ordinary belligerents, and that when captured they have extended to them the same rights as other prisoners of war; they also threaten that if such persons be punished as marauders and spies they will retaliate be executing our prisoners of war in their possession. I particularly request your views on these questions.

Source: U.S. War Department, *War of the Rebellion: Official Records of the Union and Confederate Armies,* 128 vols. (Washington, D.C.: Government Printing Office, 1880–1901), ser. 3, vol. 2, 301.

APPENDIX B: GUERRILLA PARTIES CONSIDERED WITH REFERENCE TO THE LAWS AND USAGES OF WAR, BY DR. FRANCIS LIEBER

Responding to Gen. Henry W. Halleck's request for legal guidelines in the guerrilla war, Dr. Francis Lieber provided the government with the following document. It became the basis for his later, more broadly based, "laws of war," issued to the Union army as General Orders No. 100. Indeed, without his essay on guerrillas, "Lieber's code," as it became known, may never have been written.

The position of armed parties loosely attached to the main body of the army, or altogether unconnected with it, has rarely been taken up by writers on the law of war. The term guerrilla is often inaccurately used, and its application has been particularly confused at the present time. From these circumstances arises much of the difficulty which presents itself to the publicist and martial jurist in treating of guerrilla parties. The subject is substantially a new topic in the law of war, and it is, besides, exposed to the mischievous process, so often employed in our day, of throwing the mantle of a novel term around an old and well-known offense, in the expectation that a legalizing effect will result from the adoption of a new word having a technical sound; an illustration of which occurred in the introduction of the Latin and rarer term repudiation to designate the old practice of dishonestly declining the payment of debts—an offense with which the world has become acquainted ever since men united in the bonds of society. We find that self-constituted bands in the South, who destroy the cotton stored by their own neighbors, are styled in the journals of the North as well as in those of the South guerrillas; while in truth they are, according to the common law—not of war only, but that of every society—simply armed robbers, against whom every person is permitted, or is duty bound, to use all the means of defense at his disposal; as, in a late instance, even General Toombs, of Georgia, declared to a certain committee of safety of his State that he would defend the planting and producing of his cotton; though, I must own, he did not call the self-constituted committee guerrillas, but, if memory serves me right, scoundrels.

The term guerrilla is the diminutive of the Spanish word guerra, war, and means petty war; that is, war carried on by detached parties, generally in the mountains. It means, further, the party of men united under one chief engaged in petty war, which, in the eastern portion of Europe and the whole Levant is called a capitanery, a band under one capitano. The term guerrilla, however, is not applied in Spain to a single man of the party; such a person is called guerrillero, or more frequently partida, which means partisan. Thus Napier, in speaking of the guerrilla in his History of the Peninsular War, uses, with rare exception, the term partidas for the chiefs and men engaged in the petty war against the French. It is worthy of notice that the dictionary of the Spanish academy gives, as the first meaning of the word guerrilla, "A party of light troops for reconnaissance, and opening the first skirmishers." I translate from an edition of 1826, published, therefore, long after the Peninsular war, through which the term guerrilla has passed over into many other European languages. Self-constitution is not a necessary element of the meaning given by the Spaniards or by many writers of other nations to the word guerrilla, although it is true that the guerrilla parties of the Peninsular war were nearly all self-constituted, since the old government had been destroyed; and the forces which had been called into existence by the provisional government were no more acknowledged by the French as regular troops than the self-constituted bands under leading priests, lawyers, smugglers, or peasants; because the French did not acknowledge the provisional Junta or Cortes. Many of the guerrilleros were shot when made prisoners, as the guerrilla chiefs executed French prisoners in turn. It is the state of things these bands almost lead to, according to their inherent character; yet, when the partidas of Mina and Empecinado had swelled to the imposing number of twenty thousand and more, which fact of itself implies a certain degree of discipline, Mina made a regular treaty with the French for the passage of certain French goods through the lines, and on these the partisan leaders levied regular duties according to a tariff agreed upon between the belligerents arrayed against one another in fierce hostility.

What, then, do we in the present time understand by the word guerrilla. In order to ascertain the law or to settle it according to elements already existing, it will be necessary ultimately to give a distinct definition; but it may be stated here that whatever may be our final definition, it is universally understood in this country at the present time that a guerrilla party means an irregular band of armed men, carrying on an irregular war, not being able, according to their character as a guerrilla party, to carry on what the law terms a regular war. The irregularity of the guerrilla party consists in it origins, for it is either self-constituted or constituted by the call of a single individual, not according to the general law of levy, conscription, or volunteering; it consists in its disconnection with the army as to its pay, provision, and movements, and it is irregular as to the permanency of the band, which may be dismissed and called again together at any time. These are, I believe, constituent ideas of the term guerrilla as now used. Other ideas are associated with the term, differently by different persons. Thus many persons associate the idea of pillage with the guerrilla band, because, not being connected with the regular army, the men cannot provide for themselves, except by pillage, even in their own country—acts of violence with which the Spanish guerrilleros sorely afflicted their own countrymen in the Peninsular war. Others connect with it the idea of intentional destruction for the sake of destruction, because the guerrilla chief cannot aim at any strategic advantages or any regular fruits of victory. Others, again, associate with it the idea of the danger with which the spy surrounds us, because he that to-day passes you in the garb and mein of a peaceful citizen, may to-morrow, as a guerrillaman, fire your house or murder you from behind a hedge. Others connect with the guerrillero the idea of necessitated murder, because guerrilla bands cannot encumber themselves with prisoners of war; they have, therefore, frequently, perhaps generally, killed their prisoners, and of course have been killed in turn when made prisoners, thus introducing a system of barbarity which becomes intenser in its democratization as its spreads and is prolonged. Others, again, connect the ideas of general and heinous criminality, of robbery and lust with the term, because the organization of the party being but slight and the leader utterly dependent upon the band, little discipline can be enforced, and where no discipline is enforced in war a state of things results which resembles far more the wars recorded in Froissart, or Comines, or the thirty-years' war, and the religious war in France, then the regular wars of modern times. And such a state of things results speedily, too; for all growth, progress, and rearing, moral or material, are slow; all destruction, relapse, and degeneracy fearfully rapid. It requires the power of the Almighty and a whole century to grow an oak tree; but only a pair of arms, an ax, and an hour or two to cut it down.

History confirms these associations, but the law of war as well as the law of peace has treated many of these and kindred subjects—acts justifiable, offensive, or criminal—under acknowledged terms, namely: The freebooter, the marauder, the brigand, the partisan, the free corps, the spy, the rebel, the conspirator, the robber, and especially the highway robber, the rising en masse, or the "arming of peasants."

A few words on some of these subjects will aid us in coming to a clearer understanding of the main topic which occupies our attention.

Freebooter is a term which was in common use in the English language at no very remote period; it is of rare use now, because the freebooter makes his appearance but rarely in modern times, thanks to the more regular and efficient governments and to the more advanced state of the law of war. From the freebooter at sea arose the privateer, for the privateer is a commissioned freebooter, or the freebooter taken into the service of the government by the letter of marque. The sea-gueux, in the revolution of the Netherlands, were generally freebooters at sea, and they were always treated when captured simply as freebooters. Wherever the freebooter is taken, at sea or on land, death is inflicted upon him now as in former times, for freebooters are nothing less than armed robbers of the most dangerous and criminal type, banded together for the purposes of booty and of common protection.

The brigand is, in military language, the soldier who dispatches himself from his troop and commits robbery, naturally accompanied in many cases with murder and other crimes of violence. His punishment, inflicted even by his own authorities, is death. The word brigand, derived as it is from briguer, to beg, meant originally beggar, but it soon came to be applied to armed strollers, a class of men which swarmed in all countries in the middle ages. The term has, however, received a wider meaning in modern military terminology. He that assails the enemy without or against the authority of his own government is called, even though his object should be wholly free from any intention of pillage, a brigand, subject to the infliction of death if captured. When Major von Schill, commanding a Prussian regiment of huzzars, marched in the year 1809 against the French without the order of the government, for the purpose of causing a rising of the people in the north of Germany, while Napoleon was occupied in the south with Austria, Schill was declared by Napoleon and his brother a brigand, and the King of Westphalia, Jerome Bonaparte, offered a reward of 10,000 francs for his head. Schill was killed in battle; but twelve young officers of his troop, taken prisoners, were carried by the French to the fortress Wesel, where a court-martial declared them prisoners of war. Napoleon quashed the finding, ordered a new court-martial, and they all were shot as brigands. Napoleon is not cited here as an authority in the law of war; he and many of his generals frequently substituted the harshest violence for martial usages. The case is mentioned as an illustration of the meaning attached to the word brigand in the law of war, and of the fact that death is the acknowledged punishment for the brigand.

The terms partisan and free corps are vaguely used. Sometimes, as we shall see further on, partisan is used for a self-constituted guerrillero; more frequently it has a different meaning. Both partisan corps and free corps designate bodies detached from the main army; but the former term refers to the action of the troop, the latter to the composition. The partisan leader commands a corps whose object is to injure the enemy by action separate from that of his own main army; the partisan acts chiefly upon the enemy's lines of connection and communication, and outside of or beyond the lines of operation of his own army, in the rear and on the flanks of the enemy. Rapid and varying movements and surprises are the chief means of his success; but he is part and parcel of the army, and, as such, considered entitled to the privileges of the law of war, so long as he does not transgress it. Free corps, on the other hand, are troops belonging to the regular army, consisting of volunteers, generally raised by individuals authorized to do so by the government, used for petty war, and not incorporated with the *ordre de bataille.* They were known in the middle ages. The French *compagnies franches* were free corps; but this latter term came into use only in the eighteenth century. They were generally in bad repute, given to pillage and other excesses; but this is incidental. There were many free corps in Germany opposed to Napoleon when the country rose against the French, but the men composing them were entitled to the benefits of the law of war, and generally received them when taken prisoner. These free corps were composed in many cases of high-minded patriots. The difficulty regarding free corps and partisans arises from the fact that their discipline is often lax, and used to be so especially in the last century, so that frequently they cannot cumber themselves with prisoners; and that even for their own support they are often obliged to pillage or to extort money from the places they occupy. They are treated, therefore, according to their deserts, on the principle of retaliation; but there is nothing inherently lawless or brigand-like in their character.

The spy, the rebel, and conspirator deserve notice in this place simply with reference to persons acting as such, and belonging to the population of the country or district occupied by a hostile force. A person dwelling in a district under military occupation and giving information to the government of which he was subject, but which has been expelled by the victorious invader, is universally treated as a spy—a spy of a peculiarly dangerous character. The most patriotic motives would not shield such a person from the doom of the spy. There have been high-minded and self-sacrificing spies, but when captured, even if belonging to the armies themselves, they have never been treated otherwise than as common spies. Even mere secret correspondence of a person in an occupied district with the enemy, though the contents of the correspondence may have been innocent, has subjected the correspondent to serious consequences, and sometimes to the rigor of martial law, especially if the offense be committed after a proclamation to the contrary. Prince Hatzfeld was appointed by the King of Prussia, on his leaving the capital after the battle of Jena, to conduct public affairs in Berlin until the city should be occupied by the French, and to send a report to the king every morning until the occupation by the enemy should have taken place. Prince Hatzfeld sent such a report to his own government, giving the number of the French who had arrived at Potsdam on the 24th of October, at 5 o'clock a.m.—that is, seven hours before the French vanguard entered Berlin. The letter fell into the hands of Napoleon. It is well known that the emperor, or the supplication of the princess, allowed her husband to escape the penalty of a spy. Whatever may be thought of the question, whether the prince, by sending the letter at the hour mentioned became a spy or not, no one has ever doubted that, had he secretly corresponded with his government after the occupation of Berlin by the French, giving information of the occupants, the French would have been justified in treating him as a spy. The spy becomes, in this case, peculiarly dangerous, making hostile use of the protection which by the modern law of war the victor extends to the persons and property of the conquered. Similar remarks apply to the rebel, taking the word in the primitive meaning of rebellare—that is, to return to war after having been conquered; and to conspiracies—that is, secret agreements leading to such resumption of arms in bands of whatever number, or, which is still worse, plans to murder from secret places.

The war-rebel, as we might term him, this renewer of war within an occupied territory, has been universally treated with the utmost rigor of military law. The war-rebel exposes the occupying army to the greatest danger, and essentially interferes with the mitigation of the severity of war, which it is one of the noblest objects of the modern law of war to obtain. Whether the war-rebel rises on his own account, or whether he has been secretly called upon by his former government to do so, would make no difference whatever. The royalists who recently rose in the mountains of Calabria against the national government of Italy, and in favor of Francis, who had been their king until within a recent period, were treated as brigands and shot, unless, indeed, pardoned on prudential grounds.

The rising en masse, or "the arming of peasants," as it used to be called, brings us nearer to the subject of the guerrilla parties. Down to the beginning of the first French revolution, toward the end of the last century, the spirit which pervaded all governments of the European continent was, that the people were rather the passive substratum of the State than as essential portion of it. The governments were considered to be the State; wars were chiefly cabinet wars, not national wars—not the people's affairs.

Moser, in his *Contributions to the Latest European Law of Nations in Times of War* (a German work, in 3 vols., from 1779–81), gives remarkable instances of the claims which the conqueror was believed to have on the property and on the subjects of the hostile country. They were believed to be of so extensive a character that the French, when in Germany, during the seven-years' war, literally drafted Germans for the French army, and used them as their own soldiers—although, it must be added, loud complaints were made, and the French felt themselves obliged to make some sort of explanation. The same work contains instances of complaints being made against arming the peasants, or of levies en masse, as contrary to the law of nations; but Moser also shows that the Austrians employed the Tyrolese (always familiar with the use of the rifle) in war without any complaint of the adversary.

Since that time most constitutions contain provisions that the people have a right to posses and use arms; everywhere national armies have been introduced, and the military law of many countries puts arms into the hands of all. Austria armed the people as militia in 1805; Russia in 1812; and Prussia introduced the most comprehensive measure of arming the people in 1813. The militia proper in the landwehr, and those who were too old for service in the landwehr were intended to form the landsturm—citizens armed as well as the circumstances might permit, and to be used for whatever military service within their own province they might be found fit. It is true that the French threatened to treat them as brigands—that is to say, not to treat them as prisoners of war if captured. The French, however, were expelled from Germany and no opportunity was given to test their threat.

I believe it can be said that the most recent publicists and writers on international law agree that the rising of the people to repel invasion entitles them to the full benefits of the law of war, and that the invader cannot well inquire into the origins of the armed masses opposing him—that is to say, he will be obliged to treat the captured citizens in arms as prisoners of war so long as they openly oppose him in respectable numbers and have risen in the yet uninvaded or unconquered portions of the hostile country.

Their acting in separate bodies does not necessarily give them a different character. Some entire wars have been carried on by separate bands or capitaneries, such as the recent war of independence of Greece. It is true, indeed, that the question of the treatment of prisoners was not discussed in that war, because the Turkish Government killed or enslaved all prisoners; but I take it that a civilized government would not have allowed the fact that the Greeks fought in detached parties and carried on mountain guerrilla to influence its conduct toward prisoners.

I may here observe that the question how captured guerrilleros ought to be treated was not much discussed in the last century and, comparatively, the whole discussion in the law of war is new. This will not surprise us when we consider that so justly celebrated a publicist as Bynkershoeck defended, as late as the beginning of last century, the killing of common prisoners of war.

It does not seem that, in the case of a rising en masse, the absence of a uniform can constitute a difference. There are cases, indeed, in which the absence of a uniform may be taken as very serious prima facie evidence against an armed prowler or marauder, but it must be remembered that a uniform dress is a matter of impossibility in a levy en masse; and in some cases regulars have had no uniforms, at least for a considerable time. The Southern prisoners made at Fort Donelson, whom I have seen at the West, had no uniforms. They were indeed dressed very much alike, but it was the uniform dress of the countrymen in that region. Yet they were treated by us as prisoners of war, and well treated, too. Nor would it be difficult to adopt something of a badge, easily put on and off, and call it a uniform. It makes a great difference, however, whether the absence of the uniform is used for the purpose of concealment of disguise, in order to get by stealth within the lines of the invader, for the destruction of life or property, or for pillage, and whether the parties have no organization at all, and are so small that they cannot act otherwise than by stealth. Nor can it be maintained in good faith, or with any respect for sound sense and judgment, that an individual—an armed prowler—(now frequently called a bushwhacker) shall be entitled to the protection of the law of war simply because he says that he has taken up his gun in defense of his country, or because his government or his chief has issued a proclamation by which he calls upon the people to infest the bushes and commit homicides which every civilized nation will consider murders. Indeed, the importance of writing on this subject is much diminished by the fact that the soldier generally decides these cases for himself. The most disciplined soldiers will execute on the spot an armed and murderous prowler found where he could have no business as a peaceful citizen. Even an enemy in the uniform of the hostile army would stand little chance of protection if found prowling neat the opposing army, separate from his troop at a greater than picket distance, and under generally suspicious circumstances. The chance would, of course, be far less if the prowler is in the common dress worn by the countrymen of the district. It mat be added here that a person proved to be a regular soldier of the enemy's army found in citizens' dress within the lines of the captor is universally dealt with as a spy.

It has been stated that the word guerrilla is not only used for individuals engaged in petty war, but frequently as an equivalent of partisan. General Halleck, in his International Law, or Rules Regulating the Intercourse of States in Peace and War, San Francisco, 1861, page 386 *et seq.*, seems to consider partisan troops and guerrilla troops as the same, and seems to consider "self-constitution" a characteristic of the partisan; while other legal and military writers define partisan as I have stated, namely, a soldier belonging to a corps which operates in the manner given above. I beg the reader to peruse that passage, both on account of its own value and of the many more important and instructive authorities which he will find there. They are collected with that careful industry which distinguishes the whole work.

Dr. T. D. Woolsey, page 299 *et seq.*, of his Introduction to the Study of International Law, Boston, 1860, says:

> The treatment which the milder modern usage prescribes for regular soldiers is extended also to militia called out by public authority. Guerrilla parties, however, do not enjoy the full benefit of the laws of war. They are apt to fare worse than either regular troops or an armed peasantry. The reasons for this are, that they are annoying and insidious; that they put on and off with ease the character of a soldier, and that they are prone themselves to treat their enemies who fall into their hands with great severity.

If the term partisan is used in the sense in which I have defined it, it is not necessary to treat it specially. The partisan in this sense is, of course, answerable for the commission of those acts to which the law of war grants no protection, and by which the soldier forfeits being treated as a prisoner of war if captured.

It is different if we understand by guerrilla parties, self-constituted sets of armed men in times of war, who form no integrant part of the organized army, do not stand on the regular pay-roll of the army, or are not paid at all, take up arms and lay them down at intervals, and carry on petty war (guerrilla) chiefly by raids, extortion, destruction, and massacre, and who cannot encumber themselves with many prisoners, and will therefore generally give no quarter.

They are peculiarly dangerous because they easily evade pursuit, and by laying down their arms become insidious enemies; because they cannot otherwise subsist than by rapine, and almost always degenerate into simple robbers or brigands. The Spanish guerrilla bands against Napoleon proved a scourge to their own countrymen, and became efficient for their own cause only in the same degree in which they gradually became disciplined. The royalists in the north of France during the first Revolution, although setting out with sentiments of loyal devotion to their unfortunate king, soon degenerated into bands of robbers, while many robbers either joined them or assumed the name of Royalists. Napoleon states that their brigandage gave much trouble and obliged the Government to resort to the severest measures.

For an account of the misdeeds and want of efficiency of the Spanish guerrilleros, the reader is referred to Napier's Peninsular War, and especially to Chapter II, Book XVII, while he will find, in Guizot's Memoirs, Volume IV, page 100 *et seq.,* that in the struggle between the Christinos and Carlists the guerrilla parties under Mina and Zumalacarreguy regularly massacred their mutal prisoners, until the evil became so revolting to the Spaniards themselves that a regular treaty was concluded between the parties, stipulating that the exchange of prisoners immediately after being made. How the surplus on the one or the other side was dealt with I do not know, but the treaty, concluded after the butchering of prisoners had been going on for a long time, is mentioned in all the histories of that period.

But when guerrilla parties aid the main army of a belligerent it will be difficult for the captor of guerrillamen to decide at once whether they are regular partisans, distinctly authorized by their own government; and it would seem that we are borne out by the conduct of the most humane belligerents in recent times, and by many of the modern writers, if the rule be laid down, that guerrillamen, when captured in fair fight and open warfare, should be treated as the regular partisan is, until special crimes, such as murder, or the killing of prisoners, or the sacking of places, are proved upon them, leaving the question of self-constitution unexamined.

The law of war, however, would not extend a similar favor to small bodies of armed country people, near the lines, whose very smallness shows that they must resort to occasional fighting and the occasional assuming of peaceful habits, and to brigandage. The law of war would still less favor them when they trespass within the hostile lines to commit devastation, rapine, or destruction. Every European army has treated such persons, and it seems to me would continue, even in the improved state of the present usages of war, to treat them as brigands, whatever prudential mercy might decide upon in single cases. This latter consideration cannot be discussed here; it does not appertain to the law of war.

It has been stated already that the armed prowler, the so-called bushwhacker, is a simple assassin, and will thus always be considered by soldier and citizen; and we have likewise seen that the armed bands that rise in a district fairly occupied by military force, or in the rear of an army, are universally considered, if captured, brigands, and not prisoners of war. They unite the fourfold character of the spy, the brigand, the assassin, and the rebel, and cannot—indeed, it must be supposed, will not—expect to be treated as a fair enemy of the regular war. They know what a hazardous career they enter upon when they take up arms, and that were the case reversed they would surely not grant the privileges of regular warfare to persons who should thus rise in their rear.

I have thus endeavored to ascertain what may be considered the law of war or fair rules of action toward so-called guerrilla parties. I do not enter upon a consideration of their application to the civil war in which we are engaged, nor of the remarkable claims recently set up by our enemies, demanding us to act according to certain rules which they have signally and officially disregarded toward us. I have simply proposed to myself to find a certain portion of the law of war. The application of the laws and usages of war to wars of insurrection or rebellion is always undefined, and depends upon relaxations of the municipal law, suggested by humanity or necessitated by the numbers engaged in the insurrection. The law of war, as acknowledged between independent belligerents, is at times not allowed to interfere with the municipal law of rebellion, or is allowed to do so only very partially, as was the case in Great Britain during the Stuart rebellion, in the middle of the last century; at other times, again, measures are adopted in rebellions, by the victorious party or the legitimate government, more lenient even than the international law of war. Neither of these topics can occupy us here, not does the letter prefixed to this tract contain the request that I should do so. How far rules which have formed themselves in the course of time between belligerents might be relaxed with safety toward the evil-doers in our civil war, or how far such relaxation or mitigation would be likely to produce a beneficial effect upon an enemy who in committing a great and bewildering wrong seems to have withdrawn himself from the common influences of fairness, sympathy, truth, and logic—how far this ought to be done at the present moment must be decided by the executive power, civil and military, or possibly by the legislative power. It is not for me in this place to make the inquiry. So much is certain, that no army, no society engaged in war, any more than a society at peace, can allow unpunished assassination, robbery, and devastation without the deepest injury to itself and disastrous consequences which might change the very issue of the war.

Source: U.S. War Department, *War of the Rebellion: Official Records of the Union and Confederate Armies,* 128 vols. (Washington, D.C.: Government Printing Office, 1880–1901), ser. 3, vol. 2, 301–09.

APPENDIX C: GENERAL ORDERS NO. 100: "LIEBER'S CODE"

The sections and particulars of General Orders No. 100, "Lieber's Code," dealing with irregular warfare, as issued to the Union army on April 24, 1863.

SECTION IV.—Partisans—Armed enemies not belonging to the hostile army—Scouts–Armed prowlers—War-rebels.

81. Partisans are soldiers armed and wearing the uniform of their army, but belonging to a corps which acts detached from the main body for the purpose of making inroads into the territory occupied by the enemy. If captured they are entitled to all privileges of the prisoner of war.

82. Men, or squads of men, who commit hostilities, whether by fighting, or inroads for destruction or plunder, or by raids of any kind, without commission, without being part and portion of the organized hostile army, and without sharing continuously in the war, but who do so with intermitting returns to their homes and avocations, or with the occasional assumption of the semblance of peaceful pursuits, divesting themselves of the character or appearance of soldiers–such men, or squads of men, are not public enemies, and therefore, if captured, are not entitled to the privileges of prisoners of war, but shall be treated summarily as highway robbers or pirates.

83. Scouts or single soldiers, if disguised in the dress of the country, or in the uniform of the army hostile to their own, employed in obtaining information, if found within or lurking about the lines of the captor, are treated as spies, and suffer death.

84. Armed prowlers, by whatever names they may be called, or persons of the enemy's territory, who steal within the lines of the hostile army for the purpose of robbing, killing, or of destroying the mail, or of cutting the telegraph wires, are not entitled to the privileges of the prisoner of war.

85. War-rebels are persons within an occupied territory who rise in arms against the occupying or conquering army, or against the authorities established by the same. If captured, they may suffer death, whether they rise singly, in small or large bands, and whether called upon to do so by their own, but expelled, government or not. They are not prisoners of war; nor are they if discovered and secured before their conspiracy has matured to an actual rising or to armed violence.

SECTION V.—Safe-conduct—Spies–War-traitors—Captured messengers–Abuse of the flag of truce.

86. All intercourse between the territories occupied by belligerent armies, whether by traffic, by letter, by travel, or in any other way, ceases. This is the general rule, to be observed without special proclamation.

    Exceptions to this rule, whether by safe-conduct or permission to trade on a small or large scale, or by exchanging mails, or by travel from one territory into the other, can take place only according to agreement approved by the Government or by the highest military authority.

    Contraventions of this rule are highly punishable.

87. Ambassadors, and all other diplomatic agents of neutral powers accredited to the enemy many receive safe-conducts through the territories occupied by the belligerents, unless there are military reasons to the contrary, and unless they may reach the place of their destination conveniently by another route. It implies no international affront if the safe-conduct is declined. Such passes are usually given by the supreme authority of the state and not by subordinate officers.

88. A spy is a person who secretly, in disguise or under false pretense, seeks information with the intention of communicating it to the enemy.

    The spy is punishable with death by hanging by the neck, whether or not he succeed in obtaining the information or in conveying it to the enemy.

89. If a citizen of the United States obtains information in a legitimate manner and betrays it to the enemy, be he a military or civil officer, or a private citizen, he shall suffer death.

90. A traitor under the law of war, or a war-traitor, is a person in a place or district under martial law who, unauthorized by the military commander, gives information of any kind to the enemy, or holds intercourse with him.

91. The war-traitor is always severely punished. If his offense consists in betraying to the enemy anything concerning the condition, safety, operations, or plans of the troop holding or occupying the place or district, his punishment is death.

92. If the citizen or subject of a country or place invaded or conquered gives information to his own government, from which he is separated by the hostile army, or to the army of his government, he is a war-traitor, and death is the penalty of his offense.

93. All armies in the field stand in need of guides, and impress them if they cannot obtain them otherwise.

94. No person having been forced by the enemy to serve as guide is punishable for having done so.

95. If a citizen of a hostile and invaded district voluntarily serves as a guide to the enemy, or offers to do so, he is deemed a war-traitor and shall suffer death.

96. A citizen serving voluntarily as a guide against his own country commits treason, and shall be dealt with according to the law of his country.

97. Guides, when it is clearly proved that they have misled intentionally, may be put to death.

98. All unauthorized or secret communication with the enemy is considered treasonable by the law of war.

    Foreign residents in an invaded or occupied territory or foreign visitors in the same can claim no immunity from this law. They may communicate with foreign parts or with the inhabitants of the hostile country, so far as the military authority permits, but no further. Instant expulsion from the occupied territory would be the very least punishment for the infraction of this rule.

99. A messenger carrying written dispatches or verbal messages from one portion of the army or from a besieged place to another portion of the same army or its government, if armed, and in the uniform of his army, and if captured while doing so in the territory occupied by the enemy, is treated by the captor as a prisoner of war. If not in uniform nor a soldier, the circumstances connected with his capture must determine the disposition that shall be made of him.

100. A messenger or agent who attempts to steal through the territory occupied by the enemy to further in any manner the interests of the enemy, if captured, is not entitled to the privileges of the prisoner of war, and may be dealt with according to the circumstances of the case.

101. While deception in war is admitted as a just and necessary means of hostility, and is consistent with honorable warfare, the common law of war allowed even capital punishment for clandestine or treacherous attempts to injure an enemy, because they are so dangerous, and it is difficult to guard against them.

102. The law of war, like the criminal law regarding other offenses, makes no difference on account of the differences of sexes, concerning the spy, the war-traitor, or the war-rebel.

103. Spies, war-traitors, and war-rebels are not exchanged according to the common law of war. The exchange of such persons would require a special cartel, authorized by the Government, or, at a great distance from it, by the chief commander of the army in the field.

104. A successful spy or war-traitor, safely returned to his own army, and afterward captured as an enemy, is not subject to punishment for his acts as a spy or war-traitor, but he may be held in closer custody as a person individually dangerous.

Source: U.S. War Department, *War of the Rebellion: Official Records of the Union and Confederate Armies*, 128 vols. (Washington, D.C., 1880–1901), ser. 3, vol. 3, 157–59.

NOTES

CHAPTER 1

1. William K. Scarborough, ed., *The Diary of Edmund Ruffin,* 3 vols. (Baton Rouge: Louisiana State University Press, 1972–1989), II: 18–19, 23–24, 38, 42, 61; George Fitzhugh, "The Times and the War," *DeBow's Review* 31 (July 1861): 2–4.

2. Hila Appleton Richardson, "Raleigh County, West Virginia, in the Civil War," *West Virginia History,* 10 (April 1949): 228; Jonathan Newcomb to John Letcher, June 17, 1861, Virginia Governor Executive Papers: Letcher, Virginia State Library, Richmond.

3. Christopher Phillips, *Missouri's Confederate: Claiborne Fox Jackson and the Creation of the Southern Identity in the Border West* (Columbia: University of Missouri Press, 2000), 259–60; Lynda L. Crist et al., eds., *The Papers of Jefferson Davis,* 11 vols. (Baton Rouge: Louisiana State University Press, 1971–), VII: 188–89.

4. Donald M. Murray and Robert M. Rodney, eds., "The Letters of Peter Bryant, Jackson County Pioneer," *Kansas Historical Quarterly* 27 (Autumn 1961): 348; Albert Castel, *Civil War Kansas: Reaping the Whirlwind* (1958; Lawrence: University Press of Kansas, 1997), 39–42; James L. Montgomery to George L. Stearns, June 21, July 5, 1861, George L. and Mary E. Stearns Papers, Kansas State Historical Society, Topeka.

5. Roy P. Basler, ed., *The Collected Works of Abraham Lincoln,* 8 vols. (New Brunswick, NJ: Rutgers University Press, 1953), IV: 532.

6. John S. Daniel Jr., "Special Warfare in Middle Tennessee and Surrounding Areas, 1861–62" (MA thesis, University of Tennessee, 1971), 35; Jonathan M. Johnson to Beriah

Magoffin, May 31, 1861, Jonathan A. Gardner to Johnson, June 1, 1861, V. Finnell to Magoffin, June 10, 1861, Kentucky Governor Papers: Magoffin, Kentucky Department of Libraries and Archives, Frankfort.

7. William James Smith to Leroy Pope Walker, June 3, 1861, Letters Received by Confederate Secretary of War, War Department Collection of Confederate Records, RG 109, National Archives, Washington, D.C.; W. W. Herbert to Messrs. Woodrow, Boylston and McCants, December 3, 161, McCants Family Papers, South Carolinian Library, University of South Carolina, Columbia.

8. D. M. Washington to Jefferson Davis, May 19, 1861, W. R. Rightor to Leroy Pope Walker, July 15, 1861, Letters Received by Confederate Secretary of War; J. C. Spurlin to Joseph E. Brown, June 17, 1861, William A. McDonald to Brown, September 10, 1861, George Governor Correspondence: Brown, Georgia Department of Archives and History, Atlanta.

9. Barnes F. Lathrop, "The Lafourche District in 1861–1862: A Problem in Local Defense," *Louisiana History* 1 (Spring 1960): 99–101, 107–10; Richard A. Baker to Joseph E. Brown, August 29, 1861, Georgia Governor Correspondence; S. Oliver to John J. Pettus, May 2, 1861, F. R. Wittes to Pettus, July 23, 1861, John J. Pettus Papers, Mississippi Department of History and Archives, Jackson.

10. David Paul Smith, *Frontier Defense in the Civil War: Texas' Rangers and Rebels* (College Station: Texas A&M University Press, 1992), 21–40; W. T. Harris to Leroy Pope Walker, July 9, 1861, Letters Received by Confederate Secretary of War.

11. Isaac M. David to Joseph E. Brown, May 10, 1861, William Moore to Brown, April 28, 1861, Georgia Governor Correspondence; Donald B. Dodd and Wynelle S. Dodd, *Winston: An Antebellum and Civil War History of a Hill County of North Alabama* (Birmingham, AL: Oxmoor Press, 1972), 81–83.

12. William H. Phillips to Joseph E. Brown, June 2, 1861, Georgia Governor Correspondence.

13. H. N. Lavaskin to Joseph E. Brown, March 25, 1861, Georgia Governor Correspondence.

14. James L. Sandler to Madison Perry, May 4, 1861, Nathaniel Wilde et al. to Perry, April 29, 1861, Incoming Correspondence, Florida Governor Papers, Florida State Archives, Tallahassee; B. A. Terry to John J. Pettus, April 30, 1861, Pettus Papers.

15. William R. Strachan to Simon Cameron, July 17, 1861, Letters Received by Secretary of War: Irregular Series, 1861–1866, Records of the Office of the Secretary of War, RG 107 (M492), National Archives, Washington, D.C.

16. Lowndes H. Davis to Mary Davis, June 28, 1861, Lowndes Henry Davis Papers; Edward Bates to Hamilton R. Gamble, July 16, 1861, Hamilton R. Gamble Papers, Julian Bates to Edward Bates, July 15, 1861, Bates Family Papers, all in Missouri Historical Society, St. Louis.

17. Kenneth W. Noe, "Who Were the Bushwhackers?: Age, Class, Kin, and Western Virginia's Confederate Guerrillas, 1861–1862," *Civil War History* 49 (March 2003): 5–31.

18. Kirby Ross, ed., *Autobiography of Samuel S. Hildebrand: The Renowned Missouri Bushwhacker* (Fayetteville: University of Arkansas Press, 2005), xiii–xvi; Deposition of William Monks, May 12, 1864, Union Provost Marshals' File of Papers Relating to Two or More Citizens, War Department Collection of Confederate Records, RG 109 (M416), National

Archives, Washington, D.C.; Mark W. Geiger, *Financial Fraud and Guerrilla Violence in Missouri's Civil War, 1861–1865* (New Haven, CT: Yale University Press, 2010), 100–14; Charles W. Porter, *In the Devil's Dominions: A Union Soldier's Adventures in "Bushwhacker Country,"* ed. Patrick Brophy (Nevada, MO: Vernon County Historical Society, 1998), 7–8.

19. Jay Anthony Prier, "Under the Black Flag: The Real War in Washington County, Arkansas, 1861–1865" (MA thesis, University of Arkansas, 1998), 54–62, 83, 86; Young F. Allison, "Sue Munday: An Account of the Terrible Kentucky Guerrilla of Civil War Times," *Register of the Kentucky Historical Society* 57 (October 1959): 301–2.

20. Mary Elizabeth Dickison, *Dickison and His Men: Reminiscences of the War in Florida* (1890; Jacksonville, FL: San Marco Bookstore, 1962), 197–98.

21. Jonathan M. Berkey, "Fighting the Devil with Fire: David Hunter Strother's Private Civil War," in John C. Inscoe and Robert C. Kenzer, eds., *Enemies of the Country: New Perspectives on Unionists in the Civil War South* (Athens: University of Georgia Press, 2001), 21–23; Porter, *In the Devil's Dominion,* 51.

22. R. W. Stevenson to Leroy Pope Walker, May 14, 1861, E. M. Seago to Walker, April 17, 1861, H. V. Keep to Walker, July 14, August 2, 1861, Letters Received by Confederate Secretary of War.

23. H. E. Matheny, *Wood County, West Virginia, in Civil War Times* (Parkersburg, WV: Joseph E. Sakach, Jr., 1987), 47–52; Edward E. Leslie, *The Devil Knows How to Ride: The True Story of William Clarke Quantrill and His Confederate Raiders* (New York: Random House, 1996), 186–90; Clara B. Eno, "Activities of the Women of Arkansas during the War between the States," *Arkansas Historical Quarterly* 3 (Spring 1944): 16; Elizabeth D. Leonard, *All the Daring of a Solider: Women of the Civil War Armies* (New York: W. W. Norton, 1999), 88–93.

24. T. Lindsay Baker, ed., *Confederate Guerrilla: The Civil War Memoir of Joseph Bailey* (Fayetteville: University of Arkansas Press, 2007), 39–40; Thomas F. Fisher to Leroy Pope Walker, May 1, 1861, Letters Received by Confederate Secretary of War; George T. Maddox, *Hard Trials and Tribulations of an Old Confederate Soldier,* ed. Richard T. Norton and Troy Massey (1897; Springfield, MO: Oak Hills Publishing, 1997), 9; J. Marshall Crawford, *Mosby and His Men* (New York: G. W. Carleton, 1867), 14.

25. H. T. Harrison to Leroy Pope Walker, April 19, 1861, I. W. Garrott to Walker, June 5, 1861, T. L. Faulkner to Walker, June 26, 1861, Owen L. Davis to William B. Ogletree, July 12, 1861, A. L. Pridemore to John Fletcher, July 30, 1861, Letters Received by Confederate Secretary of War; Joe M. Scott, *Four Years' Service in the Southern Army* (1897; Fayetteville, AR: Washington County Historical Society, 1958), 40–41; R. H. Williams, *With the Border Ruffians: Memories of the Far West,* ed. E. W. Williams (London: John Murray, 1897), 303.

26. O. S. Barton, *Three Years with Quantrill: A True Story Told by His Scout John McCorkle* (1914; Norman: University of Oklahoma Press, 1992), 52.

CHAPTER 2

1. Evelyn A. Benson, comp., *With the Army of West Virginia, 1861–1864: Reminiscences and Letters of Lt. James Abraham Lancaster* (Lancaster, PA: Evelyn A. Benson, 1974), 65.

2. Charles R. Williams, ed., *Diary and letters of Rutherford B. Hayes,* 5 vols. (Columbus: Ohio State Archeological and Historical Society, 1922–26), II: 60, 63–70.

3. James I. Robertson Jr., ed., *Solider of Southwestern Virginia: The Civil War Letters of Captain John Preston Sheffey* (Baton Rouge: Louisiana State University Press, 2004), 93.

4. George W. Carvill to sister, September 10, 1861, George W. Carvill Letters, Western Manuscripts and Historical Collection, University of Missouri, Columbia. For the complex political situation in Kentucky, see James W. Finck, *Divided Loyalties: Kentucky's Struggle for Armed Neutrality in the Civil War* (El Dorado Hills, CA: Savas Beatie, 2012).

5. Basil Duke, *A History of Morgan's Cavalry,* ed. Fletcher Holland (Bloomington: Indiana University Press, 1960), 183. The best biographies of Ferguson are Thomas D. Mays, *Cumberland Blood: Champ Ferguson's Civil War* (Carbondale: Southern Illinois University Pres, 2008) and Brian D. McKnight, *Confederate Outlaw: Champ Ferguson and the Civil War in Appalachia* (Baton Rouge: Louisiana State University Press, 2011).

6. For Morgan and Forrest, see James A. Ramage, *Rebel Raider: The Life of General John Hunt Morgan* (Lexington: University Press of Kentucky, 1986) and Brian Steel Wills, *The Confederacy's Greatest Cavalryman: Nathan Bedford Forrest* (New York: HarperCollins, 1992).

7. For Ashby, see Paul Christopher Anderson, *Blood Image: Turner Ashby in the Civil War and the Southern Mind* (Baton Rouge: Louisiana State University Press, 2002).

8. Cases of Ephraim D. Harris (NN8333) and Israel Young (LL716), Court-Martial Cases, 1809–94, Judge Advocate General Records, RG 153, National Archives, Washington, D.C.

9. Stephen Z. Starr, *Jennison's Jayhawkers: A Civil War Cavalry Regiment and Its Commander* (Baton Rouge: Louisiana State University Press, 1973), 87–88.

10. Alvira A. (Weir) Scott Diary, July 21, 1862, Western Historical Manuscript Collection, University of Missouri, Columbia.

11. For Anderson, see Albert Castel and Thomas Goodrich, *Bloody Bill Anderson: The Short, Savage Life of a Civil War Guerrilla* (Mechanicsburg, PA: Stackpole Books, 1998).

12. Quoted in Larry Wood, *Other Noted Guerrillas of the Civil War in Missouri* (Joplin, MO: Hickory Press, 2007), 184.

13. James E. Moss, ed., "A Missouri Confederate in the Civil War: The Journal of Henry Martyn Cheavens, 1862–1863," *Missouri Historical Review* 57 (October 1962): 18–27.

14. Samuel C. Trescott to cousin, May 1, 1862, Samuel C. Trescott Correspondence, Ohio Historical Society, Columbus; S. S. Marrett to wife, May 31, 1862, S. S. Marrett Papers, Special Collections, Duke University Libraries, Durham, NC.

15 U.S. War Department, *War of the Rebellion: Official Records of the Union and Confederate Armies,* 128 vols. (Washington, D.C.: Government Printing Office, 1880–1901), ser. 1, vol. 13, 396 (cited hereafter as *OR*).

16. Diane Neal and Thomas W. Kremm, *Lion of the South: General Thomas C. Hindman* (Macon, GA: Mercer University Press, 1993), 127–28; *OR,* vol. 13, 36, 835.

17. *OR,* ser. 1, vol. 13, 108; Drury Connally to wife, June 28, 1862, War Letters of Drury Connally, Special Collections, University of Arkansas Libraries, Fayetteville.

18. Several articles by Bruce E. Mahan in *Palimpsest* 5 (June 1924); Larry Cox, "Hawkeye Heroes: The Iowa Southern Border Militia and the Civil War," copy in Iowa Historical Library and Archives, Iowa City; and Samuel J. Kirkwood Papers, Iowa Historical Library and Archives.

19. See, generally, Yates Family Collection, Illinois Historical Society Library, Springfield; Indiana Adjutant General Records, Indiana Historical Society, Indianapolis; Ohio Adjutant General Records, Ohio Historical Society, Columbus.

20. Daniel E. Sutherland, "Guerrilla Warfare, Democracy, and the Fate of the Confederacy," *Journal of Southern History* 68 (May 2002): 273–78.

21. William Howard Russell, *My Diary North and South*, ed. Eugene H. Berwanger (New York: Alfred A. Knopf, 1988), 126.

22. Lynda L. Crist, et al., eds., *The Papers of Jefferson Davis*, 11 vols. (Baton Rouge: Louisiana State University Press, 1971–), VII:201; A. T. Bledsoe to Levi W. Lawler, June 28, 1861, Bledsoe to Burwell G. Curry, July 1, 1861, Letters Sent by Confederate Secretary of War, War Department Collection of Confederate Records, RG 109 (M522), National Archives, Washington, D.C.; Carl E. Grant, "Partisan Warfare, Model 1861–65," *Military Review* 38 (November 1958): 42.

23. A. T. Bledsoe to A. D. Prentiss, August 10, 1861, Letters Sent by Confederate Secretary of War; *OR*, ser. 4, vol. 1, 475, 491.

24. Sutherland, "Guerrilla Warfare," 281–83.

25. "Proceedings of First Confederate Congress," *Southern Historical Society Papers*, New Series VII (May 1925): 122, 128–29, 152–53 160–61; John Scott, *Partisan Life with Col. John S. Mosby* (New York: Harper & Brothers, 1867), ix–x.

26. A. T. Bledsoe to Richard Ewell, April 30, 1862, George W. Randolph to Ivermont Ward, May 15, 1862, Letters Sent by Confederate Secretary of War.

27. Riley Bock, ed., "Confederate Col. A. C. Riley, His reports and Letters: Part II," *Missouri Historical Review* 85 (April 1981): 264–65.

28. John G. Barrett, *The Civil War in North Carolina* (Chapel Hill: University of North Carolina Press, 1963), 59, 174–76.

29. John C. Inscoe and Gordon B. McKinney, *The Heart of Confederate Appalachia: Western North Carolina in the Civil War* (Chapel Hill: University of North Carolina, 2000), 105–38; James Wilse and Captain Dial to Quill Hunter, July 29, 1863, Wilse Dial Letter, Southern Historical Collection, University of North Carolina, Chapel Hill.

30. Andrew Brown, "The First Mississippi Partisan Rangers, C.S.A." *Civil War History* 1 (December 1955): 371–76; Victor Hoar, "Colonel William C. Falkner in the Civil War," *Journal of Mississippi History* 27 (February 1965): 50–53.

31. *OR*, ser.1, vol.6, 653–54, 885–90, vol.15, 508–09.

CHAPTER 3

1. For some of the other Missouri bands, see Larry Wood, *Other Noted Guerrillas of the Civil War in Missouri* (Joplin, MO: Hickory Press, 2007).

2. John W. Munson, *Reminiscences of a Mosby Guerrilla* (New York: Moffat, Yard & Co., 1906), 25; A. J. Walker, *Recollections of Quantrill's Guerrillas* (1910; Shawnee Mission, KS: Two Trails, 1996), 22; Joanne Chiles Eakin, ed., *The Little Gods: Union Provost Marshals in Missouri, 1861–1865*, 2 vols. (Independence, MO: Two Trails, 1996), II: 82.

3. William Elsey Connelley, *Quantrill and the Border Wars* (Cedar Rapids, IA: Torch Press, 1910), 317–18. For an elaborate, if sometimes strained, discussion of the significance of this garment, see Joseph M. Beilein Jr., "The Guerrilla Shirt: A Labor of Love and the Style of Rebellion in Civil War Missouri," *Civil War History* 58 (June 2012): 151–79. For photographs of Quantrill's men, see Carl W. Breihan, *The Killer Legions of Quantrill* (Seattle, WA: Superior Publishing, 1971).

4. Quoted in Wood, *Other Noted Guerrillas,* 129–30.

5. Photographs of Mosby's men are included in James J. Williamson, *Mosby's Rangers* (New York: Ralph B. Kenyon, 1896).

6. Hamp B. Watts, *The Babe of the Company* (1913; Springfield, MO: Oak Hills Publishing, 1996), 4; Eakin, *Little Gods,* II:82; statement by Edward Williams, December 19, 1863, (3250), Case Files of Investigations by Levi C. Turner and Lafayette C. Baker, Records of Adjutant General's Office, RG 94 (M979), National Archives, Washington, D.C.; Walker, *Recollections,* 41.

7. Watts, *The Babe of the Company,* 4; Munson, *Reminiscences,* 13–14.

8. Williamson, *Mosby's Rangers,* 23.

9. Nancy Chappelear Baird, ed., *Journals of Amanda Virginia Edmonds: Lass of the Mosby Confederacy, 1859–1867* (Stephens City, VA: Commercial Press, 1984), 147.

10. Quoted are Joe M. Scott, *Four Years' Service in the Southern Army* (1897; Fayetteville, AR: Washington County Historical Society, 1958), 39; George T. Maddox, *Hard Trials and Tribulations of an Old Confederate Soldier,* ed. Richard L. Norton and J. Troy Massey (Springfield, MO: Oak Hills Publishing, 1997), 30–31.

11. Munson, *Reminiscences,* 22–25.

12. J. Marshall Crawford, *Mosby and his Men* (New York: G. W. Carleton, 1867), 145; John S. Mosby, *The Memoirs of Colonel John S. Mosby* (Boston, MA: Little, Brown and Co., 1917), 284–86.

13. Walker, *Recollections,* 22; A. H. McLaws to Leroy Pope Walker, April 16, 1861, E. M. Seago to Walker, April 17, 1861, Henry E. Colton to Jefferson Davis, April 17, 1861, Letters Received by the Confederate Secretary of War, War Department Collection of Confederate Records (M437), RG 109, National Archives, Washington, D.C.

14. Connelley, *Quantrill and the Border Wars,* 318–19.

15. Cole Younger, *The Story of Cole Younger by Himself* (1903; Houston, TX: Frontier Press, 1955), 19; L. C. Miller Memoir, 10, Western Manuscripts and Historical Collection, University of Missouri, Columbia.

16. A. V. Reiff, "History of a 'Spy' Company, Raised at Fayetteville, Ark." in E. R. Hutchins, compl., *The War of the 'Sixties* (New York: Neale Publishing, 1912), 168.

17. Jasper Sutherland statement of January 15, 1930, Elihu J. Sutherland Papers, Wyllie Library, Clinch Valley College of the University of Virginia at Wise.

18. U.S. War Department, *War of the Rebellion: Official Records of the Union and Confederate Armies,* 128 vols. (Washington, D.C.: Government Printing Office, 1880–1901), ser. 1, vol. 8, 637; Richard L. Norton, ed., *Behind Enemy Lines: The Memoirs and Writings of Brigadier General Sidney Drake Jackman* (Springfield, MO: Oak Hills Publishing,1997), 35–37.

19. John M. Porter Memoirs, 45, 59, Civil War Collection, Box 14, f.11, Tennessee State Library and Archives, Nashville; Jonathan Dean Sarris, *A Separate Civil War: Communities in the Mountain South* (Charlottesville: University of Virginia Press, 2006), 123.

20. Munson, *Reminiscences,* 31, 37; Walker, *Recollections,* 23.

21. T. Lindsay Baker, ed., *Confederate Guerrilla: The Civil War Memoir of Joseph Bailey* (Fayetteville: University of Arkansas Press, 2007), 43–44, 47.

22. Charles W. Porter, *In the Devil's Dominions: A Union Soldier's Adventures in "Bush-whacker Country,"* ed. Patrick Brophy (Nevada, MO: Vernon County Historical Society, 1998), 86–87, 97–98, 104–105.

23. *OR,* ser. 1, vol. 22, pt. 1, 661; quote in Wood, *Other Noted Guerrillas,* 73.

24. Munson, *Reminiscences,* 21; John Scott, *Partisan Life with Col. John S. Mosby* (New York: Harper & Brothers, 1867), 394–95; Baird, *Journals of Edmonds,* 152.

25. Joanne Chiles Eakin, ed., *Warren Welch Remembers: A Guerrilla Fighter from Jackson County, Missouri* (Shawnee Mission, KS: Two Trails, 1997), 21.

26. Eakin, *Little Gods,* II:2.

27. B. H. Greathouse, "Women of Northwest Arkansas," *Confederate Veteran* 20 (April 1912): 169.

28. Munson, *Reminiscences,* 232–35;

29. Eakin, *Little Gods,* II: 82, 84.

30. William W. Garig Diary, January 14, 1864, February 11, 1864, Special Collections, Louisiana State University Libraries, Baton Rouge.

31. Williamson, *Mosby's Rangers,* 272.

32. Walker, *Recollections,* 31; Baker, *Confederate Guerrilla,* 43; Maddox, *Hard Trials and Tribulations,* 12.

33. Munson, *Reminiscences,* 35, 38, 238; Mosby, *Memoirs,* 332–33.

34. Williamson, *Mosby's Rangers,* 18–19.

35. Munson, *Reminiscences,* 227–28; Mosby, *Memoirs,* 262.

36. Eakin, *Little Gods,* II: 84.

37. Watts, *Babe of the Company,* 5–6; Baker, *Confederate Guerrilla,* 57; Eakin, *Little Gods,* II:87.

38. Miller Memoir, 11; Baker, *Confederate Guerrilla,* 40.

39. Miller Memoir, 10, 11.

40. Walker, *Recollections,* 49; Watts, *Babe of the Company,* 6–7.

41. Kirby Ross, ed., *Autobiography of Samuel S. Hildebrand: The Renowned Missouri Bush-whacker* (Fayetteville: University of Arkansas Press, 2005), 102–103.

42. Statement of Mr. Thorp, October 26, 1863, J. D. Hines to J. D. Cox, March 3, 1862, Union Provost Marshals' File of Papers Relating to Two or More Citizens, War Department Collection of Confederate Records, RG 109 (M416), National Archives, Washington, D.C.

43. Case of Henry Simpson (3365), Case Files of Investigations by Levi C. Turner and Lafayette C. Baker, Records of Adjutant General's Office (M797), RG 94, National Archives, Washington, D.C.

44. Statement of James T. Smith, in cases of L. E. Miles et al. (LL777), U.S. War Department, Court-Martial Cases, 1809–94, Judge Advocate general Records, RG 153, National Archives, Washington, D.C.

CHAPTER 4

1. Evelyn A. Benson, comp., *With the Army of West Virginia, 1861–1864: Reminiscences and Letters of Lt. James Abraham Lancaster* (Lancaster, PA: Evelyn A. Benson, 1974), 65.

2. Kenneth W. Noe, "Exterminating Savages: The Union Army and Mountain Guerrillas in Southern West Virginia, 1861–1862," in Noe and Shannon H. Wilson, eds., *Civil War in Appalachia: Collected Essays* (Knoxville: University of Tennessee Press, 1997), 107–09; U.S. War Department, *War of the Rebellion: Official Records of the Union and Confederate Armies,* 128 vols. (Washington, D.C.: Government Printing Office, 1880–1901), ser. 1, vol. 2, 195–96, vol. 5, 575–77 (cited hereafter as *OR*).

3. *OR,* ser. 1, vol. 3, 403–04, 415–18, 421–24, 427, ser. 2, vol. 1, 195–203.

4. Ibid., ser. 1, vol. 3, 133, 458–59, ser. 2, vol. 1, 204–06, 214–15, 218–19; Charles Gibson to Hamilton R. Gamble, August b8, 1861, Robert N. Smith to Gamble, August 12, 1861, Hamilton R. Gamble Papers, Missouri Historical Society, Saint Louis.

5. *OR,* ser. 1, vol. 3, 449–51.

6. Michael E. Banasik, ed., *Missouri in 1861: The Civil War Letters of Franc B. Wilkie, Newspaper Correspondent* (Iowa City, IA: Camp Pope Bookshop, 2001), 104 n.167, 129; *OR,* ser. 1, vol. 2, 196–97, Benson, *With the Army of West Virginia,* 65–66.

7. *OR,* ser. 1, vol. 3, 466–67.

8. Barton Bates to Edward Bates, September 8, 1861, Bates Family Papers, Missouri Historical Society, Saint Louis.

9. Elisha Leaming to wife, November 11, 1861, Elisha Leaming Letters, Iowa State Historical Library; Iowa City; Edward F. Noyes to R. H. Stephenson, September 21, 1861, Nathaniel Wright Family Papers, Library of Congress, Washington, D.C.

10. *OR,* ser. 1, vol. 3, 469, 477–78, 485, 553–54.

11. Ibid, 693.

12. Quoted in Larry Wood, *Other Noted Guerrillas of the Civil War in Missouri* (Joplin, MO: Hickory Press, 2007), 186–87.

13. *OR,* ser. 2, vol. 1, 233–35, 237, 240–43, 247.

14. Ibid., 255–56, 258–59.

15. Ibid., 281.

16. *OR,* ser. 1, vol. 13, 104–09, 119; U.S. Navy Department, *Official Records of the Union and Confederate Navies in the War of the Rebellion,* 35 vols. (Washington, D.C.: Government Printing Office, 1894–1927), ser. 1, vol. 23, 176 (cited hereafter as *ORN*).

17. *OR,* ser. 1, vol. 15, 25, 504.

18. *ORN,* ser. 1, vol. 18, 516, 520–21, 534.

19. *OR,* ser. 1, vol. 17, pt. 1, 39–40.

20. Joseph W. Keifer to wife, March 4, 10, 14, 16, April 12, 1862, Joseph Warren Keifer Papers, Library of Congress, Washington, D.C.

21. John Y. Simon, ed., *The Papers of Ulysses S. Grant,* 26 vols. (Carbondale: Southern Illinois University Press, 1967–), V: 190–91.

22. Leroy P. Graf et al., eds, *The Papers of Andrew Johnson,* 16 vols. (Knoxville: University of Tennessee Press, 1967–2000), V: 237, 241 n. 52–53, 257–59, 286–87, 312–13, 434, 478–79.

23. Ibid., VI: 666–67, VII: 262, 306; James A. Ramage, *Rebel Raider: The Life of General John Hunt Morgan* (Lexington: University Press of Kentucky, 1986), 101.

24. See Richard O. Curry and F. Gerald Ham, eds., "The Bushwhackers' War: Insurgency and Counter-Insurgency in West Virginia," *Civil War History* 10 (December 1964): 416–33; and Virginia Governor Executive Papers: Francis Harrison Pierpont, Virginia State Library, Richmond.

25. Emory S. Foster to Lucien J. Barnes, April 7, 1862, Union Provost Marshal's Files Relating to Two or More Citizens, War Department Collection of Confederate Records, RG 109 (M416), National Archives, Washington, D.C.

26. Amanda McDowell Diary, July 24, 25, 1863, Curtis McDowell Papers, Tennessee State Archives and Library, Nashville; Graf, *Papers of Andrew Johnson,* VI: 48–49, 626–27.

27. Quoted in Jonathan Dean Sarris, *A Separate Civil War: Communities in Conflict in the Mountain South* (Charlottesville: University of Virginia Press, 2006), 139–40.

28. *OR,* ser. 1, vol. 17, pt. 1, 144–45, pt. 2, 235–36, 261, 279–81, 285, 287–89.

29. *OR,* ser. 1, vol. 17, 287–88, 860.

30. *ORN,* ser. 1, vol. 23, 451–52.

31. Lisa M. Brady, *War Upon the Land: Military Strategy and the Transformation of Southern Landscapes during the American Civil War* (Athens: University of Georgia Press, 2012), 22–23.

32. Bela T. St. John Diaries, May 15, 1863, Library of Congress, Washington, D.C.

33. *ORN,* ser. 1, vol. 23, 309–18, 322, vol. 24, 39, 59, 62–65, 71–72, 75, 84, 86–87, vol. 25, 159–60, 204–05.

34. George C. Bradley and Richard L. Dahlen, *From Conciliation to Conquest: The Sack of Athens and the Court-Martial of Colonel John B. Turchin* (Tuscaloosa: University of Alabama Press, 2006), 104–25; John Beatty, *The Citizen Soldier; or, Memoirs of a Volunteer* (Cincinnati, OH: Wilstach, Baldwin & Co., 1879), 138–43; *OR,* ser. 1, vol. 10, pt. 2, 156.

35. Daniel E. Sutherland, "Abraham Lincoln and the Guerrillas," *Prologue* 42 (Spring 2010): 21–22.

36. Daniel E. Sutherland, "Abraham Lincoln, John Pope, and the Origins of Total War," *Journal of Military History* 56 (October 1992): 574–79.

37. Roy P. Basler, ed., *The Collected Works of Abraham Lincoln,* 8 vols. (New Brunswick, NJ: Rutgers University Press, 1953), V: 342–43.

38. Stephen D. Engle, *Don Carlos Buell: Most Promising of All* (Chapel Hill: University of North Carolina Press, 1999), 247–49, 326–36; *OR,* ser. 1, vol. 16, pt. 1, 8–9; Beatty, *Citizen Soldier,* 152.

39. Lynda L. Crist et al., eds., *The Papers of Jefferson Davis,* 11 vols. (Baton Rouge: Louisiana State University Press, 1971–), VIII: 292, 309–11.

CHAPTER 5

1. U.S. War Department, *War of the Rebellion: Official Records of the Union and Confederate Armies,* 128 vols. (Washington, D.C.: Government Printing Office, 1880–1901), ser. 1, vol. 22, pt. 1, 860–66 (cited hereafter as *OR*).

2. Ibid., ser. 1, vol. 13, 769–70.

3. Vivian Kirpatrick McLarty, ed., "The Civil War Letters of Colonel Basil F. Lazear: Part I," *Missouri Historical Review* 44 (April 1950): 268–69, 272.

4. Daniel E. Sutherland, "Abraham Lincoln, John Pope, and the Origins of Total War," *Journal of Military History* 56 (October 1992): 584–85; *OR*, ser. 3, vol. 2, 301.

5. *OR*, ser. 3, vol. 2, 301–09.

6. Ibid., 307.

7. Francis Lieber to Dear General, November 13, 1862, Francis Lieber Papers, South Caroliniana Library, University of South Carolina, Columbia.

8. Ibid., ser. 3, vol. 3, 148–64; Mark Grimsley, *The Hard Hand of War: Union Military Policy Toward Southern Civilians, 1861–1865* (New York: Cambridge University Press, 1995), 149–51; Burris M. Carnahan, "Lincoln, Lieber and the Laws of War: The Origins and Limits of the Principle of Military Necessity," *American Journal of International Law* 92 (April 1998): 218–31; Matthew J. Mancini, "Francis Lieber, Slavery, and the 'Genesis' of the Law of War," *Journal of Southern History* 77 (May 2011): 325–48. For Lieber on Pope, see Joshua E. Kastenberg, *Law in War, War as Law: Brigadier General Joseph Holt and the Judge Advocate General's Department in the Civil War and Early Reconstruction, 1861–1865* (Durham, NC: Carolina Academic Press, 2011), 235. The most recent book on Lieber's Code is John Fabian Witt, *Lincoln's Code: The Laws of War in American History* (New York: The Free Press, 2012).

9. *OR*, ser. 3, vol. 3, 157.

10. Ibid.; Francis Lieber, *The Miscellaneous Writings of Francis Lieber,* 2 vols. (Philadelphia, PA: J. B. Lippincott, 1880), II: 292.

11. *OR*, ser. 3, vol. 3, 160.

12. John F. Marszaleck, *Commander of All Lincoln's Armies: A Life of General Henry W. Halleck* (Cambridge, MA: Harvard University Press, 2004), 178–79; Allan Nevins, ed., *Diary of Battle: The Personal Journals of Colonel Charles S. Wainwright, 1861–1865* (New York: Harcourt, Brace & World, 1962), 184.

13. *OR*, ser. 1, vol. 22, pt. 2, 327–44; Ethan Allen Hitchcock to Francis Lieber, December 15, 1863, Lieber Papers.

14. Robert T. McMahan Diary, March 16, 1863, Western Historical Manuscript Collection, University of Missouri, Columbia; Barry Popchock, ed., *Soldier Boy: The Civil War Letters of Charles O. Musser, 29th Iowa* (Iowa City, IA: University of Iowa Press, 1995), 54; Minos Miller to mother, July 14, 1863, Minos Miller Papers, Special Collections, University of Arkansas Libraries, Fayetteville.

15. Samuel W. Pruitt to Bettie Pruitt, April 20, 1863, Samuel W. Pruitt Papers, Filson Club, Louisville, KY; Edward P. Standfield to father [February 1863], Edward P. Standfield Correspondence, Indiana Historical Society, Indianapolis; E. P. Sturges to Folks, August 9, 1862, E. P. Sturges Papers, Ohio Historical Society, Columbus.

16. Samuel T. Wells to Lizzie, May 2, 1863, Samuel T. Wells Papers, Filson Club, Louisville, Kty.; Loren J. Morse, ed., *Civil War Diaries and Letters of Bliss Morse* (Tahlequah, OK: Heritage printing Company, 1985), 46; L. P. Deatherage Proclamation to the People of Kentucky, August 13, 1862, Edward Henry Hobson Papers, Filson Club, Louisville, KY.

17. W. E. Merrill, "Block-houses for Railroad Defense in the Department of the Cumberland," *Military Order of the Loyal Legion of the United States*, 3 (1888), 416–21; Henry _____ to parents, August 25, 1862, Filson Club, Henry Letters, Louisville, KY.

18. Popchock, *Solider Boy*, 32–37; William E. Corbin, *A Star for Patriotism: Iowa's Outstanding Civil War College* (Monticello, IA: n.p., 1972), 402–04.

19. General Orders No.2 and 4, in "Orders," (Lord Division) Eltinge-Lord Family Papers, Special Collection, Duke University Libraries, Durham, NC; "Journal of Occurrences during the War of the Rebellion," 424–25, 433–34, David Dixon Porter Papers, Library of Congress, Washington, D.C.

20. Chester G. Hearn, *Ellet's Brigade: The Strangest Outfit of All* (Baton Rouge: Louisiana State University Press, 2000), 151–84.

21. Lynda L. Crist et al., eds., *The Papers of Jefferson Davis*, 11 vols. (Baton Rouge: Louisiana State University Press, 1971–), VIII: 508.

22. *OR*, ser. 1, vol. 24, pt. 2, 683.

23. Thomas A. Wiggenton et al., *Tennesseans in the Civil War*, 2 vols. (Nashville, TN: Civil War Centennial Commission, 1964), I: 80–82; *OR*, ser. 1, vol. 24, pt. 1, 423–26, pt.3, 111, 176–78, 654, 656, 658, 696–97, 757.

24. *OR*, ser. 4, vol. 2, 71–72, 82–83, 113, 206–07, 301–04, 359, 639.

25. James A. Ramage, *The Life of Col. John Singleton Mosby* (Lexington, KY: University Press of Kentucky, 1999), 46–57, 73; Jeffry D. Wert, *Mosby's Rangers* (New York: Simon & Schuster, 1990), 73–76; Nancy C. Baird, ed., *Journals of Amanda Virginia Edmonds: Lass of Mosby's Confederacy, 1859–1867* (Stephens City, VA: Commercial Press, 1984), 152.

26. John S. Mosby, *The Memoirs of Colonel John S. Mosby* (Boston, MA: Little, Brown and Company, 1917), 157.

27. Ruth A. Gallagher, ed., "Peter Wilson in the Civil War, 1863–1865," *Iowa Journal of History and Politics* 40 (October 1942): 363–65; McLarty, "Civil War Letters of Colonel Lazear," 270–71.

28. A. J. Wright to Thomas W. Ewing Jr., November 20, 1862, Thomas Ewing Family Papers, Library of Congress, Washington, D.C.

29. John Michael Foster Jr., "'For the Good of the Cause and Protection of the Border': The Service of the Indiana Legion in the Civil War, 1861–1865," *Civil War History* 55 (March 2009): 31–55.

30. Henry L. Stone to father, July 8, 1863, Henry L. Stone Papers, Indiana Historical Society, Indianapolis.

31. James A. Ramage, *Rebel Raider: The Life of General John Hunt Morgan* (Lexington: University Press of Kentucky, 1986), 158–82.

32. Thomas Goodrich, *Bloody Dawn: The Story of the Lawrence Massacre* (Kent, OH: Kent State University Press, 1991), 118, 122.

33. Thomas Carney to John Schofield, August 24, 1863, Thomas Carney Letters, Kansas State Historical Society, Topeka.

34. Thomas Ewing Jr to Thomas Ewing Sr, July 24, 1863, August 15, 1863, Ewing Family Papers; Albert Castel, *Winning and Losing in the Civil War: Essays and Stories* (Columbia: University of South Carolina Press, 1996), 51–62.

35. Kip Lindberg and Matt Matthews, "'It Haunts Me Day and Night': The Baxter Springs Massacre," *North & South* 4 (June 2001): 42–53.

36. Ibid., 52; Edward E. Leslie, *The Devil Knows How to Ride: The True Story of William Clarke Quantrill and His Confederate Raiders* (New York: Random House, 1996), 282–301; Albert E. Castel, *William Clarke Quantrill: His Life and Times* (1962; Norman: University of Oklahoma Press, 1999), 155–68.

37. Leslie, *Devil Knows How to Ride,* 293–95.

38. *OR,* ser. 1, vol. 29, pt. 1, 914–15, pt. 2, 596; Edward A. Wild to John T. Elliott (draft), December 17, 1863, Wild to Willis Sanderlin (draft), December 22, 1863, Edward Augustus Wild Papers, Southern Historical Collection, University of North Carolina, Chapel Hill.

39. Frontis W. Johnston and Joe A. Mobley, eds., *The Papers of Zebulon Baird Vance,* 2 vols. (Raleigh: North Carolina Division of Archives and History, 1963–95), II: 357; J. G. de Roulhac Hamilton, ed., *The Papers of Thomas Ruffin,* 4 vols. (Raleigh, NC: Edwards & Broughton, 1918–20), III: 348.

CHAPTER 6

1. U.S. War Department, *War of the Rebellion: Official Records of the Union and Confederate Armies* (Washington, D.C.: Government Printing Office, 1880–1901), ser. 3, vol. 2, 307 (cited hereafter as *OR*).

2. Quoted in Larry Wood, *Other Noted Guerrillas of the Civil War in Missouri* (Joplin, MO: Hickory Press, 2007), 75–77.

3. Ibid., 79–80.

4. *OR,* ser. 3, vol. 3, 159, 164.

5. Ibid., 157, Lieber quotation in Matthew J. Mancini, "Francis Lieber, Slavery, and the 'Genesis' of the Laws of War," *Journal of Southern History* 77 (May 2011): 335.

6. James J. Williamson, *Mosby's Rangers* (New York: Ralph B. Kenyon, 1896), 105–06.

7. Quoted is Robert R. Mackey, *The Uncivil War: Irregular Warfare in the Upper South, 1861–1865* (Norman: University of Oklahoma Press, 2004), 59, who also describes the Arkansas provost marshal system, 58–61; "List of Bushwhackers and Guerrillas, Home Guards, Union men, and Persons taking Oaths of Allegiance 1863–64," Department of Arkansas, v.110/360, Records of U.S. Army Continental Commands, RG 393, National Archives, Washington, D.C.; Barry Popchock, ed., *Soldier Boy: The Civil War Letters of Charles O. Musser, 29th Iowa* (Iowa City, IA: University of Iowa Press, 1995), 85.

8. Daniel Anderson to Captain, February 27, 1864, Provost Marshal Correspondence, Department of Arkansas, Letters Sent, 1863–64, v.108/353, Records of U.S. Army Continental Commands, RG 393, National Archives, Washington, D.C.

9. Files on Elbridge M. Ball and Benjamin R. Fortenberry (NN1800, NN1453), U.S. War Department, Court-Martial Cases, 1809–1894, Judge Advocate Records, RG 153, National Archives, Washington, D.C.

10. Popchock, *Soldier Boy,* 112–13.

11. Ibid., 161; Joe M. Scott, *Four Years' Service in the Southern Army* (1897; Fayetteville, AR: Washington County Historical Society, 1958), 33; From L. D. Bennett, May 1, 1864, Provost Marshal Correspondence, Department of Arkansas, Letters Received, 1864–66, v. 110/361.

12. J. L. Chandler to Dodd Patterson, September 27, 1864, Provost Marshal Correspondence, Department of Arkansas, Letters Sent, v. 108/354.

13. Case of J. K. Blair (NN1487), Court-Martial Cases.

14. Case of Nelson Cook (LL778), Court-Martial Cases.

15. Cases of James M. Fraley (MM1298) and Hugh Lawson Bell (NN1126), Court-Martial Cases.

16. Cases of Joseph T. Robinson (3106), Peter Brissey (3249), Elijah Kase and Edward Williams (3250), Thomas Wine (4072), Case Files of Investigations by Levi C. Turner and Lafayette C. Baker, Records of Adjutant General's Office (M797), RG 94, National Archives, Washington, D.C.

17. Beating incident told in Joshua E. Kastenberg, *Law in War, War as Law: Brigadier General Joseph Holt and the Judge Advocate General's Department on the Civil War and Early Reconstruction, 1861–1865* (Durham, NC: Carolina Academic Press, 2011), 229–30; case of John P. Rotchford (NN1799), Court-Martial Cases.

18. *OR,* ser. 3, vol. 3, 159.

19. Emory S. Foster to Lucian J. Barnes, April 7, 1862, statement by Julia Martin, September 20, 1864, Union Provost Marshals' File of Papers Relating to Two or More Civilians, War Department Collection of Confederate Records RG 109 (M416), National Archives, Washington, D.C.; Eakin, II:35–36, 41–42, 63–65, 70–72, 80–81.

20. Don Schaefer, ed., "The Civil War Letters of Corporal David W. Badger," *Flashback* 47 (February 1997): 26; J. Mont Wilson, "Killing of Three Brothers: Something of Warfare in Arkansas in 1863," *Confederate Veteran* V (April 1897): 156.

21. Vivian Kirkpatrick McLarty, ed., "The Civil War Letters of Colonel Bazel F. Lazear," *Missouri Historical Review* 44 (April 1950): 271, and "The Civil War Letters of Colonel Bazel F. Lazear: Part III," *Missouri Historical Review* 45 (October 1950): 50–51.

22. Case of George M. Elliott (NN1137), Courts-Martial Cases.

23. Case of L. E. Miles et al. (LL777), Court-Martial Cases.

24. Case of Gideon D. Bruce (LL1938), Court-Martial Cases.

25. Cases of T. H. Covington and S. T. Stone (3295), Newman, Cornelius, and Thomas Beach (3260), G. N. Davis (3847), Case Files of Turner and Baker.

CHAPTER 7

1. Louis Fusz Diary, August 4, 21, 1864, Missouri Historical Society, Saint Louis.

2. James O. Broadhead to Edward Bates, July 24, 1864, James O. Broadhead Papers, Missouri Historical Society, Saint Louis; Thomas Ewing Jr. to father, June 3, 1864, Thomas Ewing Family papers, Library of Congress, Washington, D.C.

3. Kirby Ross, ed., *Autobiography of Sam Hildebrand: The Renowned Missouri Bushwhacker* (Fayetteville: University of Arkansas Press, 2005), 29.

4. U.S. War Department, *War of the Rebellion: Official Records of the Union and Confederate Armies,* 128 vols. (Washington, D.C.: Government Printing office, 1880–1901), ser. 1, vol. 41, pt. 2, 75–77.

5. Albert Castel and Thomas Goodrich, *Bloody Bill Anderson: The Short, Savage Life of a Civil War Guerrilla* (Mechanicsburg, PA: Stackpole Books, 1998), 69–86, 111–24.

6. Thomas Goodrich, *Black Flag: Guerrilla Warfare on the Western Border, 1861–1865* (Bloomington: Indiana University Press, 1995), 141–42.

7. *OR,* ser. 1, vol. 34, pt. 3, 179–80 (cited hereafter as *OR*).

8. Jeffrey L. Patrick and Michael L. Price, eds., "Life with the Mountain Feds: The Civil War Reminiscences of William McDowell, 1st Arkansas Cavalry," *Arkansas Historical Quarterly* 64 (Autumn 2005): 306–07.

9. W. E. Montgomery to Charles Clark, November 25, 1863, January 24, February 1, August 7, 1864, Charles Clark Papers, Mississippi Department of Archives and History, Jackson.

10. Petition of John B. Rodgers, in LL3293, Court-Martial Cases, 1809–94, Judge Advocate General Records, RG 153, National Archives, Washington, D.C.

11. Ephraim Brown to Prusilla and Calphurnia, April 28, 1864, Ephraim Brown Papers, Ohio Historical Society, Columbus.

12. U.S. Navy Department, *Official Records of the Union and Confederate Navies in the War of the Rebellion,* 35 vols. (Washington, D.C.: Government Printing Office, 1894–1927), ser. 1 vol. 21, 360–61, vol. 26, 374–75, 745–47, 762 (cited hereafter as *ORN*); Richard L. Kiper, ed., *Dear Catherine, Dear Taylor: The Civil War Letters of a Union Soldier and His Wife* (Lawrence: University Press of Kansas, 2002), 213–14.

13. T. Lindsay Baker, ed., *Confederate Guerrilla: The Civil War Memoir of Joseph Bailey* (Fayetteville: University of Arkansas Press, 2007), 56–57; Goodrich, *Black Flag,* 43–44; Brian D. McKnight, *Confederate Outlaw: Champ Ferguson and the Civil War in Appalachia* (Baton Rouge: Louisiana State University Press, 2011), 147–50.

14. Quoted in McKnight, *Confederate Outlaw,* 152.

15. OR, ser. 1, vol. 39, pt. 2, 144–54, pt. 3, 321–22, 456–57.

16. West Virginia Historical Survey, *Calendar of the Arthur I. Boreman Letters* (Charleston, SC: Historical Survey, 1940), 9, 12, 16, 19, 22–23, 26; Nancy Hunt to Mr. and Mrs. Hoppings, September 28, 1863, May 29, 1864, Nancy Hunt Letters, West Virginia Regional History Collection, West Virginia University Libraries, Charleston.

17. E. D. Rushing to Isaac Murphy, June 7, 1864, printed in [*Little Rock*] *Constitutional Union,* June 16, 1864.

18. Leroy P. Graf et al., eds., *The Papers of Andrew Johnson,* 16 vols. (Knoxville: University of Tennessee Press, 1967–2000), VI: 399, 625, VII: 153–54, 159–60, 173, 200–01, 259–62, 268–69.

19. Donald F. Tingley, "The Clingman Raid," *Journal of Illinois State Historical Society* 56 (Summer 1963): 350–63.

20. Lazarus Noble to Thomas E. Bramlette, July 2, 3, 1864, Military Correspondence, Kentucky Governor's Papers: Bramlette, Kentucky Department for Archives and History,

Frankfort; Citizens of Harrison County to Oliver P. Morton [June 1864], Box 2, Indiana Legion Papers, Indiana Adjutant General Records, Indiana Historical Society, Indianapolis.

21. *OR,* ser. 1, vol. 41, pt. 1, 398–99.

22. Michael A. Hughes, "Wartime Gristmill Destruction in Northwest Arkansas and Military Farm Colonies," in Anne J. Bailey and Daniel E. Sutherland, eds., *Civil War Arkansas: Beyond Battles and Leaders* (Fayetteville: University of Arkansas Press, 2000), 31–45; Diane Neal and Thomas W. Kremm, "An Experiment in Collective Security: The Union Army's Use of Armed Colonies in Arkansas," *Military History of the Southwest* 20 (Fall 1990): 169–81.

23. Richard L. Troutman, ed., *The Heavens are Weeping: The Diaries of George Richard Browder, 1852–1886* (Grand Rapids, MI: Zondervan Publishing, 1987), 140–41; James C. Howard to Thomas E. Bramlette, September 10, 1864, Nat Gaither et al. to Daniel W. Lindsey, December 7, 1864, Kentucky Adjutant General Records, Military History Museum, Frankfort.

24. Margaret M. Frazier, trans., *Missouri Ordeal, 1862–1864: Diaries of Willard Hall Mendenhall* (Newhall, CA: Carl Boyer, 1985), 163–64; R. H. Powell to Harris Flanagin, May 5, 1863, T. H. Hill to Flanagin, June 1, 1863, F. J. Boston to Flanagin, August 17, 1863, Kie Oldham Papers, Arkansas History Commission, Little Rock.

25. U.S. Provost Marshal Files, Department of Arkansas, Vol.110/360, 2–5, 14–17, 22–23, 28–29, 32–35, 62–63, 72–73, RG 393, National Archives, Washington, D.C.

26. Cases of Cyrus Lee Cathey et al. (NN1368), Court-Martial Cases.

27. J. A. Little to D. C. Pearson, July 15, 1864, Confederate Conscript Bureau Papers, Southern Historical Collection, University of North Carolina, Chapel Hill; To My Dear Sir, November 2, 1864, Alexander Hamilton Stephens Papers, Special Collections, Duke University Libraries, Durham, NC; Docton Warren Bagley Diary, August 22, 1864, Duke University Libraries.

28. Michael A. Davis, "The Legend of Bill Dark: Guerrilla Warfare, Oral History, and the Unmaking of an Arkansas Bushwhacker," *Arkansas History Quarterly* 58 (Winter 1999): 414–29; John Hallum, *Reminiscences of the Civil War,* 2 vols. (Little Rock, AR: Tunnah and Pittard, 1903), I: 96–104.

29. *OR,* ser. 1, vol. 34, pt. 2, 972–77, vol. 53, 900–901; Nathaniel Cheairs Hughes, ed., *Liddell's Record: St. John Richardson Liddell* (Baton Rouge: Louisiana State University Press, 1997), 172–74.

30. *OR,* ser. 1, vol. 34, pt. 2, 944.

31. Priscilla Munnikhuysen Bond Diary, March 6, April 26, May 3, 1864, Special Collections, Louisiana State University Libraries, Baton Rouge.

32. *OR,* ser. 1, vol. 34, pt. 2, 962–67, 977, 1025; Carl Brasseaux, "Ozème Carrière and the St. Landry Jayhawkers," in Arthur Bergeron Jr., ed., *The Civil War in Louisiana* (Lafayette: Center for Louisiana Studies, 2002), 640–46.

33. David Paul Smith, *Frontier Defense in the Civil War: Texas' Rangers and Rebels* (College Station: Texas A&M University Press, 1992), 74–86, 106–10.

34. George E. Buker, *Blockaders, Refugees, and Contrabands: Civil War on Florida's Gulf Coast, 1861–1865* (Tuscaloosa: University of Alabama Press, 1993), 98–114, 183–87.

35. Mary Elizabeth Dickison, *Dickison and His Men: Reminiscences of the War in Florida* (1890; Jacksonville, FL: San Marco Bookstore, 1962), 53; *OR,* ser. 1, vol. 35, pt. 1, 398.

36. Jonathan Dean Sarris, *A Separate Civil War: Communities in Conflict in the Mountain South* (Charlottesville: University of Virginia Press, 2006), 136.

37. Raab, *With 3rd Wisconsin Badgers,* 244–45.

CHAPTER 8

1. U.S. War Department, *War of the Rebellion: Official Records of the Union and Confederate Armies,* 128 vols. (Washington, D.C.: Government Printing Office, 1880–1901), ser. 1, vol. 32, pt. 2, 486, vol. 39, pt. 2, 135–36 (cited hereafter as *OR*).

2. *OR,* ser. 1, vol. 39, pt. 2., 213.

3. Michael Bradley and Milan Hill, "Shoot If You Can by Accident," *North & South* 3 (November 1999): 33–46.

4. Case of James M. Johnson (MM1345), Court-Martial Cases, 1809–94, Judge Advocate General Records, RG 153, National Archives, Washington, D.C.

5. *OR,* ser. 1, vol. 24, pt. 3, 274–75. More broadly for Grant's destructive bent during the Vicksburg campaign, see Lisa M. Brady, *War Upon the Land: Military Strategy and the Transformation of Southern Landscapes during the American Civil War* (Athens: University of Georgia Press, 2012), 49–71.

6. John William Brown Diary, November 13, 16, December 11, 31, 1863, March 21, April 8, May 6, July 22, December 23, 1864; Sarah Bevens Kellogg to Sister Eva, February 29, April 4, 1864, Robert R. Kellogg Papers, Ohio Historical Society, Columbus; Lucy Virginia French Diaries, August 30, 1863, Tennessee State Library and Archives, Nashville; John S. Mosby to F. W. Powell et al., February 4, 1863, Mosby to James E. B. Stuart, February 4, 1863, John Singleton Mosby Papers, Library of Congress, Washington, D.C.

7. Walter J. Lemke, ed., "A Confederate Soldier Writes to His Wife in Washington County," *Flashback* 2 (October 1952): 5–6; D. D. McBrien, ed., "Letters of an Arkansas Confederate Soldier: Pt. III," *Arkansas Historical Quarterly* 2 (September 1943): 278, 281.

8. *OR,* ser. 1, vol. 33, 1081–83, 1124, 1252–53, ser. 4, vol. 3, 194.

9. Ibid., ser. 1, vol. 33, 1113; John S. Mosby, *Memoirs of Colonel John S. Mosby* (Boston, MA: Little, Brown and Company, 1917), 269–70.

10. Everard H. Smith, "Chambersburg: Anatomy of a Confederate Reprisal," *American Historical Review* 96 (April 1999): 432–55; Philip H. Sheridan, *The Personal Memoirs of Philip H. Sheridan* (New York: C. L. Webster, 1888), 265–67.

11. James A. Ramage, *Gray Ghost: The Life of John Singleton Mosby* (Lexington: University Press of Kentucky, 1999), 184–200, 209–12; Jeffrey D. Marshall, *A War of the People: Vermont Civil War Letters* (Hanover, NH: University Press of New England, 1999), 264–65.

12. Jeffry D. Wert, *Mosby's Rangers* (New York: Simon and Schuster, 1990), 262; *OR,* ser. 1, vol. 43, pt. 2, 679; Howard M. Smith to D. M., December 4, 1864, February 20, 1865, Howard Malcolm Smith Papers, Library of Congress, Washington, D.C.

13. Sheridan, *Personal Memoirs,* 267.

14. *OR,* ser. 1, vol. 32, pt. 3, 246.

15. Ibid., ser. 1, vol. 38, pt. 5, 140–41; Robert Winn to sister, July 28, August 1, September 5, 1864, Winn-Cook Family Papers, Filson Club, Louisville, KY; James S. Thompson

Journal, September 10, October 15, 24, 1864, Indiana Historical Society, Indianapolis; Samuel S. Pruitt to Bettie Pruitt, September 13, 1864, Pruitt to Martha Pruitt, October 1, 1864, Samuel W. Pruitt Papers, Filson Club, Louisville, KY.

16. *OR,* ser. 1, vol. 39, pt. 3, 162, 357–58, 378; quote from Brady, *War Upon the Land,* 107.

17. *Ibid.,* ser. 1, vol. 39, pt. 2, 480, 503.

18. John H. Parrish to Henry Watson, November 9, 1863, Henry Watson Jr. Papers, Special Collections, Duke University Libraries, Durham, NC; A. C. Bean to Thomas H. Watts, November 30, 1864, Alabama Governor Papers: Watts, Alabama Department of Archives and History, Montgomery.

19. Sarah R. Espy Diary, September 8, 12–18,1863, July 22, 29–30, August 19, 1864, Alabama Department of Archives and History, Montgomery; James W. Silver, ed., "The Breakdown of Morale in Central Mississippi in 1864: Letters of Judge Robert S. Hudson," *Journal of Mississippi History* 16 (April 1954): 106–07, 115.

20. Annette Koch to C.D. Koch, September 26, October 3, November 14, 1864, Christian D. Koch Family Papers, Special Collections, Louisiana State University Libraries, Baton Rouge.

21. *OR,* ser. 1, vol. 46, pt. 3, 1383.

22. Clifford Dowdey and Louis H. Manarin, eds., *The Wartime Papers of R. E. Lee* (New York: Bramhall House, 1961), 939.

23. *OR,* vol. 47, pt. 3, 806–07, 823–24.

24. Nancy C. Baird, ed., *Journals of Amanda Virginia Edmonds: Lass of Mosby's Confederacy, 1859–1867* (Stephens City, Va.: Commercial Press, 1984), 220; Lee C. Drickamer and Karen D. Drickamer, *Fort Lyon to Harper's Ferry: On the Border of North and South with "Rambling Jour"* (Shippensburg, PA: White Mane, 1987), 233.

25. *OR,* ser. 1, vol. 48, pt. 2, 872.

26. Case of Oscar Scarborough (NN1452), Court-Martial Cases.

27. Malcolm C. McMillan, ed., *The Alabama Confederate Reader* (Tuscaloosa: University of Alabama Press, 1963), 439; *OR,* ser. 1, vol. 49, pt. 2, 505.

28. *OR,* ser. 2, vol. 8, 325.

29. Edmund Fontaine to Richard H. Meade, April 23, 1865, Meade Family Papers, Virginia Historical Society, Richmond.

CHAPTER 9

1. T. J. Stiles, *Jesse James: Last Rebel of the Civil War* (New York: Alfred A. Knopf, 2002); Fellman, *In the Name of God and Country,* 97–142.

2. Eliza Sivley to Jane Sivley, Jane Sivley Papers, Southern. Historical Collection, University of North Carolina, Chapel Hill.

3. Cole Younger, *The Story of Cole Younger by Himself* (1903; Houston, TX: Pioneer Press, 1955), 56.

4. George T. Maddox, *Hard Trials and Tribulations of an Old Confederate Soldier,* ed. Richard L. Norton and J. Troy Massey (1897; Springfield, MO: Oak Hills Publishing, 1997),

77; T. Lindsay Baker, ed., *Confederate Guerrilla: The Civil War Memoir of Joseph Bailey* (Fayetteville: University of Arkansas Press, 2007), 47.

5. Joe M. Scott, *Four Years' Service in the Southern Army* (1897; Fayetteville, AR: Washington County Historical Society, 1962), 31–32.

6. Kirby Ross, ed., *Autobiography of Samuel S. Hildebrand: The Renowned Missouri Bushwhacker* (Fayetteville: University of Arkansas Press, 2005), 2; Hamp B. Watts, *The Babe of the Company* (1913; Springfield, MO: Oak Hills Publishing, 1996), 5.

7. W. J. Courtney, "Guerrilla Warfare in Missouri," *Confederate Veteran* 29 (March 1921): 104.

8. Quotations from Michael Fellman, *Inside War: The Guerrilla Conflict in Missouri during the American Civil War* (New York: Oxford University Press, 1989), 253–54.

9. R. D. Chapman, "A Georgia Soldier, C.S.A." *Confederate Veteran* 37 (July 1930): 270–71.

10. V. Y. Cook, "Scouting Expedition by Forrest's Men," *Confederate Veteran* 17 (January 1909): 41; B. F. Nelson, "A Boy in the Confederate Cavalry," *Confederate Veteran* 36 (October 1928): 374; Basil W. Duke, *A History of Morgan's Cavalry*, ed. Cecil Fletcher Holland (1906; Bloomington: Indiana University Press, 1960), 232; Anderson Chenault Quisenberry, "The Eleventh Kentucky Cavalry, C.S.A.," *Southern Historical Society Papers* 35 (1907): 261.

11. Paul F. Hammond, "Campaigns of General E. Kirby Smith in Kentucky, in 1862," *Southern Historical Society Papers* 9 (May 1881): 227–28. This description was supposedly written in 1863, but it bears all the signs of having been crafted after the war.

12. Wade Pruitt, compl., *Bugger Saga: The Civil War Story of Guerilla and Bushwhacker in Lauderdale County, Alabama* (Columbia, TN, P-Vine Press, 1976), 2, 57.

13. B. L. Ridley, "Champ Ferguson," *Confederate Veteran* 7 (October 1899): 442–43; Duke, *History of Morgan's Cavalry,* 416–17.

14. Scott, *Four years' Service,* 36.

15. Maddox, *Hard Trials and Tribulations,* 77.

16. Watts, *Babe of the Company,* 6; John P. Burch, *Charles W. Quantrill: A True Story of His Guerrilla Warfare . . . As Told by Captain Harrison Trow* (Vega, TX: J. P. Burch, 1923), 25.

17. John S. Watson, "The Guerrilla Chief Quantrell," *Confederate Veteran* XV (May 1907): 238.

18. O. S. Barton, *Three Years with Quantrill: A True Story Told by his Scout John McCorkle* (1914; Norman: University of Oklahoma Press, 1992), 49; Burch, *Charles W. Quantrill,* 25.

19. "Henry W. Ridder," *Confederate Veteran* 23 (November 1915): 511; "Jared Lee Jackson," *Confederate Veteran* 30 (February 1922): 70; "Capture of the Federal Steamer *Maple Leaf,*" *Southern Historical Society Papers* 24 (1896): 169–70.

20. J. Mont Wilson, "Killing of Three Brothers: Something of Warfare in Arkansas in 1863," *Confederate Veteran* 5 (April 1897): 155–56.

21. John W. Munson, *Reminiscences of a Mosby Guerrilla* (New York: Moffat, Yard, & Co., 1906), 5; L. C. Miller Memoir, 8, Western Manuscripts and Historical Collection, University of Missouri, Columbia.

22. Miller Memoir, 8; James J. Williamson, *Mosby's Rangers* (New York: Ralph B. Kenyon, 1896), 105.

23. Elmira F. Snodgress, "Reminiscences of the Old South," in United Confederate Veterans of Arkansas, *Confederate Women of Arkansas, 1861–65: Memorial Reminiscences* (P. H. Pugh, 1907), 128–29; Fellman, *Inside War,* 256–59;

24. Miller Memoir, 17.

25. "Monument to Mosby's Men," *Southern Historical Society Papers* XXVII (1899): 270–71; Adele H. Mitchell, ed., *The Letters of John S. Mosby* (2nd ed.; Clarksburg, VA: Stuart-Mosby Historical Society, 1986), 100. See also Paul Ashdown and Edward Caudill, *The Mosby Myth: A Confederate hero in Life and Legend* (Wilmington, DE: Scholarly Resources, 2002).

26. John S. Mosby, *The Memoirs of Colonel John S. Mosby* (New York: Little, Brown and Company, 1917), 371–72.

27. Adam Rankin Johnson, *The Partisan Rangers of the Confederate States* (Louisville, KY: G. G. Fetter, 1904), i, 121.

28. Joanne Chiles Eakin, ed., *Warren Welch Remembers: A Guerrilla Fighter from Jackson County, Missouri* (Independence, MO: Two Trails, 1997), 17–18.

29. Thomas D. Mays, *Cumberland Blood: Champ Ferguson's Civil War* (Carbondale: Southern Illinois University Press, 2008), 144; Kirby Ross, ed., *Autobiography of Samuel S. Hildebrand: The Renowned Missouri Bushwhacker* (Fayetteville: University of Arkansas Press, 2005), 2.

30. Ross, *Autobiography of Hildebrand,* 29, 51.

31. Walter Williams, "Battle at Centralia, Mo.," *Confederate Veteran* 17 (January 1909): 31.

32. Ibid., 30.

33. Barton, *Three Years with Quantrill,* 162–66.

34. Ibid., 120–26.

35. Miller Memoir, 15–16; Younger, *Story of Cole Younger,* 45.

36. Baker, *Confederate Guerrilla,* 59–61.

37. Johnson, *Partisan Rangers,* 120–21.

38. Fellman, *Inside War,* 249, 260; Matthew C. Hulbert, "Constructing Guerrilla Memory: John Newman Edwards and Missouri's Irregular Lost Cause," *Journal of the Civil War Era* 2 (March 2012): 58–81. Conger Beasley Jr. provides a good sketch of Edwards' career in his edited edition of John N. Edwards, *Shelby's Expedition to Mexico: An Unwritten Leaf of the War* (1872; Fayetteville: University of Arkansas Press, 2002), xiii–xxxvii.

39. John Newman Edwards, *Noted Guerrillas* (Saint Louis, MO: Bryan, Brand, & Co., 1877), 19.

40. "Discussion of Jayhawkers," f. 21, Dandridge McRae Papers, Arkansas History Commission, Little Rock.

41. Younger, *Story of Cole Younger,* 56–57; Watts, *Babe of the Company,* 24; Baker, *Confederate Guerrilla,* 66–67.

42. Edwards, *Noted Guerrillas,* 13.

43. "Monument to Mosby's Men," 250–53; Mitchell, *Letters of Mosby,* 214–15. Ten granite markers were erected in Clarke County, Virginia, in the 1890s to commemorate actions by Mosby's Rangers in 1864–65, but they are simple affairs, no larger than tombstones. An

impressive monument to Mosby alone was erected in Fauquier County in 1920, but it is a tribute to him as both a lawyer and a soldier. Timothy S. Sedore, *An Illustrated Guide to Virginia's Confederate Monuments* (Carbondale: Southern Illinois University Press, 2011), 32–36, 38–39, 169.

44. Virgil Carrington Jones, *Gray Ghosts and Rebel Raiders: The Daring Exploits of the Confederate Guerillas* (New York: Henry Holt and Company, 1956), vii.

BIBLIOGRAPHICAL ESSAY

INTRODUCTION

For trends in scholarly interpretation of the guerrilla war, see Daniel E Sutherland, "Sideshow No Longer: A Historiographical review of the Guerrilla War," *Civil War History* 46 (March 2000): 5–23 Since that article was published, a new wave of historians has probed the complexity of the guerrilla conflict in ever more sophisticated ways Most recent inquiries focus, as they have generally done, on particular geographical regions or selected issues. These works will be cited, where appropriate, in the end notes , but see also James A. Ramage, "Recent Historiography of Guerrilla Warfare in the Civil War—A Review Essay," *Register of the Kentucky Historical Society* 103 (Summer 2005): 517–41, and Keith Poulter et al., "Irregular warfare, 1861–1865," *North & South* 11 (June 2009): 16–29. Daniel E. Sutherland, *A Savage Conflict: The Decisive Role of Guerrillas in the American Civil War* (Chapel Hill: University of North Carolina Press, 2009), provides the broadest survey. For the historical context of America's guerrilla war, see Peter Mansoor, ed., *Hybrid Warfare: The Struggle of Military Forces to Adapt to Complex Opponents from the Ancient World to the Present* (Cambridge, U.K.: Cambridge University Press, 2012), and Stig Forster and Jorg Nagler, eds., *On the Road to Total War: The American Civil War and the German Wars of Unification* (Cambridge, U.K.: Cambridge University Press, 1997). The latest assessment of wartime deaths is given in J. David Hacker, "A Census-Based Count of the Civil War Dead," *Civil War History* 57 (December 2011): 307–48, and for the broadest implications of wartime loss and destruction, see Megan Kate Nelson, *Ruin Nation: Destruction and the American Civil War* (Athens: University of Georgia Press, 2012), and Lisa M. Brady, *War Upon the land: Military Strategy and the Transformation of Southern Landscapes during the American Civil War* (Athens: University of Georgia Press, 2012). The book that mistakenly discounted guerrillas as terrorists was Caleb Carr, *The Lessons of Terror: A History of Warfare Against Civilians: Why It Has Failed and Why It Will Fail Again* (New York: Random House, 2002). For a corrective, and a provocative look at the legacy of guerrilla insurgencies as terrorism in American history, see Michael Fellman, *In The Name of God and Country: Reconsidering Terrorism in American History* (New Haven, CT: Yale University Press, 2010).

CHAPTER ONE

The prewar background of the Trans-Mississippi is explained by Nicole Etcheson in *Bleeding Kansas: Contested Liberty in the Civil War Era* (Lawrence: University Press of Kansas, 2004) and Jeremy Neely, *The Border Between Them: Violence and Reconciliation on the Kansas-Missouri Line* (Columbia: University of Missouri Press, 2007). Neely is also useful for the war years, but more authoritative are Michael Fellman, *Inside War: The Guerrilla Conflict in Missouri during the American Civil War* (New York: Oxford University Press, 1989) and Albert Castel, *Civil War Kansas: Reaping the Whirlwind* (1958; Lawrence: University Press of Kansas, 1997). The richest sources for understanding the widespread enthusiasm for organizing guerrilla bands, cited several times in the notes, are Letters Received by Confederate Secretary of War, War Department Collection of Confederate Records, RG 209, National Archives, Washington, D.C. Besides the writings of individual guerrillas, good examples of the efforts to understand the motivations and identity of guerrillas are Kenneth W. Noe, "Who Were the Bushwhackers?: Age, Class, Kin, and Western Virginia's Confederate Guerrillas, 1861–1862," *Civil War History* 49 (March 2003): 5–31; Don R. Bowen, "Guerrilla War in Western Missouri, 1862–1865: Historical Extensions of the Relative Deprivation Hypothesis," *Comparative Studies in Society and History* 19 (January 1977): 30–51, and "Quantrill, James, Younger, et al.: Leadership in a Guerrilla Movement, Missouri, 1861–1865," *Military Affairs* 41 (February 1977): 42–48; Mark E. Geiger, *Financial Fraud and Guerrilla Violence in Missouri's Civil War, 1861–1865* (New Haven, CT: Yale University Press, 2010).

CHAPTER TWO

For the symbiotic relationship between Kentucky and Tennessee, see Benjamin Franklin Cooling, *Fort Donelson's Legacy: War and Society in Kentucky and Tennessee,*

1862–1862 (Knoxville: University of Tennessee Press, 1997); Cooling, *To the Battles of Franklin and Nashville and Beyond: Stabilization and Reconstruction in Tennessee and Kentucky, 1864–1866* (Knoxville: University of Tennessee Press, 2011); and Kent T. Dollar et al., eds., *Sister States, Enemy States: The Civil War in Kentucky and Tennessee* (Lexington: University Press of Kentucky, 2009). The situation in West Virginia is vividly conveyed in Richard O. Curry and F. Gerald Ham, eds., "The Bushwhackers' War: Insurgency and Counter-Insurgency in West Virginia," *Civil War History* 10 (December 1964): 416–33. For the delicate political situation in the border states, from Missouri to Maryland, see William C. Harris, *Lincoln and the Border States: Preserving the Union* (Lawrence: University Press of Kansas, 2011). The total military situation in Missouri is treated in Louis S. Gerteis, *Civil War Missouri: A Military History* (Columbia: University of Missouri Press, 2012). For Arkansas, see Thomas A. DeBlack, *With Fire and Sword: Arkansas, 1861–1874* (Fayetteville: University of Arkansas Press, 2003). The best sources for understanding the panic caused by the guerrilla war in the Midwest are the correspondence of the governors and adjutant generals of those states, but see, as examples of the secondary literature, Russell Corder, *The Confederate Invasion of Iowa* (Unionville, IA: n.p., 1997); Scott Roller, "Business as Usual: Indiana's Response to the Confederate Invasions of the Summer of 1863," *Indiana Magazine of History* 88 (March 1992): 1–25; Carl L. Stanton, comp., *They called It Treason: An Account of Renegades, Copperheads, Guerrillas, Bushwhackers and Outlaw Gangs That Terrorized Illinois during the Civil War* (Bunker Hill, IL: n.p., 2002). For the occupation of the South, and the complex relationships this created among Confederates, Unionists, and the Union army, see Stephen V. Ash, *When the Yankees Came: Conflict and Chaos in the Occupied South, 1861–1865* (Chapel Hill: University of North Carolina Press, 1995).

CHAPTER THREE

For firsthand accounts of a guerrilla life, one must go to the published and unpublished recollections and memoirs of the guerrillas themselves, or, as suggested in the narrative, to legal proceedings and military reports that had cause to inquire into guerrilla operations. Numerous examples of these sources are provided in the notes, but see, too, Sutherland, *A Savage Conflict,* and the works cited below about the lives of individual guerrillas. Those records seem to be especially plentiful for Missouri and Virginia, and so the concentration in this chapter is on those two states. The indispensable primary sources for details about the careers of individual rebel guerrillas are the transcripts of their trials by military commissions, in Courts-Martial Cases, 1809–1894, Judge Advocate General Records, RG 153, National Archives, Washington, D.C.

CHAPTER FOUR

For the Union response to the guerrilla war, see specifically Robert R. Mackey, *The Uncivil War: Irregular Warfare in the Upper South, 1861–1865* (Norman: University of Oklahoma Press, 2004); Clay Mountcastle, *Punitive War: Confederate Guerrillas and Union Reprisals* (Lawrence: University Press of Kansas, 2009); and Andrew J. Birtle, *U.S. Army Counterinsurgency and Contingency Operations and Doctrine, 1861–1941* (Washington, D.C.: Center for Military History, 2003). A fine study of Southern Unionists in blue is James Alex Baggett, *Homegrown Yankees: Tennessee's Union Cavalry in the Civil War* (Baton Rouge: Louisiana State University Press, 2009). A more general discussion of the changes in Union military policy may be found in Mark Grimsley, *The Hard Hand of War: Union Military Policy Toward Southern Civilians, 1861–1865* (New York: Cambridge University Press, 1995). Burrus Carnahan, *Acts of Justice: Lincoln's Emancipation Proclamation and the Law of War* (Lexington: University Press of Kentucky, 2007), considers that issue, although he provides none of the valuable historical context found in Mackey, Mountcastle, and Grimsley. Also useful in parts is Dennis K. Bowman, *Lincoln and Citizens' Rights in Civil War Missouri: Balancing Freedom and Security* (Baton Rouge: Louisiana State University, 2011). William T. Sherman, a pivotal figure for understanding the response of the Union army to the guerrilla war, is examined in Michael Fellman, *Citizen Sherman* (New York: Random House, 1995) and John Marszalek, *Sherman: A Soldier's Passion for Order* (New York: Free Press, 1993). For the internal war in Alabama, see Margaret M. Storey, *Loyalty and Loss: Alabama's Unionists in the Civil War and Reconstruction* (Baton Rouge: Louisiana State University Press, 2004), and specifically for events in this chapter, George C. Bradley and Richard L. Dahlen, *From Conciliation to Conquest: The Sack of Athens and the Court-Martial of Colonel John B. Turchin* (Tuscaloosa: University of Alabama Press, 2006) and Joseph W. Danielson, *War's Desolating Scourge: The Union Occupation of North Alabama* (Lawrence: University Press of Kansas, 2012). The evolution of Lincoln's thinking is found in two article by Daniel E. Sutherland, "Abraham Lincoln, John Pope, and the Origins of Total War," *Journal of Military History* 56 (October 1992): 567–86 and "Abraham Lincoln and the Guerrillas," *Prologue* 42 (Spring 2010): 20–25. More broadly, see William Marvel, *Lincoln's Darkest Year: The War in 1862* (Boston: Houghton Mifflin, 2008). Two good examples of recent efforts to address the reasons for and implications of the physical destruction of the South are, again, Brady, *War Upon the Land* and Nelson, *Ruin Nation*.

CHAPTER FIVE

Burris Carnahan, *Lincoln on Trial: Southern Civilians and the Law of War* (Lexington: University Press of Kentucky, 2010), addresses the political and legal issues caused by the guerrilla war, although, for context, see Grimsley, *Hard Hand of War,* Sutherland, *Savage Conflict,* Matthew J. Mancini, "Francis Lieber, Slavery, and the 'Genesis' of the Law of War," *Journal of Southern History* 77 (May 2011): 325–48; and L. Lynn Hogue, "Lieber's Military Code and Its legacy," in Charles R. Mack and Henry H. Lesene, eds., *Francis Lieber and the Culture of the Mind* (Columbia: University of South Carolina Press, 2005). Barton A. Myers, *Executing Daniel Bright: Race, Loyalty, and Guerrilla Violence in a Coastal Carolina Community, 1861–1865* (Baton Rouge: Louisiana State University Press, 2009) expands on the consequences of the Wild raid. Judkin Browning, *Shifting Loyalties: The Union Occupation of Eastern North Carolina* (Chapel Hill: University of North Carolina Press, 2011), provides the broader context. For an interesting use of the concept of military necessity to analyze Confederate military policies, see Paul D. Escott, *Military Necessity: Civil-Military Relations in the Confederacy* (Westport, CT: Praeger Security International, 2006).

CHAPTER SIX

In addition to the courts-martial records, other important legal sources from the Union side are the records of the provost martial offices in each state. Some examples are given in the notes, but a fuller array may be found in the National Archives Records of U.S. Army Continental Commands, RG 393. Two excellent surveys of the legal process during the Civil War are Joshua E. Kastenberg, *Law in War, War as Law: Brigadier General Joseph Holt and the Judge Advocate General's Department in the Civil War and Early Reconstruction, 1861–1865* (Durham, NC: Carolina Academic Press, 2011) and Stephen C. Neff, *Justice in Blue and Gray: A Legal History of the Civil War* (Cambridge, MA: Harvard University Press, 2010), although neither book has a very firm grasp of the guerrilla problem. Useful for the broader implications of Lieber's Code, though less authoritative for the war years, is John Fabian Witt, *Lincoln's Code: The Laws of War in American History* (New York: The Free Press, 2012). For the operation of the military commission system, see the splendidly erudite Elizabeth D. Leonard, *Lincoln's Forgotten Ally: Judge Advocate General Joseph Holt of Kentucky* (Chapel Hill: University of North Carolina Press, 2011).

CHAPTER SEVEN

A variety of internal Southern conflicts are explored in Daniel E. Sutherland, ed., *Guerrillas, Unionists, and Violence on the Confederate Home Front* (Fayetteville: University of Arkansas Press, 1998); John C. Inscoe and Robert C. Kenzer, eds., *Enemies of the Country: New Perspectives on Unionists in the Civil War South* (Athens: University of Georgia Press, 2001); Jonathan Dean Sarris, *A Separate Civil War: Communities in Conflict in the Mountain South* (Charlottesville: University of Virginia

Press, 2006); Sean Michael O'Brien, *Mountain Partisans: Guerrilla Warfare in the Southern Appalachians, 1861–1865* (Westport, CT: Praeger, 1999); David Pickering and Judy Falls, *Brush Men and Vigilantes: Civil War Dissent in Texas* (College Station: Texas A&M Press, 2000); Daniel L. Schafer, *Thunder on the River: The Civil War in Northeast Florida* (Gainesville: University Press of Florida, 2010); and Victoria E. Bynum, *The Long Shadow of the Civil War: Southern Dissent and Its Legacies* (Chapel Hill: University of North Carolina Press, 2010). Inscoe and Gordon B. McKinney explore an important part of North Carolina in *The Heart of Confederate Appalachia: Western North Carolina in the Civil War* (Chapel Hill: University of North Carolina Press, 2000). For Louisiana, see Samuel C. Hyde Jr., *Pistols and Politics: The Dilemma of Democracy in Louisiana's Florida Parishes, 1810–1899* (Baton Rouge: Louisiana State University Press, 1996). The perspective of Southern Unionists is found most resoundingly in the documentation they submitted to the government for financial compensation after the war. See U.S. House of Representatives, Southern Claims Commission Case Files, 1877–1883, Records of the Government Accounting Office, Records of the Third Auditor's Office, RG 217, National Archives, College Park, MD, and U.S. House of Representatives, Claims Disallowed by Commissioners of Claims (Southern Claims Commission), Records of the House of Representatives, 1871–1880, RG 233, National Archives, Washington, D.C.

CHAPTER EIGHT

Events in the Shenandoah Valley and northern Virginia are covered in David Coffey, *Sheridan's Lieutenants: Phil Sheridan, his Generals, and the Final Year of the Civil War* (Wilmington, DE: Rowman and Littlefield, 2005) and John L. Heatwole, *The Burning: Sheridan in the Shenandoah Valley* (Charlottesville: University of Virginia Press, 1998). Sherman's Georgia and Carolinas campaigns are explored by Richard M. McMurry, *Atlanta 1864: Last Chance for the Confederacy* (Lincoln: University of Nebraska Press, 2000); Joseph T. Glatthaar, *The March to the Sea and Beyond: Sherman's Troops in the Savannah and Carolinas Campaigns* (New York: New York University Press, 1985); and Jacqueline Glass Campbell, *When Sherman Marched North from the Sea: Resistance on the Confederate Home Front* (Chapel Hill: University of North Carolina Press, 2003). For the dying days of the Confederacy and the possibilities of a continuing guerrilla war, see William C. Davis, *An Honorable Defeat: The Last Days of the Confederate Government* (New York: Harcourt, 2001); Jay Winik, *April 1865: The Month That Saved America* (New York: Harper-Collins, 2001); and Mark Grimsley and Brooks D. Simpson, eds., *The Collapse of the Confederacy* (Lincoln: University of Nebraska Press, 2001). Several dimensions of the postwar Confederate exodus are discussed in Daniel E. Sutherland, *The Confederate Carpetbaggers* (Baton Rouge: Louisiana State University Press, 1988); Andrew Rolle,

The Lost Cause: The Confederate Exodus to Mexico (Norman: University of Oklahoma Press, 1965); and Cyrus B. Dawsey and James M. Dawsey, eds., *The Confederadoes: Old South Immigrants in Brazil* (Tuscaloosa: University of Alabama Press, 1995).

EPILOGUE

Paul A. Cimbala and Randall M. Miller, eds., *The Great Task Remaining Before Us: Reconstruction as America's Continuing Civil War* (New York: Fordham University Press, 2010) provides a sampling of the type of postwar violence that prevailed, as does the aforementioned Fellman, *In the Name of God and Country*. For more on the image of the guerrilla as soldier, see Daniel E. Sutherland, "Forgotten Soldiers: Civil War Guerrillas," *Hallowed Ground* 2 (Summer 2001): 20–24. The number of books dealing with memory and the Civil War has exploded in recent years, with ever more doctoral dissertations also pursuing that theme. However, several good essays that link our interpretation of the past directly to the guerrilla war may be found in John C. Inscoe, *Race, War, and Remembrance in the Appalachian South* (Lexington: University Press of Kentucky, 2008). Other efforts of that sort have generally been confined to the biographies of individual partisans, including Anderson's *Blood Image;* Ashdown and Caudill, *The Mosby Myth;* McKnight, *Confederate Outlaw;* Ramage, *Rebel Raider;* Michael A. Davis, "The Legend of Bill Dark: Guerrilla Warfare, Oral History, and the Unmaking of an Arkansas Bushwhacker," *Arkansas Historical Quarterly* 58 (Winter 1999): 414–29; and LeeAnn Whites, "The Tale of Three Kates: Outlaw Women, Loyalty, and Missouri's Long Civil War," in Stephen Berry, ed., *Weirding the War: Stories from the Civil War's Ragged Edges* (Athens: University of Georgia Press, 2011), 73–94.

FINAL THOUGHTS

Readers familiar with the other volumes in the *Reflections on the Civil War Era* series will have noticed that this contribution has relied more than most others on primary sources rather than on the secondary literature. The reason for that has been suggested elsewhere in both my narrative and other parts of this bibliography. It was not until the 1980s that historians began to consider the guerrilla conflict as an important part of the larger American Civil War, at least in any sort of sophisticated or systematic way. While that neglect has been remedied, that is far from saying we know the complete story. Certain patterns in the guerrilla war have been fairly well identified. We know, for instance, quite a bit about how and why so many Americans, and especially Southerners, embraced guerrilla warfare. We know much more than once we did about their identity and modes of operation. Yet, in order to push these boundaries farther, students and scholars who research and write about the irregular

war must still rely on contemporary correspondence, military reports, public records, newspapers, and periodicals if they are to unearth fresh evidence or new clues
about the conduct of that conflict.

The two topics most in need of deeper exploration and comparative study are the
questions of what motivated people to become irregular fighters and who exactly
joined these guerrilla bands, the latter issue to be measured by social–economic pro-
files of their members. It remains necessary, as well, to explore these questions at the
community level. My attempt to understand the war, as explored in *A Savage Conflict*,
was the first attempt to embrace the totality of the guerrilla's role, but it was dependent on (and therefore much limited by) the work done by other scholars in local,
state, and regional studies. Since one of the most firmly established truisms about the
irregular war is that it was really a series of intense local struggles, more such studies
are necessary before we can be confident of understanding the big picture.

That said, it may also be time to place America's guerrilla war of 1861–1865 in a
broader context. Some steps have already been taken with that object in mind, most
recently by Murray and Mansoor in *Hybrid Warfare*. However, it would be even more
useful, and perhaps revealing, to place events of the Civil War within the context of
U.S. history. Anthony James Joes, *America and Guerrilla Warfare* (Lexington: University Press of Kentucky, 2000), which looks at the nation's irregular conflicts from
the American Revolution to our involvement in Afghanistan in the 1980s, attempted
this more than a decade ago. Unfortunately, his very constricted understanding of the
Civil War—centered almost exclusively on the examples of Virginia and Missouri—
could not complement the breadth of his study. Far more effective in some respects is
Fellman's *In the Name of God and Country*, although that book is too inward looking.
While Fellman uses the construct of terrorism to good effect in analyzing the Civil
War, Reconstruction, and the Haymarket riot, he ignores the American Revolution
(for him, John Brown is the first American terrorist) and Mexican War, and his application of the theme outside the United States extends only to American involvement
in the Philippines. Consequently, the study of America's broader experience in irregular warfare remains segregated, with the best books on the subject, such as Mark V.
Kwasny, *Washington's Partisan War, 1775–1783* (Kent, Ohio: Kent State University
Press, 1996), Paul Foos, *A Hort, Offhand, Killing Affair: Soldiers and Social Conflict
during the Mexican-American War* (Chapel Hill: University of North Carolina Press,
2002), and Brian McAllister Linn, *The Philippine War, 1899–1902* (Lawrence: University Press of Kansas, 2000), dealing with single conflicts.

INDEX

ABOUT THE AUTHOR

DANIEL E SUTHERLAND is a Distinguished Professor of History at the University of Arkansas, Fayetteville. He is the author or editor of 13 books on 19th-century U.S. history, including *A Savage Conflict: The Decisive Role of Guerrillas in the American Civil War* (Chapel Hill, 2009), *Guerrillas, Unionists, and Violence on the Confederate Home Front* (Fayetteville, 1999), and *Seasons of War: The Ordeal of a Confederate Community, 1861–1865* (New York, 1995).